NETWORK SENSE

METHODS FOR
VISUALIZING A DISCIPLINE

#WRITING

Series Editor: Cheryl E. Ball

The #writing series publishes open-access digital and low-cost print editions of monographs that address issues in digital rhetoric, new media studies, digital humanities, techno-pedagogy, and similar areas of interest.

The WAC Clearinghouse, Colorado State University Open Press, and the University Press of Colorado are collaborating so that books in this series are widely available through free digital distribution and in a low-cost print edition. The publishers and the series editor are committed to the principle that knowledge should freely circulate. We see the opportunities that new technologies have for further democratizing knowledge. And we see that to share the power of writing is to share the means for all to articulate their needs, interest, and learning into the great experiment of literacy.

NETWORK SENSE

METHODS FOR VISUALIZING A DISCIPLINE

By Derek N. Mueller

The WAC Clearinghouse
wac.colostate.edu
Fort Collins, Colorado

University Press of Colorado
upcolorado.com
Louisville, Colorado

The WAC Clearinghouse, Fort Collins, Colorado 80523

University Press of Colorado, Lousville, Colorado 80027

ISBN 978-1-64215-012-4 (PDF) | 978-1-64215-013-1 (ePub) | 978-1-60732-862-9 (pbk.)

Printed in the United States of America

Library of Congress Cataloging-in-Publication Data

Names: Mueller, Derek N., 1974– author.
Title: Network sense methods for visualizing a discipline / by Derek N. Mueller.
Description: Fort Collins, Colorado : WAC Clearinghouse, [2018] | Series: #writing
  | Includes bibliographical references and index.
Identifiers: LCCN 2017059421| ISBN 9781607328629 (pbk. : alk. paper) | ISBN
  9781642150131 (epub)
Subjects: LCSH: English language—Rhetoric—Study and teaching (Higher) |
  English language—Composition and exercises. | Digital humanities—Methodology.
Classification: LCC PE1404 .M84 2018 | DDC 808/.042072—dc23 LC record available at
https://lccn.loc.gov/2017059421

Copyeditors: Lydia Welker, Sarah Truax, and Kasey Osborne
Designer: Mike Palmquist
Cover Design: Than Saffel
Series Editor: Cheryl E. Ball

This book is printed on acid-free paper.

The WAC Clearinghouse supports teachers of writing across the disciplines. Hosted by Colorado State University, and supported by the Colorado State University Open Press, it brings together scholarly journals and book series as well as resources for teachers who use writing in their courses. This book is available in digital formats for free download at wac.colostate.edu.

Founded in 1965, the University Press of Colorado is a nonprofit cooperative publishing enterprise supported, in part, by Adams State University, Colorado State University, Fort Lewis College, Metropolitan State University of Denver, Regis University, University of Colorado, University of Northern Colorado, Utah State University, and Western State Colorado University. For more information, visit upcolorado.com. The Press partners with the Clearinghouse to make its books available in print.

For my son and daughter, Phillip and Isabel,
in no particular order (I love you both the most).

Contents

Interactive Media

Acknowledgments

As all books build up—such a wondrous alignment of setups!—this book has taken shape following an elaborate tangle of interactions; copious questions and suggestions; and a well of generative, thoughtful conversations. For their gestures of kindness, support, and encouragement, I am indebted to many people. The kernel of this book began in the dissertation, which was generously shaped during my doctoral studies in Syracuse University's Composition and Cultural Rhetoric program by Collin Brooke, Louise Wetherbee Phelps, Rebecca Moore Howard, Alex Reid, and Anne Wysocki. Chapter Four, a version of which was published in *College Composition and Communication's* research methodologies special issue in 2012, found refined shape through revisions guided by editor Kathleen Blake Yancey and two anonymous reviewers. Shortly after that article appeared, I was fortunate to continue conversations as a guest presenter and respond to many thoughtful questions posed by students in classes taught by Laurie Gries at the University of Florida, Jeff Pruchnic at Wayne State University, and Seán McCarthy at James Madison University. For their attentiveness and genuine curiosity, this book is also a credit to engaged conference-goers as well as the intellectual communities that have coalesced around several conferences, including the Western States Rhetoric and Literacy Conference, the Conference on College Composition and Communication, Writing Research Across Borders, HASTAC, Computers & Writing, and WIDE-EMU. Colleagues and graduate students in written communication at Eastern Michigan University also gave much to this book's development with their expressions of curiosity and interest, offerings of intellectual acuity, and sustaining friendship. To faculty colleagues, Steve Krause and Chalice Randazzo, and to former and current graduate students Jana Rosinski, Joe Torok, Chris Stuart, Gabe Green, Thomas Passwater, Brianne Radke, and Ja'La Wourman, I can think of few more valuable professional gifts than the conversations we've had when we were wondering together about what on earth I was working on. To Eastern Michigan University and the Department of English Language and Literature, I am grateful for a Winter 2016 sabbatical that created clearings sufficient to finish drafting the book. I owe a special thank you to Kate Pantelides, who invited me to present on Chapter Three and to lead a workshop at Middle Tennessee State University as the 2016 Peck Composition Series presenter while I was on sabbatical and whose collegiality and limitless cheer are one of a kind. For reading and offering feedback on the early drafts of the proposal, for reminding me to heed as a life principle the road sign on the Trans-Canada Highway near Kenora,

Ontario, and always to drive according to conditions, and for persistently urging me along throughout the trickiest parts of the book's development, I am grateful to Jen Clary-Lemon. This would have been a diminished undertaking absent such steadfast reassurances. To my family, I am thankful for unwavering support, good humor, and everyday motivation. Finally, the book attests to the support and guidance from #writing series editor Cheryl Ball and reviewers Bill Hart-Davidson and Madeleine Sorapure, whose timely feedback and smart questions pushed late-stage writing so thoughtfully along.

NETWORK SENSE

METHODS FOR
VISUALIZING A DISCIPLINE

Introduction: The Distant and Thin of Disciplinarity

> An inventive culture requires the broadest possible criteria for what is relevant. (Ulmer, 1994, p. 6)

At its heart, this is a book about research methodologies: Its central arguments, premises, and motivations adapt, extend, and apply two recently named methodologies, *distant reading*, introduced in 2000 by Franco Moretti, a scholar of literary history and the evolution of literary forms, and *thin description*, theorized by literary scholar Heather Love and set in sharp relief against anthropologist Clifford Geertz's well-known and widely adopted approach to ethnography, *thick description*. Weaving together these two methodological orientations—the distant and the thin—I argue for their convergence as suited to theoretically underpinning a suite of methods used to visualize patterns indicative of the ongoing growth and maturation of an academic discipline: rhetoric and composition/writing studies.[1] Distant and thin treatments foster primary, if tentative and provisional, insights into what I refer to as a *network sense*—incomplete but nevertheless vital glimpses of an interconnected disciplinary domain focused on relationships that define and cohere widespread scholarly activity. When inquiring into disciplinary emergence and maturation, network sense names a facility for recognizing and tracing relationships, for engaging in focused reading and exploratory reading, and for noticing connections among programs and people, publications and conferences, activities and their material castings, difficult questions and myriad stakeholders. When this pursuit of network sense is fortuitous, disciplinary patterns—the field *itself*—become ever more evident to those who identify their work with it, to newcomers, such a graduate students, and to diverse stakeholders, including higher education policy makers. Accepting the invitation to read this work is accepting an invitation to consider the epistemological value of *network sense*. By way of description and example, the book demonstrates ways that a distant–thin methodology renders dynamic disciplinary patterns obvious.

---

1   Throughout the book, I refer to the field as "rhetoric and composition/writing studies" because, although it presents somewhat inelegantly at times, it matches with the Classification of Instructional Programs (CIP) designation 23.13, as established by the National Center for Educational Statistics (NCES). This phrasing also underscores ongoing developments in the field with regard to a richer disciplinary history associated with "rhetoric and composition" and a contemporary relabeling that has taken hold unevenly under the designation "writing studies." To ease the inelegance, the phrase is often abbreviated here as RCWS.

I encourage you to imagine even more expansive applications of these approaches to under-examined areas of rhetoric and composition/writing studies (RCWS) as well as to other, yet-emerging disciplinary domains.

The questions motivating this research stem from an inventive exigency, a purpose that must be understood as epistemologically generative for how it participates in the project of making disciplinarity knowable, but knowable such that it is future-oriented, participatory, and heuristic. Rather than pursuing the production of fixed, static representations, this project promotes distant reading and thin description and celebrates them for their dynamic, generative qualities—adaptiveness, flexibility, open-endedness—and for their suitedness to making visual models that support efforts to continuously shape the field. These methods do not anchor one-time answers to the wicked problems they help us disentangle. Rather, they underscore interests in invention and provocation; the models and the data sets they build upon are living and responsive, updated as new information is added. These methodologies are highly suggestive and probabilistic. I think of them as a companion of *heuretics*, in the way Gregory Ulmer (1994) used the term to commingle aesthetic and critical qualities of inquiry—open to the eureka! moments in research. Much like heuretics, distant reading and thin description complement and, to varying degrees, even replace rational logics with networks of association that afford inquiry and discovery for newcomers and seasoned scholars alike. These inventive dimensions are among the strongest aspects of the argument advanced here. I implicitly promote these methodologies because of their potential to create an expansive range of possibilities in each encounter with an abstract visual model: new forms of knowledge, new insights, new questions. The visual models are not proofs, finally, but provocations; not closures, but openings; not conclusions or satisfying reductions, but *clearings* for rethinking disciplinary formations—they stand as invitations to invention, to wonder, as catalysts for what Ulmer described as "theoretical curiosity" (p. xii).

So that you have a vivid though admittedly cursory illustration of the network sense that coalesces between distant reading and thin description, consider the tag cloud of this project presented in Figure 1. Leaving aside for now some of the subtler distinctions addressed in Chapter Three's elaboration of semantic networks, the tag cloud simply presents a cluster of key words and phrases that appear most frequently in a selected text or set of texts. A tag cloud resembles the list of indexical keywords commonly assigned to an article by an editor, but it is different because of its condensed visual presentation. Tag clouds also have much in common with article abstracts, which likewise function as an abridgment of the content of the article. Tag clouds reduce and simplify a corpus (whether a single text or batch of texts), rearranging the syntactic elements (sentences and paragraphs) and, in turn, presenting words and phrases as units of data that occur repeatedly in the text itself. The word frequency cloud, or keyword confluence, is not the only variety of tag cloud, of course, but is one fairly common and pervasive use. Tag clouds, as I will demonstrate much more thoroughly in Chapter Three, constitute one variety of distant reading, one variety of thin description, and, as such, they prompt an acutely language-based instance of network sense—one impression of disciplinarity as constituted by a discoverable and traceable semantic network. These methods—and the tag cloud created with them in mind—create a *temporary clearing*, holding the text at bay so that we might see it instead as a semantic network with concentrations of terms coalescing throughout it.

abstract (97) accounts (98) activity (116) article (177) chapter (124) citation (120) collection (126) complex (85) composition (263) concepts (102) data (150) database (79) description (179) development (78) disciplinary (233) discipline (120) distant (224) field (249) figure (103) generative (85) graphs (99) index (79) journal (94) knowledge (97) list (102) locations (80) maps (295) methodological (88) methods (237) models (189) network (155) patterns (169) practices (114) presented (103) programs (94) project (123) reading (296) references (87) rhetoric (260) scale (114) sense (152) studies (257) terms (125) text (125) thin (215) turns (177) visual (167) work (205) writing (272) years (117)

Figure 1. A tag cloud of this book. Tag clouds commonly present weighted lists of terms occurring in a text, offering them as a gestalt model and alternative abstract.

Still other commonplace varieties of distant reading and thin description, like abstracts, further exemplify the methodological basis for this work. For example, consider the ways an ordinary movie trailer offers a succinct account of the full-length feature film. The trailer is a concentrated version constructed to suggest just enough of the film itself to compel prospective viewers to take in a full viewing. Movie trailers function, in one sense, as abridgments, not unlike article abstracts. Article abstracts tend to be summary-like. They reduce and simplify the full-length article, offering a version adequate for providing just enough sense of what the article holds so that we can make a semi-informed leap. Movie trailers tend to rely on explicitly promotional enticements more so than do scholarly article abstracts, but they function similarly: By deliberately reducing something complex (i.e., the movie, the article) into something simpler (i.e., the trailer, the abstract), they provide thinned out, yet adequate, insight to decide how to proceed or whether to proceed at all. The point here is that we can identify a number of everyday examples where distant reading and thin description already do their thin–distant work in the world: from tables of contents, indexes, and the notes on a book jacket to product packaging and nutritional labels or from weather maps and forecasts to scatterplots of economic data.

The purpose of this book is to articulate a set of methods appropriate to investigating aspects of the disciplinary maturation of RCWS from the mid-1980s to the mid-2010s. While in part I will be drawing on the methodological precedents for distant reading initiated in Moretti's scholarship and thin description sketched in Love's work, I seek here both to enrich the methodology and to suggest its adequacy for revisiting some of the ways in which the discipline of RCWS has been depicted in the scholarship of the field. As the discipline grows increasingly complex and ever more acutely specialized, we share a need for operations that will assist us (all of us, but particularly newcomers) in apprehending some of the prevailing patterns that have characterized the field up to the present moment. This relates to one of the project's key concerns: When scholarship and conversations are piling up *en masse*, how does one grasp the insurmountable complexity sufficient to participate in disciplinary conversations? There are any number of plausible responses to this question, the most commonplace of which involves vague truisms about diligent attentiveness and hard work. No one would argue that being an active, engaged reader by conventional methods is anything short of requisite to a life as a rigorous scholar. But such a time-honored adage as "read everything" or "read steadily" (i.e., all day, every day) does little to acknowledge the unbridled accumulation of disciplinary materials—the too-muchness of entering conversations that started many decades (even centuries) ago and that, therefore, demand back-reading while also tuning in to current conversations and, ultimately, preparing to participate knowingly and responsibly in them. Underlying the hard-work approach so pervasive in the American academy are highly differentiated repertoires of tacit skills in reading and selecting what to read as well as determining the degree of investment with which to read it. Distant reading and thin description acknowledge that there are constantly new challenges involved in making sense of a vast store of materials—materials that are diverse, challenging, and continuously produced. Further, if successful, distant reading should allow us to bolster (and better understand) the skills necessary for keeping abreast of disciplinary currents, both in their antecedent and contemporary trajectories.

These methodologies will not ultimately eliminate the need to reconcile personal knowledge with the influx of scholarly disciplinary materials—a quandary I refer to as the *reading problem*, which is a matter I will address in Chapter One and return to in Chapter Six. Distant reading and thin description do, however, combine to provide a basis for enacting an expanded set of abstracting practices that culminate in scalable visual models, a suite of patterned images useful for stirring questions about disciplinary trends and relationships.[2] Specifically, this project is concerned with three types of visual models: word clouds, citation frequency graphs, and maps of scholarly activity. Each of these models is dealt with substantially in Chapters Three through Five. Without question, there are more visual models that might be of interest to those whose work with data constructs tangible iterations of the field, but these three models provide an initial selection and a right-sized sample. The data that grounds these visual models comes from numerous sources: from more than 500 articles published in *College Composition and Communication* between 1987 and 2013[3] and from survey data gathered by the Master's Degree Consortium of Writing Studies Specialists and a study of Canada–U.S. interdependencies. Data sources are always unavoidably limited, but these are sufficient to demonstrate some of the ways distant reading and thin description methodologies might be applied to well-known disciplinary data sets in the interest of pattern-finding and its epistemological corollary, network sense, a concept I delineate in Chapter Six. While this project, if successful, gives distant reading and thin description methodologies a concentrated push, the prosperity of these heuretical, experimental methods beyond this limited demonstration will continue to be settled in the future as we perpetually reconcile the field's maturation, its growing complexity, and its means of substantiation and sustainability.

Thin Descriptions of the Chapters

Chapter One, "Methods for Visualizing Disciplinary Patterns," establishes the contemporary exigence for the integrated methodology that defines network

---

2   "Patterned images" names a class of visual objects that allow us to reckon with trends in large collections of data and metadata. Patterned images are generated with the aid of computational processes. This phrase is an admittedly slight variation on "data visualization," and I use it primarily to emphasize the constructedness of the visual images, their rhetoricity, and the interests in pattern-seeking that motivate their development.

3   Bibliometric data informing Chapter Four was drawn from *CCC* articles between 1987 and 2011. Semantic data used as the basis of Chapter Three comes from a 25-year set of *CCC* articles published from 1989–2013. These slightly different timeframes are due to the sequence of the research as it developed and my preference for working within a 25-year timeframe in both cases.

sense. The chapter begins by locating 1987 as a moment of complexity when distinct shifts in publishing hinted at conditions of continuing growth that meant it would be increasingly difficult to keep up with the expanding arena of scholarly publication. Stephen North's (1987) well-known methodological portrait, *The Making of Knowledge in Composition*, surfaced as the first theoretical monograph in the field. Changes in the peer review process and citation format for *College Composition and Communication*, one of the field's prominent journals, also signal a shift in the late 1980s to disciplinary activity at a broader scale. Since 1987, scholars have continued to produce discipliniographies, or accounts of the field, but such accounts have resorted in large measure to localized cases and, as such, have accorded with close and thick methodologies. In this chapter, I argue that important aspects of the field's formation are differently available when massive collections of disciplinary materials are subjected to distant reading and thin description.

Chapter Two, "Patterned Images of a Discipline: Database, Scale, Pattern," sketches three foundational concepts for network sense: database, scale, and pattern. Treating each concept in turn, I first revisit a tension between narrative and *database* that is well documented by Lev Manovich (2001) and N. Katherine Hayles (2007). I contend that, although they have been tremendously important, hyper-local, narrative-based accounts of disciplinary emergence operate more powerfully when paired with data-based accounts. In addition to composing narrative accounts, scholars must also begin to build and curate the field's databases more systematically (e.g., program profile data, directories of programs, journal indexes, etc.). Second, I examine the importance of *scale* as a quality, naming the possibility that aspects of disciplinary formation become evident at different orders of magnitude, from the nano to the macro. With this in mind, network sense is constituted by what I characterize as *planeury*, an aerial, altitude-minded alternative to Michel de Certeau's (1988) walking *flaneur*, who knows a city by foot. In the context of scale, planeury names a gliding, bird's-eye sensibility that seeks the right distance while attending to the ways perspective shifts across distances. Finally, Chapter Two discusses *pattern* as a visual-representational articulation with great promise for orienting newcomers and stakeholders to the field. Visualized patterns intervene into discipliniography as an important epistemic technology whose thin, distant qualities provide handles on complex, distributed disciplinary activity. Understood in this way, pattern intervenes as rhetorically *descriptive*, in the Latourian sense of the word, which refers to prospective, future-oriented script-making (Johnson, 1988; Latour, 2007). In other words, semantic, bibliographic, and geolocative patterns surfaceable from materials and activities *describe* and in effect set up ways of knowing and participating in an emerging disciplinary future. Database, scale, and pattern coalesce as three concepts vital for understanding the illustrations of network sense featured in the following three chapters.

Chapter Three. "Turn Spotting: The Discipline as a Confluence of Words," focuses on the relationship between the keywords that surface and circulate in scholarship and the notion of *turns*, or widespread attention events that indicate concentrated interest and curiosity (e.g., interpretive turn, new materialist turn, global turn). Methods for corroborating turns are only beginning to catch up with the frequency of turns being announced nowadays. I contend that turns ought to be evidence-based and that they manifest gradually, first as patterned phenomena discernible across scales. The chapter features a Google motion chart that displays a sample of 25 keywords across 25 years as they rise and fall in usage frequency within more than 400 articles published in *College Composition and Communication* since 1989. The installation, which amounts to an animated index, foregrounds an aspect of network sense located in a lexicon rendered from published scholarship. I extend this to considerations of the relationship among projects such as *Keywords in Writing Studies* (Heilker & Vandenberg, 2015), emerging studies of threshold concepts (Adler-Kassner & Wardle, 2015), and the vocabularies that substantiate them. As such, I not only claim in this chapter that so-called turns must be methodologized but also show how distant reading and thin description contribute distinctly to this undertaking. The chapter also explores the relationship between turns and threshold concepts, suggesting that attention to the evolving character of a disciplinary lexicon provides insight into the temporal nature of these discursive events.

Chapter Four, "Graphs: The Thin, Long Tail of *CCC* Citation Frequency," features a bibliometric report on more than 15,000 citations in *College Composition and Communication* over 25 years. Figures whose work was frequently cited (e.g., Linda Flower, Peter Elbow, Patricia Bizzell, David Bartholomae, and James Berlin) reflect influence, affinity, and concentrations of interest circulating in the journal, and yet tallying *only* the most frequently cited figures provides a small part of the picture. A thinner, more distant treatment of the same data set, such as the graphs themselves, which are presented as static images and as a dynamic sequence (i.e., animated GIF), indicates a declining citation density within the journal. Steadily over the 25-year sample, the most frequently cited figures have trended downward, while the single, unduplicated citations have grown. Reflecting on this phenomenon using a Poisson distribution (long tail) offers compelling evidence for disciplinary diffuseness that may be framed as promising or ominous and that returns us to the necessity of continuing to share concerns for the evolving definitional basis of disciplinarity (n.b., a version of this chapter was published in *College Composition and Communication*).

Chapter Five, "Emplaced Disciplinary Networks: Toward an Atlas of Rhetoric and Composition/Writing Studies," considers the prospects of a geolocative disciplinary atlas, or collection of cartographic representations of disciplinary activity, by turning to three illustrative examples: 1) a map of the locations of doctoral, master's, and undergraduate majors consortia members, 2) a map of the hosting locations for three major conferences (Conference on College Composition and Communication, Rhetoric Society of America, and Computers & Writing), and 3) a map series modeling differently the emplaced, traversive career paths (i.e., institutional affiliations) for 55 Canadian scholars who responded to a 2014 survey inquiring about Canada–U.S. interdependencies in RCWS. The chapter contextualizes the exigencies that gave rise to each of these mapping projects and examines the specific data types (e.g., GeoJSON, geocoded Google Sheets), platforms (e.g., MapBox, Google Maps), and maintenance regimens involved in building and maintaining each of them. Recognizing the field as a North American phenomenon with trends toward internationalization hinges on an array of thin, distant, and scalable cartographic representations of disciplinary data concerned with the locations of programs and institutions, job openings, and career paths. But mapping disciplinary activity can also assist with regional coalition building, recruitment of graduate students, and strengthening local program culture by inviting as consultants and guest speakers colleagues of all ranks and specializations from nearby programs.

The book's concluding chapter, "Network Sense: Patterned Connections Across a Maturing Discipline," reiterates the rationale for visualizing disciplinary patterns, noting the timeliness of improving systematic data collection and representation both as a supplement to continuing discipliniographic efforts and as an intervention into the rising complexity of the field. In this chapter, I argue that the thin and distant methods introduced and enacted in the book facilitate *network sense*, which stands both as a loose structure of participation necessary for welcoming newcomers to the field and also as an aid to awareness that provides casual stakeholders with tools for understanding disciplinary activity in many of its divergent and distributed manifestations. In addition to reasserting the relationship between thin and distant methods and network sense, the chapter acknowledges the vital importance of methodological pluralism for understanding the rich array of activity associated with the discipline. In its concluding section, "Thickening Agents," the chapter sketches the stakeholders in the field who are well-served by network sense before finally calling attention to prospects for continuing studies of disciplinary patterns using distant and thin methods alongside close and thick methods.

Chapter 1: Methods for Visualizing Disciplinary Patterns

> If this study supplies a kind of map, it is a map of an ever-shifting, ever-moving terrain, whose shape . . . is a function of where you happen to be standing. (North, 1987, p. 6)

Rhetoric and Composition Discipliniography in the 1980s

In his 1987 monograph, *The Making of Knowledge in Composition: Portrait of an Emerging Field*, Stephen North told the story of the "methodological land-rush" (p. 317) that characterized the emergence and early stabilization of rhetoric and composition/writing studies (RCWS) in the 1980s (p. 2). With the publication of North's account, disciplinarity and the modes of studying disciplinary emergence grew *thicker*. Focusing on eight modes of inquiry, North identified his own method as anthropological because he developed insights "from the inside," that is, from the sort of "living among" that social scientists typically employ when they conduct research by means of participant-observation (p. 4). North's "ten years of 'living among' the people of Composition" (p. 4) constitute the foundation for his ethos; his insights into the discipline, its "language and rituals, histories and mythologies, ontologies and epistemologies," take root in a decade of personal professional experience (p. 4). North's approach follows closely anthropologist Clifford Geertz's (1977) *thick description*, which, as literary scholar Heather Love (2010, 2013) pointed out, pursues investigative empirical depths and provides an interpretive account, in effect regarding human activity as suited to text-like hermeneutics. North's identification with Geertz's anthropological *interpretation of culture*, I argue, provided a formidable, influential model for scholarly discipliniography in RCWS that still pervades the field to this day. Although the celebrated status of North's book did little to catalyze alternative approaches to disciplinary activity similar to Love's *thin descriptions* or other methods that are based on textual analytics and investigations into patterns.

Gauging by its reception and legacy, North's project stands out as one of the most impactful texts of the 1980s on the field's formation. *The Making of Knowledge in Composition* is well known and frequently cited; it is one of the few books to be reviewed multiple times in *College Composition and Communication* (*CCC*). And the 25-year anniversary of its publication was punctuated in 2011, with the release of an honorific collection, edited by Lance Massey and Richard Gebhardt, *The Changing of Knowledge in Composition*. Few would identify North's 1987 monograph as anything less than a highly influential landmark study that has since seeped into and even grown to be constitutive of the field's ontology. Furthermore, it was one of the first—if not the first—theoretical monographs to be published in the discipline, with Karen Burke LeFevre's (1986) *Invention as a Social Act*, James Berlin's (1987) *Rhetoric and Reality*, and Louise Wetherbee Phelps's (1991) *Composition as a Human Science* entering into circulation contemporaneous to North's *The Making of Knowledge*.

North (1987) made a direct, deliberate effort to resolve the rising disciplinary complexity of the moment—which he characterized as "chaotic and patternless" (p. 3)—with methodological trends in the scholarly research performed over the preceding two decades. Early in the study, he acknowledged "two major liabilities" resulting from the rapid growth of the previous 20 years (the span from approximately 1967 until 1987) during which modern RCWS emerged:

> The first [liability] is that the new investigators have tended to trample roughshod over the claims of previous inquirers, especially the 'indigenous' population that I will call the Practitioners. . . . Second, the growth of methodological awareness has not kept pace with this scramble for the power and prestige that go with being able to say what constitutes knowledge. Investigators often seem unreflective about their own mode of inquiry, let alone anyone else's. The predictable result within methodological communities has been disorder: investigators are wont to claim more for their work than they can or should. Between communities, it has produced a kind of inflation: in the absence of a critical consciousness capable of discriminating more carefully, the various kinds of knowledge produced by these modes of inquiry have piled up uncritically, helter skelter, with little regard to incompatibilities. The result has been an accumulated knowledge of relatively impressive size, but one that lacks any clear coherence or methodological integrity. Composition's collective fund of knowledge is a very fragile entity. (p. 3)

What's clear here is North's preference for "coherence" and "methodological integrity," timely correctives presumably dealt with by his project in response to the problems of "disorder" and "inflation." North's methodological typology with its eight modes of research activity sought to reconcile these disparate forces and divergent qualities, legitimizing lore through the use of methods generally thought to be indicative of rigorous research. North's work captured the criticality of the moment: the emerging field's phase-shift from an era of lore and all of its attachments and associations—many of them operating as a patchwork of idiosyncratic anecdotes and local insights, spanning from either 1949 or 1963 to 1987—to an era of comparable stability, legitimacy, and professionalization, which included the rise of graduate programs, tenure lines, specialization, and a greater likelihood for intra-discipline insularity or pocketing. Lore did not dissipate after North placed a spotlight on it, but a greater stratification was demonstrable and with it new trends toward specialization in the field. In 1987, these were contentious matters and serious concerns after more than two decades of helter-skelter disciplinary emergence. Had RCWS grown too large, too fast? What theories, methods, and practices cohered in this domain of study? Would it be possible to affirm the legitimacy of practitioners' tacit knowledge while at the same time strengthening methodological integrity?

North's was not the first account that sought to refine thinking about the inner workings of RCWS, but it has arguably been the one whose narrative of the field is best known and most widely heralded as *the story* for a number of reasons. I will return to this in a moment. But first I want to fold North's narrative into a broader classification of scholarly efforts in the 1980s and early 1990s to deal with disciplinarity—with the emergence, formation, and stabilization of the field we call rhetoric and composition/writing studies—a broader classification I will refer to as *discipliniography*, the writing of the discipline. In *Authoring a Discipline*, a study of nine scholarly journals in RCWS from 1950 to 1990, Maureen Daly Goggin (2000) referred to journal editors and article authors as *discipliniographers*—as those who produced the field with their scholarship. *Authoring a Discipline* is a periodic history of the development of key journals over a 40-year period; I will discuss Goggin's work in greater depth in Chapter Four. For now, I simply want to expand on the idea of discipliniography as a genre that both writes the field and is written by scholars in the field, and as such, a genre that is responsive to the growth of the field and its changing, contested state(s).

This book attempts to offer a partial intervention into the long line of disciplinary accounts of RCWS by writing the field using distant, thin methods as well as methods devised to discern patterns in large collections of words, citations, and geographic locations. As such, this work stands apart from most attempts to write the discipline that have come before it. Early accounts, including Janet Emig's 1977 (1983 reprint) essay "The Tacit Tradition: The Inevitability of a Multi-Disciplinary Approach to Writing Research," Richard Fulkerson's 1979 *CCC* essay "Four Philosophies of Composition," as well as his article a decade later, "Composition Theory in the Eighties" (1990), James A. Berlin's 1982 *College English* essay "Contemporary Composition: The Major Pedagogical Theories," and Janice Lauer's 1984 *Rhetoric Review* essay "Composition Studies: Dappled Discipline," attempted to explain the field's complexity by introducing taxonomies for organizing philosophical or pedagogical epistemologies or for explaining the extradisciplinary influences that, in part, justify a sense of patchiness and diffuseness among those who identify with RCWS. Each of these accounts of the discipline is significant in its own right, and each is a noteworthy precursor to the book-length accounts of the field by North and Phelps that were published late in the 1980s. Still other articles subsequent to the 1980s, such as Martin Nystrand, Stuart Greene, and Jeffrey Wiemelt's 1993 *Written Communication* article "Where Did Composition Studies Come From? An Intellectual History," indicated that the formal genre of discipliniography continued. And, there are still other, more recent attempts—a class of articles and monographs about the discipline that have done much to theorize and historicize the conditions contributing to its emergence while also offering newcomers devices for gaining traction on what has passed that can explain contemporary and future developments. The point here is not so much to critique discipliniography (though it does warrant asking whether such accounts stabilized the field and therefore reified certain lingering conceptions of it) but rather to acknowledge that this sort of work—the chronicling of the discipline—has always been a part of RCWS and that, from early on, discipliniography reflected methodological influence from Geertz's thick description. As Massey and Gebhardt attested in the introduction to their volume, ethnography is "our leading empirical scholarship" (p. 8).

Collectively, discipliniographical accounts seemed to peak in the late 1980s and early 1990s, shortly after the publication of North's (1987) *Making of Knowledge* and perhaps culminating with Susan Miller's (1993) *Textual Carnivals* or with Donna Burns Phillips, Ruth Greenberg, and Sharon Gibson's (1993) *CCC* article "*College Composition and Communication*: Chronicling a Discipline's Genesis." Numerous discipliniographies have been written and published since this moment of criticality, but I would argue that many of the discipliniographies attempted after 1993 have been hard-pressed to account for the fullness and richness of this expanding disciplinary complexity subsequent to 1987. As a result, we find more highly selective accounts of the discipline that zero in on a particular historical moment (viz., Joseph Harris's [1997] *A Teaching Subject*, which examined key tenets of disciplinarity through pedagogical imperatives advanced in the 1966 Dartmouth Conference), on sites (viz., Anne Ruggles Gere's [1997] *Intimate Practices*, which examined constructs of intimacy and literacy in women's clubs), on historical precursors to the post-WWII emergence of the field (viz., Thomas Masters's

[2004] *Practicing Writing* and Sharon Crowley's [1998] *Composition in the University*), and on missed opportunities (viz., Geoffrey Sirc's [2002] *English Composition as a Happening*, which argued for reimagining the field according to the performances of avant-garde artists, and Jeff Rice's [2007] *The Rhetoric of Cool*, which called for re-thinking the relationship of new media and composition by way of Marshall McLuhan and others).

There are more accounts to consider, but this list should be adequate to underscore what I am suggesting: Many disciplinary accounts, since the moment of criticality I want to locate in 1987, have become more specialized. They have done well to showcase the chaotic and patternless nature of the field's emergence and have simultaneously shown the challenges of aggregating dappledness into broadly inclusive, yet coherent, accounts. In most cases, these overt discipliniographies, by which I mean the explicit attempts to write the discipline (as mildly distinct from the implicit authoring of the discipline Goggin wrote about that happens at the hands of journal editors and authors of scholarly articles) narrowed in scope and in focus. While North called for methodological pluralism in his 1987 monograph, what followed included discipliniographic pluralism that remained beholden to anthropological ways of knowing—that is, approaches that were experientially interpretive and thick-descriptive. The field's proper emergence—this moment of criticality and phase shift I have mentioned—also ushered in a profound expansion of the field that we are still witnessing and enacting decades later. This project aims to offer a modest, contemporary response to this rising complexity, a response that urges the development of distant reading and thin description methods and expands our means of abstracting and modeling patterned images of the field's development since 1987, patterned images that will render intelligible the disciplinary materials and activities that have rapidly piled up over the past three decades.

The key proposition here is that 1987 should be regarded as a moment of criticality, after which accounts of the totality of the discipline grew ever more narrow, focused, and specialized. Hereafter, no single perspective or viewpoint could sufficiently grapple with the whole field—the discipline—as a totality of practices and activities in addition to the published record. Perhaps this observation is commonplace, so plain and so widely understood that it hardly needs to be posed as insightful once again. Yet the publication of North's monograph, followed shortly thereafter by Phelps's (1991) *Composition as a Human Science*, is not all there is to my contention that something profound happened at this transformative moment for the field. At the same time the field's "social fabric" was, according to Goggin, gaining strength (2000, p. 178); the field was creeping sidelong into other forays, interests, and specialized niches. In the following section, I will explain how formal changes to *College Composition and Communication* strengthen the case I set out for marking 1987 as a moment of criticality.

Disciplinary Catalysts: Restructuring and Accumulation

When in 1987 Richard Gebhardt assumed editorial responsibilities for *College Composition and Communication*, two significant changes to the journal were already underway. First, the journal was switching from the use of endnotes to the use of a works cited page as defined by the Modern Language Association (MLA). Second, the review of article submissions was, for the first time, conducted using a blind peer review system. While these alterations lent a sense of modernization and rigor to the journal, they were not only indications that the field itself was responsive to contemporary developments in academic publishing but also that the field was burgeoning and that its rising complexity would require new processes and new apparatuses for selecting, presenting, and circulating the journal's content.

Changing from a system of end notes to works cited was to be expected for such a prominent journal as *CCC*, given that several other journals in the field were making the same change at this time. *JAC*, for instance, used endnotes through the end of 1986 before applying MLA works cited format for bibliographic citation in 1987. *College English* and *Rhetoric Review* made the changeover early in 1985, and *Rhetoric Society Quarterly* adopted the MLA works cited style in the summer of 1986 (16.3).

Although this initial change appears at first glance to be a minor modification to the formal arrangement of reference lists, the new design for formal citations can also be understood as restructuring disciplinary discourse in ways that complement network sense. The previous system of endnotes functioned like a highly localized (i.e., article-scale) trail of only internally relevant crumbs, ordered sequentially in direct correspondence to the linear, start-to-finish progression of reading an article from its first word to its last. Each notes reference was numbered, and while this numbering preserved a logical system for cross-referencing notes and citations that appeared at the end of the article, it made the external tracing of references difficult. Independent of the article, the entangled thicket of notes and references at the end of the article was in many cases too dense, too contingent upon the context of the reference, and often even further obscured by systems of abbreviation used to use as little page space as necessary for appending the notes. The collection of listed references could not easily be glanced at in a predictably ordered, coherent location.

The adoption of MLA formatting meant for the journal articles that the works cited for a given article was listed separately from the endnotes. Notes now appeared at the end, followed by a separate listing of references appearing in the article, and they included specific design features such as alphabetical ordering by the author's last name and hanging indent, which would make the listing of references more readily accessible. With this change, the works cited could be, in some sense, *read* independent of the article. And although the system has its limitations, which include the flattening out of the extent of each reference's bearing in the article itself, the MLA works cited feature was an abstraction of the article. Works cited listings now operated as an orderly yet thin description of the article itself—a bibliographic apparatus that functioned synecdochally (part standing in for whole) and that lent itself to systematic treatments as regularized strings of data. Further, such lists made possible one kind of distant reading of the scholarly article. For illustration, consider the differences between the notes appearing at the end of T.Y. Booth's 1986 *CCC* article, "I. A. Richards and the Composing Process" (Fig. 2), and the works cited listed at the end of William F. Irmscher's, "Finding a Comfortable Identity" (Fig. 3), which was published in the next issue.

Notes

1. I. A. Richards, *So Much Nearer: Essays Toward a World English* (New York: Harcourt, Brace & World, 1968), p. 118. This book is referred to subsequently in the text as *SMN*.

2. Adrian Akmajian, Richard A. Demers, and Robert M. Harnish, *Linguistics: An Introduction to Language and Communication* (Cambridge, MA: MIT Press, 1979), p. 228.

3. Akmajian, *Linguistics,* pp. 146, 186.

4. Wilma R. Ebbitt and David R. Ebbitt (Glenview, IL: Scott, Foresman, 1982), p. 457. The above sentence about wind, trees, and ice is from p. 496, italics not reproduced.

5. Richards took the token-Type terminology from C. S. Peirce, calling each of the individual seeable letters on the page a "token" of one of the "Types" which are designated when we say there are twenty-six letters in the alphabet. Although all of us, I assert grandly, can see the distinction once it is pointed out, the difficulties of developing a philosophy which adequately deals with it have been recognized since at least as far back as the time of Socrates. See I. A. Richards, *Beyond* (New York: Harcourt, Brace, Jovanovich, 1974), pp. 5-13.

6. Jack W. Germond and Jules Witcover, "Huge March to Embody Dream of Peace," and William F. Buckley Jr., "Convict's Views on Drugs Ring Truer than Solon's," *Salt Lake Tribune,* 3 September 1985, Sec. A, p. 14.

Figure 2. CCC Notes in 1986. The listing of endnotes appearing after T.Y. Booth's 1986 article "I.A. Richards and the Composing Process" shows the way such notes followed the syntagmatic logic of the conventional reading of the article itself. Endnotes like these were used from the inception of College Composition and Communication *in 1949 through 1986.*

As the field stabilized, scholarship drew on a greater breadth of references. An attempt to visualize that shifting breadth is featured in Chapter Four, using a series of citation frequency graphs. In turn, vestiges of conversations played out in journals whose sponsorship was more explicitly grounded in shared disciplinary concerns than ever before. These concerns surfaced with great frequency in the themes of conferences and in conference keynote addresses. As a consequence of growing disciplinary engagement, there was more citation-appropriate material to work with. Goggin indicated that while there were 13 journals founded between 1950 and 1980 in RCWS, 10 more journals were founded in the 1980s alone. The separation of the works cited list at the end of each article made it much easier to trace these conversations—to glance them over and quickly apprehend connections, recurrence, and familiarity in the list: in effect, to forge a network sense of the emerging field. This would be true both for those who wanted to cross-reference an in-text citation with the works cited listing while reading the article and also for those who look over the works cited listing before reading the article. The journal now included independently organized data on the scale of individual articles—something systematic that readers of an article could, in a glance, use to know something about the article itself and its relationships to other published work. The network of citations was presented in a more orderly fashion than before; readers could more readily apprehend it. With this design adaptation, the journal as a record of scholarly activity became more portable; it was better suited for the circulation of professional scholarship, and it remains in place today, nearly two decades into the 21st century.

Works Cited

Braddock, Richard, Richard Lloyd-Jones, and Lowell Schoer. *Research in Written Composition*. Champaign: NCTE, 1963.

Burke, Kenneth. "Terministic Screens." *Language as Symbolic Action*. Berkeley: University of California Press, 1966. 44-62.

Coles, William E., Jr. *The Plural I*. New York: Holt, Rinehart and Winston, 1978.

Emig, Janet. "Inquiry Paradigms and Writing." *CCC* 33 (1982): 64-75.

———. "The Tacit Tradition: The Inevitability of a Multi-Disciplinary Approach to Writing Research" in *Reinventing the Rhetorical Tradition*. Eds. Aviva Freedman and Ian Pringle. Ottawa: Canadian Council of Teachers of English, 1980. 9-17.

Hagstrum, Jean H. Review of *Research in Written Composition*. *College English* 26 (1964): 53-56.

Hairston, Maxine. "Breaking Our Bonds and Reaffirming Our Connections." *CCC* 36 (1985): 272-282.

Hillocks, George, Jr. *Research on Written Composition*. Urbana: ERIC Clearinghouse on Reading and Communication Skills, 1986.

Lloyd-Jones, Richard. "Richard Braddock." *Traditions of Inquiry*. Ed. John Brereton. New York: Oxford University Press, 1985. 153-170.

Odell, Lee, and Dixie Goswami, eds. *Writing in Nonacademic Settings*. New York: Guilford, 1985.

Figure 3. CCC Works Cited in 1987. The works cited listing following William F. Irmscher's "Finding a Comfortable Identity" shows the conventional listing endorsed by the Modern Language Association in the late 1980s. Rather than following a sequential logic through the article itself, works cited lists introduced a substitutive logic. Each source referenced in the article would appear just once in a comprehensive listing arranged in alphanumeric order.

A second change to accompany Gebhardt's tenure as editor of *CCC*, the journal with a subscription circulation second only to *College English* among those journals identified with RCWS, was to introduce a double-blind peer review process for the screening of manuscript submissions. Before blind peer review, reviewers knew full well who was submitting an article; identities were not obscured, thus leaving uncertain just how much knowledge (familiarity, kinship, etc.) beyond the article weighed on the assessment of it as scholarship appropriate for publication in *CCC*. When a pool of readers, writers, editors, and reviewers is relatively close-knit, blind peer review would have different consequences, perhaps beset by familiarity biases. But as the field diversified, as graduate programs sprouted and the number of tenure track lines increased, there would be not only a greater number of article submissions but also a greater range of institutional perspectives, methodological preferences, and theoretical orientations as well as a lower rate of acceptance for publication. Blind peer review, for a prominent journal in an emerging field like RCWS, indicates a transition from this relatively familiar cluster of active, known participants to a broader, more heterogeneous (and potentially contentious, where representation in powerful platforms like an international journal is at stake) formation. This might also be framed metaphorically as a shift from the field as small, tight-knit cluster to a more complex constellation, partitioned and intersected by a number of attributes, including the chief cause for this *moment of criticality*: Everyone no longer knew everyone else.

The blind peer review system for *CCC* in 1987 also introduced a condition of scarcity that made the content of the journal appear at once to be rarer and more precious. In his inaugural editor's note (1987), Gebhardt wrote that "over two hundred men and women at universities, liberal arts colleges, and two-year colleges in the United States, Canada, and Australia sent me submissions" (p. 19). Even if this approximation referred to every genre included in the journal, from articles to staffroom interchanges and book reviews, it would indicate an acceptance rate of, at most, just more than 40% for the 1986 publishing cycle. Publication in *CCC* was becoming more competitive—the inevitable result of the transformation of the discipline demonstrated at this time.

Admittedly over-identifying 1987 as the stand-out year in the rising disciplinary status—from emergence to stability—risks eclipsing myriad additional transformative moments in the field's rich history. Certainly a number of other factors and happenings before and after 1987 loosen the somewhat arbitrary temporal boundaries of any given year. For example, on a panel titled "Choragraphies of Composition" at the 2009 Conference on College Composition and Communication, I spoke about 1987 as a moment of criticality, and, in addition, Jeff Rice identified 1949 as a key moment, James Brown pinpointed 1995, Michael McGinnis, 1969, and David Grant, 1994. Across such a long and divergent disciplinary archipelago, these and many additional moments are defensible as catalytic or as points marking a distinctive change. Keying in on 1987, however, my purpose has been to survey *some* of the disciplinary activities that substantiate the mid-1980s as the beginning point for data sets behind the data-visual models featured in Chapters Three and Four. Because I introduce and ultimately promote distant reading and thin description as methods for apprehending and understanding selected aspects of RCWS since 1987, I contend that the factors I have outlined so far explain the timeframe within which I am working. As I will discuss in the final section of this chapter, many of the discipliniographic methods adopted in 1987 are no longer wholly sufficient for deriving generalities about the field 30 years hence. The other conditions I have discussed so far—a burst of discipliniography related to this moment of criticality, the formal adoption of MLA Works Cited format for listing the materials referenced in a scholarly article, and the transition to anonymous peer review—coalesce to point out that with this moment of criticality, the discipline was faced with new opportunities and new challenges, some of which remain unaddressed, or perhaps under-addressed, by the field at large. Since 1987, the field of RCWS continued to witness unbridled change, presenting us with what Kathleen Yancey identified in her 2004 CCCC keynote address as a "moment" (p. 297) in which to reckon such "seismic tremors" (p. 321) in the academy and the world at-large with the changing shape of the discipline.

Accepting that the growth and complexity of the field persisted and even accelerated after 1987—after this critical lurch through one particularly important phase transition—we should begin to understand that the proliferation of the discipline would spell big changes for research methods and specifically those strategies used to make sense of this daunting pile of disciplinary materials. North's contention that "composition's collective fund of knowledge is a very fragile entity" (p. 3) can, in light of this moment of criticality, be regarded as both challenge and prophesy. At the very least, it must be regarded as a harbinger of things to come.

With this necessarily abbreviated historical gloss, this brings us to the cusp of this book's methodological intervention into the discipline. Why distant reading and thin description? Why now? We can begin to formulate a response to these questions by considering three contemporary challenges or quandaries.

First, the broadly defined data associated with the field of RCWS, though it has begun to take shape in recent years, remains generally piecemeal and impoverished. This first problem, then, keys on disciplinary data sets, their collection, review, circulation, and curation. We have, as of yet, few systematic approaches to the basic processes of aggregating detailed information about the people, places, and events that constitute the field and its ecology of activities. This is not to say that the field lacks any data whatsoever. The data exists in pockets; it is intermittent, scattered, and only loosely assembled, often for very specific, temporary purposes. For distant reading and thin descriptive methods to bring about and sustain network sense, the systemic gathering and assembling of data must improve. Further, claims about appreciable trends or key moments, shifts, and "turns" in the field tend to be grounded in irreproducible and laborious data-gathering efforts, on the one hand, or in glancing impressions, which typically rely overmuch on idiosyncratic data and inductive logic, on the other.

Second, as do many other disciplines, RCWS continues to face a complex, expansive reading problem that bears direct relationship to disciplinary epistemology. Accepting that the field itself is constituted significantly by writing (MacDonald, 2010, p. 5; Prior, 1998, p. 27), the discipline piles up and expands at the edges. Writing of teaching lore, Wendy Bishop (1998) extended this expansion to include not only research-based and scholarly texts but also the guides, how-to, and advice books circulating about writing more generally: "More and more of this stuff is being written and published. Lore creates more lore. There's some that's good, some that's bad. There's some that's a joy to read and some that's slow going" (p. 226). This ongoing condition—the field's perpetually being written—means that more disciplinary material is generated than any one person reading by conventional strategies alone could reasonably handle. Specialization is to credit, in part, for this burgeoning, and specialization carries with it hazards of *homophily bias*—the condition observed in networks where small clusters of like-minded people partition themselves off in an echo chamber and tend to proliferate in-group assent. Scholarly materials are produced and circulated in niche journals, both in print and online, as well as in a number of less formal venues. What we need and what distant reading and thin descriptive methods provide are devices suited to supporting those scholars in the field who desire to maintain a generalist's wherewithal—whether out of a sense of professional responsibility or a commitment to intellectual acumen. Both for materials with immediate, direct relevance to the work of the field and for materials that mix and blend, hybrid-like and multimodal as well as inter- and sub-disciplinarily, distant reading and thin descriptive methods offer a practical, viable accessory to claim-making about disciplinarity that is either too cursory and inductive to be theoretically viable or too labor-intensive to be sustained, much less reproducible.

Third, the field has sponsored numerous, ongoing attempts to chronicle its continuing emergence, and these attempts have relied primarily on ethnographic approaches to discipliniography. Scholars and researchers will continue to write the field into existence, often drawing on local knowledge and experience (often at the spatial order of program or institution or the temporal order of appointment or career) to underscore their impressions of what it means to conduct this work with some understanding of the apparatus of disciplinarity, and yet these small-world, inductive reports ought to be reconciled with broader manifestations of disciplinary conditions. Additionally, we need not re-invent the data associated with this broader order of disciplinarity each and every time we wish to comment on it. Distant reading and thin descriptive methods make it possible, in other words, to corroborate one account of the discipline with other selections of disciplinary materials. Because the discipline is sufficiently complex that no one vantage point can claim an omnipotent, ascendant view of its totality, we must not rely not on the local accounts alone but broaden out from the local accounts, re-associating them with the other perspectives on the ongoing, ever-shifting terrain.[4]

These three quandaries—data sets, a reading problem, and appropriate methods, although I have only sketched them briefly, catalyze what I will refer to through the book as the *internal problematic of disciplinarity*. I adopt the phrase "internal problematic" from Moretti (2007), who claimed that distant reading methods "enrich" the "internal problematic" of literary history (p. 2)—that is, a need to slow down, to take into account a larger record of materials than canonical forces typically allow, and to strengthen connections where alternatives to conventional criticism, such as distant reading and thin description, make such strengthening possible. The internal problematic of RCWS is considerably more complex than the three main concerns I have outlined above. Still, the phrase resonates with the pragmatic and theoretical spirits in which this pursuit is presented here as an intervention—as it calls for network sense and, to a modest degree, enacts correctives to these three quandaries.

Data-Mining and Visualization Methods for Rhetoric and Composition/Writing Studies

Late in the fall of 2005, John Unsworth stood before an audience of scholars in the humanities and library sciences where he presented the Lyman Award Lecture, "New Methods for Humanities Research." In his lecture, Unsworth argued that humanities scholars had, since the mid-1980s, witnessed a resurgence of research methods, including data mining, which he claimed

---

4   This tracing of associations may never quite bring us to a total sense of the field, but it does match with what I describe as network sense: the epistemological standpoint that accepts as viable, suggestive forms of knowledge these abstract visual models produced by distant reading and thin descriptive methods. Network sense is highly compatible with a contextualist worldview (such as that elaborated in Phelps's [1991] *Composition as a Human Science*) and with an ambient rhetoric (such as that elaborated by Thomas Rickert [2004] in his article, "In the House of Doing: Rhetoric and the Kairos of Ambience"); the tracing of associations can, relative to this framework, be understood as an instrument harmonious with the priorities of contextualism or ambient rhetorics.

complicate the sense in which humanities research has ordinarily been used to describe "the work of an individual, work that is preparatory to writing, work that results in the publication of a book" (p. 4). Unsworth acknowledged that humanities researchers had yet to sort through the fullness of what data-mining initiatives could offer. Nevertheless, he was optimistic about "profoundly collaborative" interdisciplinary initiatives that had begun exploring data-mining methods as promising paths of inquiry in the humanities. More to the point of what data mining offered, Unsworth explained:

> Data-mining delivers a new kind of evidence into the scene of reading, writing, and reflection, and although it is not easy to figure out sensible ways of applying this new research method (new, at least, to the humanities), doing so allows us to check our sense of the gestalt against the myriad details of the text, and sometimes in that process we will find our assumptions checked and altered, almost in the way that evidence sometimes alters assumptions in science. (p. 18)

Processes by which our assumptions are "checked and altered" ought to underscore the relevance of data-mining methods for RCWS, especially in such cases where something as abstract and unwieldy as a comprehensive discipline is invoked. Data mining, Unsworth pointed out, introduces more varied ways of working with texts, more highly differentiated ways of handling text-related problems. A decade later, data mining has aided researchers in understanding texts differently and in such a way that we are able to reconcile these forms of evidence, "arriv[ing] at a deeper sense of what we already know" (p. 17) and potentially leading to greater awareness of patterns that may or may not have been apprehensible to us before (e.g., see Drucker, 2010; Jockers, 2013; Moretti, 2013).

Unsworth (2005) articulated, as well, some of the ways data-mining initiatives stand apart from usual efforts to catalogue texts so that they are indexed in stable databases, such as search engines. When using databases developed for the purposes of searching digitized materials,

> we bring specific queries to collections of text and get back (more or less useful) answers to those queries; by contrast the goal of data-mining (including text-mining) is to produce new knowledge by exposing similarities or differences, clustering or dispersal, co-occurrence and trends. (p. 7)

In RCWS, CompPile is perhaps the best-known example of a discipline-specific "search-and-retrieval" system, and while it is an adequate database for users who want to enter an author's name and get a listing of all recorded scholarship associated with that name, CompPile is not, in itself, a system that does the sort of data mining modeled in this book, nor, I would argue, does it "produce new knowledge" in quite the way Unsworth described.

Unsworth's leading example of a data-mining project in the humanities was NORA, a two-year collaborative research venture involving more than 17 researchers at multiple universities between 2004 and 2006. According to Unsworth, who delivered his 2005 address at the mid-point of NORA's two-year grant, "the goal of the [NORA] project is to produce text-mining software for discovering, visualizing, and exploring significant patterns across large collections of full-text humanities resources from existing digital libraries and scholarly projects" (p. 7). Within this research cooperative, one representative application of their work can be found in the Java tool written by a Maryland graduate student that "weighted searches across multiple [Emily Dickinson] poems, so that it would be easy to see the poems in which erotic terminology, once identified, seemed to cluster" (p. 13). Data mining, at least in this case, worked at the problem of collectively visualizing semantic associations on a specific theme across the entire Dickinson corpus.

Following NORA's culmination in 2006, the project merged with related projects at a number of other universities and renewed its mission under the acronym MONK, which stands for "Metadata Offer New Knowledge." MONK expanded to involve 32 researchers and scholars at 7 North American universities, and by all indications their work will continue to focus on data-mining software designed to visualize patterns in large-scale humanities corpora, many of which tend to align with literary studies. NORA, and its successor MONK, offer formidable examples of the sort of data-mining work that potentially "delivers a new kind of evidence into the scene of reading, writing, and reflection" (Unsworth, 2005, p. 18). And although this project takes as its primary objects of study scholarly data sets related to RCWS rather than the poetic works of Emily Dickinson, Walt Whitman, or William Blake, NORA and MONK are noteworthy for the "new methods" they initiated, new methods involving data mining and visualization with considerable parallels to the distant reading and thin description demonstrated in Chapters Three through Five of this book.

Distant Reading and Thin Description: Orienting Methods

This book builds on Moretti's distant reading combined with Heather Love's thin description as orienting methods that respond distinctively to the internal problematic of disciplinarity in RCWS—a three-part problematic, as I sketched previously, constituted by

1. inadequate (i.e., partial and unsystematic) collections of data related to the field,

2. a reading problem in which relevant materials are produced at a pace far exceeding anyone's ability to keep up with them by conventional reading strategies alone (specialization is but one inevitable by-product of this condition), and

3. the persistence of disciplinary accounts that either rely on dubious, idiosyncratic evidence for making claims about the field or employ exceedingly laborious methods for surveying the field as to be at once impractical and irreproducible.

Distant reading and thin description allow us to pursue lines of inquiry related to the discipline at-large in ways distinctive from what has been done before.

Distant Reading

Franco Moretti first expressed the phrase *distant reading* in his 2000 *New Left Review* essay "Conjectures in World Literature." Moretti was concerned with means of comparing, historicizing, and apprehending the large-scale phenomenon to differentiate patterns spanning something as complex and sprawling as national literatures, while comparing these sub-categories (and the social histories wrapped up with them) in relationship to world (larger scope) and local (smaller scope) literatures. The intensive labor of such a monumental task is among the leading justifications Moretti offered as rationale for distant reading. Moretti drew a comparison between the aims of distant reading and a slogan credited to French social historian Marc Bloch: "years of analysis for a day of synthesis" (qtd. in Moretti, 2000, para. 8). The phrase underscores a radical shift in scale from something broad and inclusive to something comparably reduced. Among the problems with traditional textual analysis, Moretti noted, was the conventionalized practice of contextualizing a scholarly argument or literary critique by surveying sample after sample of text (albeit by presenting mere slivers of quotation, paraphrase, and summary) that are sufficient to represent the voluminous texts themselves. According to Moretti, much scholarly reading and writing of this variety is already *distant* in that it is filtered and synthesized by others—the concentration of years of reading into mere paragraphs or maybe a page. Distant reading names an alternative to the common practice of writing a literature review, an alternative Moretti accepted as heretical (also, I would argue, *heuristic*, in fitting with Young, Becker, and Pike's [1970] term for negotiating strictly rule-bound and free-ranging rhetorics). Moretti (2000) wrote of distant reading as a "little pact with the devil: we already know how to read texts, now let's learn how *not* to read them" (para. 10). Moretti continued:

> Distant reading: where distance, let me repeat it, *is a condition of knowledge*: it allows you to focus on units that are much smaller or much larger than the text: devices, themes, tropes—or genres and systems. And if, between the very small and the very large, the text itself disappears, well, it is one of those cases when one can justifiably say, Less is more. If we want to understand the system in its entirety, we must accept losing something. We always pay a price for theoretical knowledge: reality is infinitely rich; concepts are abstract, are poor. But it's precisely this 'poverty' that makes it possible to handle them, and therefore to know. This is why less is actually more. (para. 10)

Germinated with distant reading methods are data-mining and visualization methods that can be used to inquire into emerging shapes and patterns in an academic discipline; these, too, offer visually intensive "conditions of knowledge." A sense of the field unfolds from these practices in reduction and simplification, of quantification and aggregation that, by way of these methods, amplifies patterns in textual and extra-textual metadata (e.g., word counts, citation frequencies, and geolocative indicators, among others). Distant reading imposes granularity on the "infinitely rich" object of study. The "disappearance" of the text—one of the more prominent points of critique among skeptics of Moretti's work—is only temporary. It is a deliberate, selective maneuver that admits a broadened context for the work itself, putting the text at a different scale so that relationships may be explored. Moretti's methodology simply challenges us to accept that texts need not be read *exclusively* by the default method in English studies (one text, at the scale of what can be held in the hand) but that there is insight to be gained in differential readerly scales, scales that support inquiry into patterns produced across the largest collection of texts available. With the momentary disappearance is a re-appearance of the text (and also traditional ways of reading), but now the devices for understanding the text become plural and multifaceted, expanding by the treatments Moretti introduced.

Only in recent years, first with the 2007 publication of *Graphs, Maps, Trees: Abstract Models for a Literary Theory* and later with *Distant Reading* in 2013, has Moretti's work on distant reading become more prominent, particularly in English Studies. Both books advance Moretti's thinking about the production of abstract visual models in conjunction with data-mining and distant reading methods. *Graphs, Maps, Trees* was particularly influential on the work that follows. It delivered examples of distant reading but also offered a strange invitation, arguing implicitly for the ways similar processes might assist efforts to work with disciplinary data sets to explore patterns that, if they do not in themselves constitute disciplinarity, certainly offer a highly suggestive complement to existing efforts to chart and chronicle the emergence and maturation of RCWS. Moretti has been studying the sociology of literary forms for his entire scholarly career—a thread both noted and extended by Heather Love in her theorizing of *thin description*.

For example, Moretti (2005) worked through related questions in *Signs Taken for Wonders*, a collection of essays on literary criticism, historiography, genre, and form. He began that book's introduction with an unmistakable invocation of rhetoric. Drawing on the Burkean concept of identification, Moretti explained his interest in the observable relationship between form and "division" (p. 3), a thoroughly social matter concerned also with association and re-association. Rhetoricians have long examined the capacities of discourse to foster unity and division through identification and disidentification, generating senses of belonging, shared purpose, and consensus. I mention this way in which Moretti's work from its earliest presentation has been inflected with rhetorical principles because, although he is a scholar of literary form, he recognized that form is deeply entangled with rhetorical principles and even co-constitutive of sociality (of people and things, beyond community to network, the mobilization of a collective). He refers to the proliferation of forms as a "system of associated commonplaces" (p. 5) and as "doxai" (p. 3), which are significant indicators of consensus—the mobilization of group identification that, even while riddled with and rattled by divisive tendencies, congregates around some shared activity or interest. Moretti explained, "It is no longer a question . . . of contrasting rhetorical (or ideological) 'consent' with aesthetic 'dissent', but of recognizing that there are different moments in the development of every system of consent, and above all different ways of furthering it" (p. 8). For Moretti, he is concerned with literary historiography and forms of mass literature as the systems of consent; these systems coalesce in the novel as canonical, as definitional, as popular, and so on.

I am interested in a different system of consent: the field of RCWS as it has matured since 1987, growing in size, number, and complexity in the intervening years, and built from a fund of materials and knowledge Stephen North (1987) characterized as "a fragile entity" (p. 290). A variety of forms are relevant to this line of inquiry, but the primary form I will consider is the scholarly article—manuscripts published in *College Composition and Communication* over a 25-year period, in addition to a handful of contemporary data sets from conference locations, consortia, and an international survey. A modest collection, in the grand scheme of things, but nevertheless a suggestive beginning point for using distant reading and thin descriptive methods to engage and further provoke insights into disciplinarity.

Distant reading intentionally varies the level of detail at which readers ordinarily engage with texts. It begins with the collection and selection of text-based data (e.g., words and phrases, citations, time stamps, and geolocations), which are then re-made, often with the assistance of computational processes, into abstract visual models. In Moretti's (2013) research, the distant reading models elucidated patterns that had been difficult to apprehend because of the magnitude of materials under consideration. Graphical representations, therefore, help to clarify the large collections derived by data- and text-mining processes. Data appropriate to distant reading come in many forms, but they are typically textual. From rudimentary counts of things, such as the number of articles published in a given journal over a specific number of years, to those data sets that are not so self-evident or easy to collect, like the keyword confluences of large corpora of texts over time, distant reading names a methodology interested in the pursuit of granularity that elucidates patterns. Counting journal articles and selected attributes, laborious though it may be, can be accomplished manually (it is no less valuable for this reason, of course). But because of the enormity of the task, distant reading is most often a hybrid methodology that thoughtfully merges automatic, computational processes with the agency of the researcher whose inquiry gives shape to the project. This means that much of the data collected and produced in accordance with distant reading relies upon computer-aided aggregation and reassembly. But distant reading is best understood as a hybrid orchestration of methods, neither wholly manual in their data-gathering techniques, nor entirely technical, automatic, or uniform from one application to the next.

Thin Description

The methodology forwarded in this book pairs distant reading with thin description. Thin description has been articulated by literary theorist Heather Love as a recuperative hermeneutics that calls for humanities scholars to reconsider the value of first impressions and descriptions of texts. In "Close Reading and Thin Description," Love (2013) noted the sweeping reception of Clifford Geertz's (1977) thick description, calling attention to the ways it provided a bridge between text-interpretive hermeneutics and social anthropology by framing cultures as texts best read by immersed participant–observers. Love (2013) argued convincingly that the warm reception of thick description has operated since the mid-1970s as a variety of depth fetishism whereby interpreting deeply and more deeply still stands as the hallmark of rigorous engagement with any variety of objects of analysis, from literary texts to discourse communities. Thin description, however, interrupts this general narrative with a reminder that something of value is overlooked in the frenzy over thickness, depth, and closeness.

Love (2013) re-evaluated Clifford Geertz's use of a "turtles all the way down" methodology to loosen the association of thinness with behaviorism and functionalism. As Love pointed out, "turtles all the way down" looms as a ready, stalwart, antifoundationalist maxim. It gradually ascends to commonplace status, and as it does so, it risks skewing empirical inquiry in the human and social sciences toward unending plumbings of ever-deeper depths, ever richer richnesses. Love wrote,

> Formulas such as . . . 'it is turtles all the way down' suggest that there is no bottom slice, or at least not one that can be distinguished from the upper layers of the sandwich. Geertz's attack was aimed at traditional empiricism, the habit of thought that tendentiously identified the bottom slice as the 'factual basis' of reality. (p. 409)

While Geertz's introduction of thick description to anthropology was meant as a timely corrective of interpretation over observation, Love (2013) suggested about "surface reading" that "it is possible to translate the concept into Geertz's terms: what can we learn by looking very carefully at the topmost turtle?" (p. 412). Turned toward questions of disciplinary emergence and formation—as well as to the material basis for disciplinarity itself, which, according to Paul Prior (1998) is "centered around texts, around the literate activities of reading and writing" (p. 27)—this book pursues a comparable question: Can we begin with noticing and describing first the topmost turtle and thereby become familiar with the turtle heap as an interconnected, networked phenomenon? The pairing of distant reading and thin description offers a flexible methodological framework within which to attempt to conduct this inquiry.

Heather Love theorized *thin description* with only glancing reference to Moretti's distant reading, though her framing provided a valuable counterpart to distant reading, especially when they are paired as a methodological basis for the data-visual work that I argue is vital for contemporary discipliniography as well as for fostering a network sense of the expanding field. Thin description names Love's attempt to refocus literary studies on the positive epistemological gains located in empirical noticing, reconcilable sensory experiences, and techniques for sampling, selection, and reduction.

Such a refocusing complicates and complements disciplinary gravitation in literary studies toward deep reading and immersive ethnographic methodologies that seek to *textualize* experience, or to regard complex, worldly activity and interaction as *text-like*. Like Moretti, Love focused her methodology on the centrality of texts as well as on particular attitudes toward texts and the kinds of work worth doing with them. However, Love's thin description moved beyond the normative epistemology in literary and cultural studies that has cemented around Geert'z thick description as a way of reading culture *qua* text. Love (2013) argued for a different mindset that resists taking thin description for granted, noting as exigency and corrective that Geertz-influenced methods have "tended to overlook the importance . . . of thin description" (p. 403).

Love advanced arguments for thin description as an interest in what textual-materiality can tell us about a phenomenon rooted in texts but not necessarily beholden to language-based interpretation alone—impression–encounters, glances, and what Erving Goffman (1974) called *strips*, intentionally narrowed selections of interaction that facilitate analysis. Another way to think about this, according to Love (2013), is to "reverse the process of textualization that Geertz describes" (p. 430). This sort of move by a researcher is useful for managing scope and for contextualizing interactions; it seeks to postpone deep-destination plumbings of hermeneutical depth and investments of meaning beyond meaning *en abyme* (i.e., bottomlessly) to instead inventory what is observable. Given that her methodology has circulated in literary journals and with an audience of literary and cultural studies scholars in mind, Love's case for thin description primarily set out to navigate literary studies debates concerning the value of close reading, although she does so with the aim of counterbalancing any assumption that close reading and thick description are, unto themselves, superior to alternative engagements with objects of study. Thin description insists on the value of other ways of knowing, that, although reductive, establish first impressions and operate as important sites of initiation for further inquiry. As a literary scholar, Love's arguments are invested primarily in urging reconsideration of an empirical research tradition and its "range of potentially useful tools" (p. 219) in service of reading.

While this brief account on thin description situates Love's work in the context of her scholarship on the subject, perhaps the clearest handle on thin description is how it contributes a perspective on data visualization and graphical modeling known as *thinning practices*. The text falls away; the data falls away; and, in its place, a gloss stands in. Thinning practices, or synecdochal techniques, name a set of substitutive operations in which a right-sized (usually reduced, smaller) surrogate stands in for a more complex whole. Thin description aptly names Love's theoretical argument for humanities scholars and particularly those in literary studies to recognize the epistemological force of such practices.

Representing Distant and Thin Through Visual Epistomologies

The interdependence of distant reading, thin description, and abstract visual models necessitates a more rigorous conception of visuality appropriate to the rhetoricity of the data visualizations they work together to inform. Johanna Drucker's (2010, 2014) theorization of *graphesis* is a significant ally to Moretti's and Love's efforts and also to the data-mining methods Unsworth identified in his 2005 address. Drucker (2010) set up graphesis as a point of convergence that effectively middles the tendencies toward visualization (a *mathesis* that predominates in quantitative sciences) and art (an *aesthesis* that predominates in the arts). Graphesis is highly compatible with efforts to render abstract visual models that refashion massive collections of data for the humanities—compatible in the sense that Drucker's approach is centrally concerned with "the study of visual epistemology as a dynamic, subjective process" (p. 21).

In Drucker's 2010 work on graphesis, she emphasized a hybrid and multidisciplinary orientation to visual epistemology. Rather than assuming the "cultural authority of objectivity" (p. 3), graphesis works simply by "defining entities and their relations" (p. 19) in such a way that might enable us to trace associations and patterns among concepts without diminishing the interplay of interests, data, and aesthetics. According to Drucker, "Graphesis is premised on the idea that an image, like a text, is an aesthetic provocation, a field of potentialities, in which a viewer intervenes. Knowledge is not transferred, revealed, or perceived, but is created through a dynamic process" (p. 29). Unlike those approaches to data visualization that treat the visual mode of presentation as neutral, objective, or purely rational, Drucker's work on graphesis pushes us to reconcile visual models with the interests they serve and with the design choices that have gone into their making. In short, graphesis resituates data visualization and visual modeling in the wheelhouse of rhetoric, thereby making such abstracting practices more responsible because they are now understood to be *motivated and performative.*

With the provocations articulated by Unsworth (viz., data mining), the methodological demonstrations presented by Moretti (viz., distant reading) and Love (viz., thin description), and the theorization of visual epistemology offered by Drucker (viz., graphesis), a groundwork is in place to apply these methods to disciplinary data sets and corpora.

Network Sense: Continuations Toward Self-Understanding of a Discipline

> On what basis can we articulate an idea of composition as a discipline? (Phelps, 1991, p. 41)

The knotted relationship between distant reading and thin description methods and close reading surfaces in work by Moretti and Love, and as such, it warrants direct acknowledgement when adopting these methods. The parallels can perhaps best be addressed by turning to a pair of articles from the 2006 *College English* symposium on "What Should College English Studies Be?": one on close reading by Don Bialostosky and another on networks and new media by Jeff Rice. Read in combination, a merger formed between them, and we find another way of accounting not only for the limited distinctions between close reading, distant reading, and thin description, but we also see yet another example of how distant reading methods are inventive and generative as well as what such methods, by abstracting, concretely produce. Bialostosky makes his brief contribution to the symposium as someone whom we might identify as a cautionary advocate of close reading. In response to the question asked in his piece, "Should College English Studies be Close Reading?," Bialostosky offered a heavily qualified "yes." With this affirmative response, he explained, "I want instead to open a space for considering alternatives to New Critical close reading by marking out, without naming, a pedagogical space where we teach productive attentiveness to literary texts" (p. 113). Is this a space within which distant reading might gain further justificatory hold? Perhaps so. The chances for this happening improve once we accept (as, most assuredly, not everyone will) that distant reading methods promote and even insist upon a "productive attentiveness to . . . texts" (p. 113). The removal of "literary" here is necessary to assert rhetoric and composition's more expansive interest in writing and not exclusively literary texts. The adoption of Moretti's methods is admittedly selective in this regard. I am bringing along what I find in his methodology to be most usable and useful while also letting certain other aspects fall away (e.g., his application of evolutionary biology and his focal interest in literary genres). Bialostosky's contribution to the symposium, like the others, has a distinctive pedagogical flavor; his response, like Rice's, implied that the invitation to address "What Should College English Studies Be?" will be answered in the classroom. I address the applicability of distant reading and thin description methods to pedagogy later; however, here I invoke Bialostosky because his elaboration of close reading scrapes the concept (both as methodology and as pedagogy) free from some of the residual New Critical burdens that have accumulated over the years. Judging by the spirit of Bialostosky's argument, he would agree that close reading, distant reading, and thin description, are only helpful if they are reconciled with the question of what reading practices we consider important enough to teach.

For distant reading and thin description to be viewed as inventive and generative, as heuristic, we must read Bialostosky's expansion of close reading in tandem with Jeff Rice's (2006) contribution to the symposium. Rice answered "new media" and, more precisely, aspects of networks as connective, associative phenomenon proliferating throughout the digital, informational domains. "College English has not yet imagined or perceived itself as a network" (p. 128), Rice wrote. The ways "networks alter current understandings and rhetorical output still need unpacking and further study" (p. 132), Rice cited N. Katherine Hayles's suggestion of linking as an emerging form of expression and William Burroughs's anticipation of "the rise of the network as rhetoric" (p. 130), as we "reimagine English studies' efforts to generate a 21st century focus" (p. 130). Rice identified a key moment in the edited collection *Composition in the Twenty-First Century*, where David Bartholomae explained composition's focus on "the space on the page and what it might mean to do work there and not somewhere else" (qtd in Rice, 2006, p. 130). Rice emphasized Bartholomae's differentiation between the page and the "not somewhere else," suggesting that, in fact, new media and networks compel us toward the *somewhere else*, "the open space constructed out of connections where multiple writers engaging within multiple ideas in multiple media at multiple moments function" (p. 130). Rice's "writing as network" breaks the fixity of established knowledge typical in much of English studies (p. 129–131) and allows a space where distant reading and thin description make it possible for us to create a network sense of disciplinarity.

The combined aims of Bialostosky and Rice together form a keen lens through which distant reading and thin description become recognizable not strictly as a text-focused methodology but also an approach to unwieldy, systemic complexity of disciplinarity, of which texts are only a small part. Their pairing is especially suggestive for their shared concern in an "open space" that, for Bialostosky, offered a revision of close reading that frames it as productive attention and, for Rice, asserted the value in "somewhere else" in the rhetorical networks proliferating via digital practices of reading and writing. Distant reading and thin description render these networked "somewhere else's" traceable, conferring on large-scale data sets a granularity that makes ties observable and renders patterns visible as well as makes new forms of knowledge unavailable to us by other means. This is the way in which these methods are inventive, generative, and productive, doing something more than renewing the interpretation of existing texts. Distant reading and thin description methods and the abstract visual models produced in the second half of this project catalyze what I call *network sense*—an epistemological capacity for discerning those patterns entangled with a broad set of forces running through and beyond the text, involving matters of semantic associations, historical orientations, locations, and relationships. Distant reading and thin description advance network sense; network sense finds tangible coherence in complexity, making available a means of elucidating these discursive and extra-discursive "somewhere else's" without compromising their magnitude or downplaying their abundance. As I have claimed, distant reading and thin description afford us a contemporary methodology that, by promoting network sense, makes it possible for us to come at the internal problematic of RCWS differently than has been done before.

Up to this point, I have tried to show clear, persuasive, and informative paths leading toward a point of convergence for the two primary scholarly phenomena that motivate this book. On the one hand, this is a project interested in discipliniography; on the other hand, it is a project that has an interest in advancing new and emerging methods for engaging with the internal problematic of RCWS. Now that we have arrived at a nexus—the intersection of distant reading and thin description methods and discipliniography—there remains the task of examining more closely what happens once we are here. Some familiarity with attempts to write the discipline is helpful in this endeavor and will become evident in the final section of this opening chapter, where I offer more about the reading problem and look at two recent scholarly efforts to write the discipline, one by Wendy Hesford and another by Richard Fulkerson.

Epitomes of Rhetoric and Composition/Writing Studies

Rhetoric and composition/writing studies has grown in size and complexity since its modern emergence, rapidly folding in on itself more deeply through compound specialization and also branching in constant recombination where it meets with other disciplinary interests and formations. This point has been well established. Compared with 20 or 40 years ago, today there is more scholarship to read in the form of journal articles, monographs, and edited collections; there are more forums within which disciplinary concerns are discussed, from national and regional conferences to blogs and listservs. At the outset of this chapter, I suggested that while discipliniographic efforts have persisted since the moment of criticality I locate for RCWS in 1987, many of the more recent attempts to chronicle the discipline have grown ever more acute in the slice of the field with which they deal. Contemporary discipliniography, in other words, increasingly works in epitomes—bibliocentric slices: summaries, abridgements, and representative cases, many of which are paired with inductive methods or justified tacitly by felt sense[5] or many years of "living among," as was the case for North. Looking at two examples will further illustrate certain constraints impinging on contemporary discipliniography while also demonstrating how distant reading and thin description methods can assist in creating devices for sizing up the field *differently* through multiple, selectable layers of aggregable data and metadata, that is, through thinning practices that underscore disciplinary knowledge as network sense. These examples will also shed light on the lack of field-wide data and metadata as one ongoing challenge for the field.

Before working directly with the two cases that cap this chapter, the concept of *epitomes* deserves more extensive elaboration. The term is roughly synonymous with the representative anecdote; epitomes selectively sample from something large, unwieldy, and complex; identifying an epitome involves *a cut* (epi-), an act at once of incorporation and neglect (i.e., look at *this*, but not all of *that*). Epitomes are thin descriptions in that they do away with the bulkiness of the minute record so that they can amplify; they require separation as a function of weeding out in the interest of illustration. The very concept of epitome refers both to the cut and to a book (-tome). As a paragraph-long abstract is to a scholarly article, an epitome is to a book-length tract. These synecdochal techniques condense, yielding a tree from the dense forest. Epitomes, like other synecdochal techniques, have their limitations; they are dangerous for their neatness and partiality, and therefore they must be read back through a more comprehensive record—as comprehensive as is available.

First, consider Wendy Hesford's May 2006 *PMLA* article, "Global Turns and Cautions in Rhetoric and Composition Studies," a 10-page bibliographic essay that makes use of 102 citations. Hesford traced the *topoi* of "global studies and transnational cultural studies" back through scholarship of the field, in the interest of showing how "scholars in rhetoric and composition studies are meaningfully contributing to conversations about the pressures of globalization and the consequences of the new United States nationalism" (p. 788). Hesford concluded, based on this sizable selection of scholarly materials, that the field is turning to "national public rhetoric in the United States (Lazare) and its reception by global audiences (Booth)" (p. 797). Corroborating Hesford's conclusions, or even countering or complicating them,

---

5   *Felt sense* is a bodily epistemology informed by intuition and by wide-ranging, combinatory sensory experiences. I define it further in Chapter 6, informed by Sondra Perl and others. But here I am letting the concept stand as-is from my own thinking about felt sense.

would require not only reading the heap of texts listed in her works cited; it would require us to reconcile the proposed turn with any number of other disciplinary indicators, such as the scholarship *not* overtly about globalization and nationalism (an examination that would wonder *what other turns are there?*—a matter I will address in Chapter Three); the dissertations produced by PhDs in the field in a given year (Miller, 2014); as well as graduate course descriptions, job advertisements, and any number of other archives, many of which have not been systematically collected or, as of yet, studied. Furthermore, Hesford's bibliographic essay is relatively (i.e., recognizably) conventional for the way it works primarily with scholarly materials as an indication of some *epitomic* characteristic. This is a case where discipliniography and bibliography run parallel courses; a disciplinary turn, therefore, can be traced through the scholarship alone.

Hesford's summation is impressive for the scope of the materials she draws upon, yet she makes it clear that the article is forged from reading she did not purely of her own choice and volition but rather as a member of a book award committee. In a footnote, Hesford (2006) noted that "the major archive for this project consists of nearly 40 books nominated for the 2005 Conference on College Composition and Communication Outstanding Book Award" (p. 797). Hesford continued in the note to explain,

> Additionally, I reference several initiatives that provide critical opportunities for thinking through what the global turn means in terms of research methods, pedagogy, and theory building in rhetoric and composition studies. This self-imposed constraint has made feasible a critical bibliographic essay of this length, which serves as a barometer of the pressures of globalization on the changing profession. (p. 797)

Read almost 40 books, reconcile them with another 60 or so sources you already know, trace a theme across the full collection, and identify it as a barometer for a turn in the field—I offer this as a simplistic, though not unfair, sketch of Hesford's methods. We can (and *do*) take Hesford at her word. It helps knowing Hesford's well-deserved scholarly reputation and having read many of the books on her list, which affirms what her synthesis of them suggests. More than settling whether this synthesis is plausible, however, I am interested here in matching up what Hesford *did* with what distant reading and thin description methods *do*.

With this in mind, looking again at Hesford's work, we see that its success depended upon an intensely laborious method of collecting, reading, and reducing a heap of texts into a handful of abridgments. To reproduce her findings, one would first have to read all her sources—again, sources gathered for her and others on the book award committee by the more or less arbitrary criteria of one year's worth of scholarly monographs. Revisiting the sources alone would not be sufficient, however, because any persistent thematic pattern would then have to be reconciled with other knowledge about the field and its reach. Let me put it another way: Could distant reading and thin description methods have led us to these same conclusions? If, in addition, for these nearly 40 books, we had tag clouds, citation frequency graphs, and maps suggestive of, say, geographical interest, would the same conclusions be available to us? These questions are not easy to answer without carrying out the project (perhaps this is an undertaking worth pursuing down the line). But Hesford's brief bibliographic essay is striking for how much thin description it already does without presenting any visual models. For instance, much of her collection of resources falls away; it disappears! In place of full texts, we have quotations, titles, and some analytical stitching. How far removed is this approach from the "pact with the devil" that Moretti (perhaps jokingly) identified in 2000 with distant reading, that this is "one of those cases when one can justifiably say, Less is more" (para. 10)? The purpose of the bibliographic essay is much like Moretti's: the substitution of the default, full-text experience of reading for one's self with another variety of reading, via someone else's gloss, a variation on not reading. Yet, the genre of the bibliographic essay does not attract nearly so vocal charges of heresy as does Moretti's distant reading.

The resemblance I am suggesting between distant reading, thin description, and bibliographic work is not unique to Hesford's *PMLA* essay, epitomic though her essay is. Bibliographic essays extrapolate patterns from large, complex collections. Importantly, the practice of producing bibliographies shifted in the late 1980s. Noted rhetoric and composition bibliographer Richard Larson last published his annual "Selected Bibliography of Scholarship on Composition and Rhetoric" in the October 1988 issue of *College Composition and Communication* (*CCC*). It was a bibliography accounting for 82 works from the year 1987. Following several of the indicators I described earlier in this chapter, it stands to reason that the scope of the field was thereafter insurmountable relative to any one person's attempt to account *comprehensively* for the published record in any annual cycle. Like discipliniographies subsequent to 1987, bibliographic essays, including Hesford's, have narrowed, settling into identifiable niches and specializations. Contemporary discipliniographers have resorted to tactics other than the tracing of themes across a sampling of scholarly publications, although this method is highly effective and well recognized in most academic fields. The difficulty with bibliographic essays is that as the body of works increases, so does the intensity of the task and the degree of selectivity of the sample. It is exceedingly laborious to extrapolate patterns from such a deep well of textual material. But this not the only approach to identifying turns in the field.

A second, far more inductive method is on display in Richard Fulkerson's "Composition at the Turn of the Twenty-First Century," which appeared in the June 2005 issue of *CCC*. Fulkerson has written article-length surveys of the discipline approximately every 10 years since 1979, when *CCC* published his essay, "Four Philosophies of Composition," bridging pragmatism, mimeticism, expressivism, and objectivism with rhetoric and composition. Fulkerson's early work proceeded like so many of the early readings of the discipline in the 1980s. In "Composition Theory in the Eighties," Fulkerson (1990) revisited his "Four Philosophies" piece and concluding that consensus had started to coalesce around a "rhetorical axiology" (p. 411). As rhetoric became a shared value in the field, those viable philosophies from a decade earlier—expressivism, mimeticism, and formalism—waned. Continuing his assessment of decade-long trends in the field, Fulkerson's (2005) "Composition at the Turn of the Twenty-First Century" raises difficult questions about the adequacy of his evidence for perceiving disunity in the field and the "new theory wars" (a phrase he borrowed from Scott McLemee in *Inside Higher Ed* [2003]). Fulkerson claimed "that we have diverged again. Within the scholarship, we currently have three alternative axiologies (theories of value): the newest one, 'the social' or 'social-construction' view, which values critical cultural analysis; an expressive one; and a multifaceted rhetorical one" (p. 655). Fulkerson proceeded with "mapping Comp-landia," staking out the conceptual terrain suggestive of certain formations in the field (p. 655).

Fulkerson's chief resources for identifying the field's disconcerting pattern of divergence in the new millennium were two tables of content of edited collections on the teaching of writing: one table from *Eight Approaches to Teaching Composition*, published in 1980; another table from *A Guide to Composition Pedagogies*, published in 2001. With a cursory comparison of the two tables, Fulkerson found that the volume published in 2001 includes four titles whose related themes were not represented in the 1980 collection.

> The major difference shows up in chapters 5 to 8 of the new volume. They have no parallels in the older one. These four chapters represent variations of the major new area of scholarly interest in composition as we begin the 21st century, critical/cultural studies (CCS), showing the impact of postmodernism, critical/cultural studies, and British cultural studies. (p. 657)

With this as the identified catalyst for his argument about the field's compounding disunity, Fulkerson proceeded with an analysis of the four axiologies he perceived to be drawing the field asunder: current/tradition-al rhetoric, expressivism, critical/cultural studies, and procedural rhetoric. Fulkerson was most highly critical of the critical/cultural studies thread in the more recent pedagogy collection because he saw it as aligned not with the teaching of writing but with the political pursuit of liberation; the cur-rent-traditional axiology, on the other hand, was treated as a given and was not subject to critique in any extended, explicit way, like the others were. Fulkerson's *modus operandi* is clarified through his critique; his own critical emphasis on CCS raises questions about the ease with which these two tables of content (an alarmingly small sample of evidence for such wide-reaching claims about the field's disunity) came to light. The dubious nature of his set-up with the tables of content is further stressed by his neglect of tech-nology—a matter which, although slight in its representation in the 2001 collection (with just one essay), was not mentioned at all in the 1980 collec-tion—and one which can hardly be overlooked in anything attempting to account for field-wide axiological turns in the 21st century.

Where Hesford's bibliographic essay gives us what she identified meta-phorically as a barometer, Fulkerson's article, by his own framing, gave us a map of Comp-landia, a survey pervaded with spatial and navigational phras-es. Yet, even though Fulkerson attributed his map to the two tables of con-tent, his approach is implicated with claims based largely (if not solely) on more than 30 years of accumulated experience in the field. Keeping with the mapping metaphor, this presents a problem with *ground-truthing*, the prac-tice by which cartographers (especially digital cartographers) venture into the terrain itself in search of discordance between the map and the landscape. Beyond the principle of validation, it is a dynamic practice, one that accepts the constant transformation, fluidity, and adaptiveness of the space being rep-resented. Should a newcomer to the field pick up both edited collections iden-tified by Fulkerson, the experience of reading them might or might not match up with his conclusions because of the inferences he drew from more than 30 years of experience. In fact, Fulkerson acknowledged that the density of the bibliographic essays in the 2001 volume "frequently makes daunting reading even for old hands" (p. 657). Fulkerson's map of Comp-landia is drawn not so much from a shared (or sharable) perspective on the field as it is from local, tacit knowledge, an epitome of composition derived from the accumulated experience of "living among"—much like North's.

The connection with North is more than capricious. Fulkerson conclud-ed his article with direct reference to North's (1987) *The Making of Knowl-edge in Composition*, as follows:

> In *The Making of Knowledge in Composition*, Stephen North
> asserted that 'composition faces a peculiar methodological
> paradox: its communities cannot get along well enough to
> live with one another, and yet they seem unlikely to survive
> [. . .] without one another' (369). I suggest the paradox is
> now not just methodological, but axiological, pedagogical,
> and processual. If you think this is a dangerous situation, as
> North and I do, then early in the twentieth-first [sic] centu-
> ry, composition studies is in for a bumpy ride. (p. 681)

Here, the temporal gap—an interlude collapsed into "North and I"—deserves careful consideration. North's claims about methodological pluralism, after all, were presented nearly 20 years before Fulkerson's claims about
the trends toward disunity and fragmentation in the field. On many levels,
Fulkerson's speculative conclusion—whether it is right or not that RCWS "is
in for a bumpy ride"—affirms what I proposed at the beginning of this chapter: With the growing complexity of the field past the moment of criticality
I locate in 1987, our methods for apprehending large-scale patterns in the
scholarly materials of the discipline have fallen behind and become cum-
bersome. What were once adequate methods for sizing up the discipline
(i.e., North's 10 years of "living among") are, these 20 years later, insufficient
for grasping the complexity in such a sprawling, widespread phenomenon.
Even though Fulkerson located a suggestive artifact of the field's turn in the
comparison between the two tables of content, his method is by and large ex-
perience-based and inductive, drawing on 20 more years of "living among"
than North had when he wrote his landmark monograph. Whether or not
he is right—and he very well may be right that deep discord surrounding
good writing, writing processes, and pedagogy pervade the discipline—the
combination of his two forms of evidence nevertheless present us with no
viable means for corroborating his claims except by inference, comparing
them helter-skelter with our own perceptions of the field—an especially
compromised undertaking for readers of his work who do not share his
many years of experience in the field. Respondents (Chidsey Dickson, Jaime
Mejía, Jeffrey Zorn, and Patricia Harkin) to his essay in the June 2006 "Interchanges" section of *CCC* make this concern explicit: Jaime Mejía, for instance, questioned whether Fulkerson's commentary "realistically reflect[s]
'the composition landscape'" (p. 744); Jeffrey Zorn took exception as well,
noting, "None of [Fulkerson's framework] informs a moment of what I do in
any of my writing classes, but I'm used to that" (p. 751). The interchange is an
outpouring of local, immediate experience that contrasts with Fulkerson's
own limited view of a complex, cosmopolitan domain.

Two approaches to contemporary discipliniography, then, and two variations on how the field is known have been presented here: one by heavily sampling the scholarship in a given year as Hesford has done, and the other by comparing tables of content from edited collections at 20 years' removal and then underscoring selected differences with first-hand, experiential knowledge as Fulkerson has done. One is daunting because of the labor intensivity of the task of reading and synthesizing more than 40 books and related materials into a 10-page manuscript; the other is challenging because inductive, inferential conclusions about something so abstract as the field can, even with 30 years of experience, be at best partial and localized. Neither of the pre-conditions to knowledge-claims about the field offered by Hesford or Fulkerson is easily reproduced except by reading extensively and exhaustively or by working for many years in the field.

If I have seemed up to this point critical of their work that has not been my intention. My aim here has been to identify and describe the methods that back each of their discipliniographic accounts—accounts that present firm conclusions about turns in the field of RCWS. The works by Hesford and Fulkerson should crystallize the immensity of the internal problematic of the field in the terms I presented earlier—that field-wide data and metadata are impoverished, that claim-making about the field tends to be problematic in direct proportion to the degree such claims are (a) highly specialized (drawing on niche knowledge) or (b) highly inductive (drawing on experiential knowledge), and that (c) the unceasing proliferation of disciplinary materials makes it ever more difficult to be a generalist reader. The internal problematic—which, no doubt, extends beyond the three points of emphasis I have included here—is intractable from the complex, multifarious, dynamic organization that is the field.

Can we know such an abstract agglomeration of activities and things except by the means modeled by Hesford and Fulkerson? If, as I believe, disciplinary understanding and invention is foremost a matter of network sense—that is, of apprehending traceable connections among people, places, concepts, and values—then distant-thin methods and the abstract visual models produced by these means have much to offer. The purpose of this book is to demonstrate how such methods might make a formidable intervention into the epitomic practices of writing the discipline. The field's rising complexity has outpaced the conventional techniques available to account for it. Efforts must be expanded to render disciplinarity traceable—to envision the field as networked phenomena, phenomena that can be found in the imaged patterns that emerge over long periods of time and vast collections of materials.

Chapter 2: Patterned Images of a Discipline: Database, Scale, Pattern

Visualizing a Discipline

Over the last two decades, numerous researchers, artists, and software developers have produced work that shares basic qualities with distant reading and thin descriptive methods and that by demonstrative force add depth and credence to those methods' viability. Gathering a few of these projects—to notice them and to become more directly familiar with their designs—is useful for establishing a richer notion of the practices and operations involved with distant–thin methods. Of course, not all of these projects—a small sample of which are listed below—follow distant–thin methods *self-consciously*, nor do all of them identify with RCWS or with the digital humanities, but they nevertheless add up to a rising investment in alternative treatments of large, complex, and unwieldy textual collections—across a variety of domains, academic, popular, and public–civic. In each of the following examples, data sets were transformed into something different—a tag cloud, an interactive network visualization, a weighted list, a re-arranged film, and so on, each punctuating the recent history of distant reading and thin description and indicating an expanding methodological milieu for the 21st century that augments the traditionally privileged inquiry-proximities of the close and the thick.

- *Wordcount* by computer programmer and artist Jonathan Harris. Harris's (2004) website described WordCount as "an artistic experiment in the way we use language." The project displays all the words from the British National Corpus in a horizontal sequence based on commonness, or frequency of appearance.
- Michael J. Faris's visualizations of citation networks among queer rhetorical scholarship. The in-progress (as of October 2017) project includes six different network visualizations based on nearly 250 publications.
- The serialized, iterative publications of chapters from Franco Moretti's *Graphs, Maps, Trees* (2007) as articles in the *New Left Review*, beginning in November–December of 2003 and continuing for two

subsequent issues through the summer of 2004. Later the articles were expanded and paired with additional projects based on the methodology in *Distant Reading* (2013).

- Producer Lenka Clayton's (2002) release of the film *Qaeda, Quality, Question, Quickly, Quickly, Quiet*, which rearranged George W. Bush's 2002 State of the Union address by splicing the film into individual word-utterances before re-ordering them alphabetically.

- Jeremy Tirrell's (2012) mapped histories of online rhetoric and composition journals, which plotted locations where digital scholarship has been produced, weighted phrases as localizable themes in digital scholarship, and proposed as promising and possible many more maps that resonate with the disciplinary atlas I sketch in Chapter Five.

- Nathan Yau's (2010) Walmart Growth Map, which presents U.S.-based geolocations for new Walmart and Sam's Club stores as a map-based time series.

- The Writing Studies Tree, a collaborative data-gathering and visualization initiative that its developers (Miller, Licastro & Belli, 2016) characterize as "a crowdsourced, online, open-access, interactive database of individual scholars, educational institutions, and the disciplinary movements that connect them." The tree generates interactive network visualizations (i.e., zoomable, clickable) for more than 4,568 relationships among 1,744 people and 495 institutions indicative of multivariable disciplinary genealogies (Benjamin Miller, 2017, personal communication).

Although these seven projects range from scholarly publications and software applications to more experimental and artistic installations, they represent an eclectic collection that indicates how distant reading and thin description can be used to render apprehensible nonobvious patterns intrinsic to complex and relatively large data sets. As such, they also prime—and in the case of Faris's work, Tirrell's work, and the Writing Studies Tree *carry out*— new practices that extend distant and thin methodologies to engage with the rising complexity of RCWS. That is, taken together, these projects suggest some of the ways disciplinary activity might be rendered as visually traceable, the field thereby modeled as dynamic and complex networked phenomena.

Surveying this broader collection of precursors to *network sense*, let's consider one additional example in greater detail to understand how distant–thin methods have as a contemporary development emerged amidst visual modeling and abstracting practices, and, even more precisely, how database, scale, and pattern operate as bridging concepts for such work.

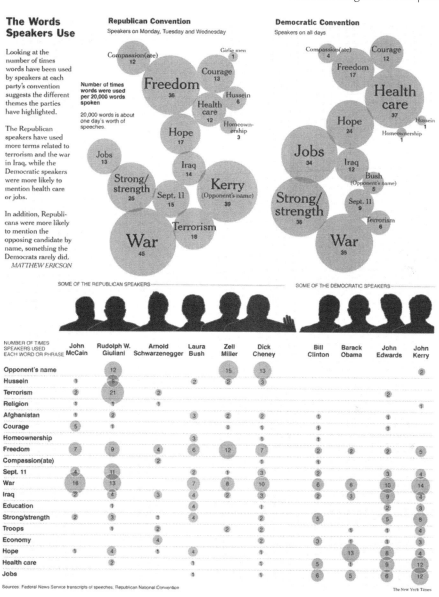

Figure 4. The New York Times infographic "The Words Speakers Use."
This infographic adopts a tabular bubble chart to highlight concentrations
of convention speakers prior to the 2004 U.S. presidential election.

On Thursday, September 2, 2004, following the Democratic and Republican National Conventions, Matthew Ericson's color infographic (see Fig. 4) appeared on the front page of *The New York Times*. Dotted with an assortment of red and blue circles, the graphic presented a bubble graph to indicate the "number of times words were used per 20,000 words spoken" by speakers at each of the national conventions leading up to the presidential elections later that fall. The infographic prompted considerable buzz in the days that followed—mentions of its memorable adaptation of bubble graphs to stand in for recurrent words and phrases stirred in conversations among those following the approaching election or those interested in the methodology of its rendering. The information graphic drew attention specifically for the way it aggregated key words from the lengthy transcripts, translating the debates into an abstract visual model—thin and distant—that concentrated several days of convention addresses into just a few column inches of front page space. Further, the information graphic boosted interest in what was at the time an expanding set of automated tools available online for processing samples of texts, from single paragraphs and simple lists to full chapters, monographs, and speech transcripts into a concordance of recurring terms.

"The Words Speakers Use" information graphic operates in this chapter as an anchoring example of data visualization techniques used to render variously scaled textual corpora. Similar processes—typically grouped under the heading of text mining or data mining—have been around for decades, but until recently, they were not so widely available for timely, inexpensive, everyday use. Data-mining methods involve varying degrees of complexity depending on which parts of text are to be treated. Historical precedents for data mining span the work of linguists and indexers and include the labor-intensive pre-digital initiatives to develop concordances for large collections of legalistic, literary, and religious texts. Undeniably these precedents have bearing for the methods carried out across this project. Rather than develop more deeply the history of generating keyword concordances, for now, I refer to "The Words Speakers Use" because it pinpoints one watershed moment for distant–thin methods circulated publicly as an infographic. As such, it also reinforces the connections among Franco Moretti's distant reading, Heather Love's thin description, and Johanna Drucker's theorization of graphesis, which I addressed in some detail in the previous chapter, and it serves as a reference point for the concepts key to the remainder of this chapter.

The presentation of transcript-based patterns (i.e., concentrations of nouns and noun phrases, comparatively aligned to see the frequency of usage by individual convention speakers and also by the collective lineups) bears resemblance to the set of visual models and abstracting practices advanced at the nexus of distant reading and thin description—a nexus this chapter sets out to orient and to deepen conceptually by anchoring these methods to three key concepts: *database*, *scale*, and *pattern*. "The Words Speakers Use" offers a thin–distant rendering of the national conventions, reproducing transcripts in the form of labeled bubble charts. The graphical presentation involves aesthetic choices. Applying a slight translucence, the bubbles are shaded with red or blue, corresponding to the arch-color associated with the primary political parties. Shadow-outlines of each of the figures suggest placeholders—silhouettes asserting that what matters more than the detailed physical appearances of the speakers are the utterances themselves. The wordcounts may be read for the collective contributions of *all* speakers at each convention or read for the recurrent terms in the speeches of *individual* speakers from either party. The graphic presentation is designed to amplify selected aspects of the data, such as the disproportionate number of references across party lines to topics like health care, war, and terrorism. Bubbles and the two-column alignment makes this much more than a simple listing of recurrent terms—"The Words Speakers Use" lays bare the focal terms in each party's language choices relative to the other's.

Ericson's *Times* infographic influenced subsequent (also increasingly interactive) infographics following the 2011 conventions and the Republican National Convention in 2012 (see, e.g., Ericson, 2011; Ericson & Bostock, 2012). Thus considering this a noteworthy precursor to the expanding milieu of infographics, I elaborate upon this example at the outset to set up the premises that ground the chapter ahead. In this chapter, I set out from the occasion of numerous data visualization projects, including those above, to discuss selected conceptual dimensions related directly to the development of abstract visual models rendered through distant reading and thin description methods. Following a gradual but intentional build-up from *concepts* to *practices* and finally to *consequences*, I sketch the importance that each of three concepts—database, scale, and pattern—has for the *visual modeling* and *abstracting practices* that I argue offer generative heuristics for a *network sense* of the discipline. Database, scale, and pattern name three concepts vital to the advancement of distant–thin methods as well as the models and practices these methods carry out in service of network sense—a capacity for knowing as interconnected divergent aspects of the field constituted by its discourses, citations, and emplaced professional activities.

Further, the conceptual–theoretical framework for distant–thin methods insists on their functioning *heuretically*, to use Gregory Ulmer's term, which emphasized the ways these models and practices destabilize commonplaces, opening up new questions, provoking insights, promoting speculation, and stimulating conversations that will encourage those invested in notions of disciplinarity—including newcomers in particular. This inventional emphasis is especially interested in revisiting long-established assumptions about RCWS leveled predominantly by the problematic processes identified in Chapter One: anecdotal/experiential, local, and predominantly invested in ethnographic methods, underpinned by fixations on deep, close reading and thick description. For the complementary alternatives laid out ahead, I have included mention of heuretics to ensure that the scalable, abstract visual models assembled function as considerably more than representations. While they are representative, they are also open-ended, adaptive, and subject to updates; they are not static, final statements but concentrations of data and metadata with a high degree of tolerance for keeping up with the inevitably shifting terrain of the field—for inciting those who make them and who interact with them to anticipate, speculate, wonder, and project a generative curiosity onto a future horizon.

To deepen the emphasis on generativity across these distant–thin practices, consider again the ways thin description functions to describe, and just what describing *does*. By assigning language to experience, description makes experience accessible (albeit *partially* accessible) and durative (albeit *limitedly* durative), setting experience into rhetorical circulation. This accomplishes, strictly speaking, a mediated shifting-out, and although the shift-out is beholden to what is and what was, the description itself functions as an act of becoming for the ways it shapes a future horizon. As such, description is generative, a heuretical intervention. Description participates in setting up what is next just as much as it freezes in representational amber what was or what has been. This recognition of description as generative is influenced by Bruno Latour, who wrote (in a pseudonymous essay) that

> descriptions are always in words and appear very much like semiotic commentaries on a text or like a programming language. They define actors, endow them with competences and make them do things, and evaluate the sanction of these actions very much like the narrative program of semioticians. (Johnson, 1988, p. 306)

In this context, description sets a script that participates in a gradual transformation of agency, action, and materials in the world.

Consider Ericson's infographic once more in these terms: It represents the discourses of each convention, but, by reducing, aggregating, and simplifying those discourses, it reduces complexity *temporarily* to the semantic patterns intrinsic to each party's platform. Thus, understood as rhetorical constructs, perhaps abstract visual models like this can, in turn, influence the future discourses they sponsor. The distant–thin infographic is both descriptive and generative. In what follows, I will address each of three concepts key to distant–thin methods—database, scale, and pattern—so that the elaboration of specific models in the second half of this project will be enriched.

6

Because the distant–thin methods demonstrated in this book are both data-driven and in service of network sense, the case for them cannot proceed responsibly without acknowledging the availability of suitable data sets and the related matter of disciplinary databases, their sporadic curation, and their perilous sustainability. The previous chapter established that numerous discipliniographic accounts have been built on testimonial and ethnographic methods. They have relied upon thick description, tended toward archival methods and local–historical cases, and adopted narrative—storytelling—as the predominant discursive mode. A well-documented attachment to thick-descriptive and narrativistic approaches among discipliniographic accounts is worth reconsidering because it cannot help but elicit the issues I address here on the status of disciplinary databases, the interdependence of database and narrative, and the importance of revitalizing what I call *database infrastructure* for RCWS in service of stabilizing disciplinary trajectories cognizant of newcomers, divergent stakeholders, and discipliniographic accounts capable of involving durable data sets and narrativistic impulses. I contend that, although they have been tremendously important, hyperlocal, narrative-based accounts of disciplinary emergence operate more powerfully when paired with data-based accounts. In addition to composing narrative accounts, scholars must also begin to systematically build and curate the field's databases (e.g., program profile data, directories of programs, journal indexes, etc.).

Contemporary definitions of databases often foreground the record-like storage of electronic objects (or object-markers that stand in for physical objects, such as would be the case for an inventory spreadsheet). In "The Database as System and Cultural Form," Christiane Paul (2007) distinguished five types of databases: hierarchical, network, relational, client/server, and object-oriented (p. 96). Hierarchical and network databases privilege predictable

---

6   Chapter Two's arrangement presents as section breaks a series of five iconic graphic organizers retrieved in 2017 from *The Noun Project*: "Database" by Ed Jones, "Scale" by Oliviu Stoian, "Pattern" by Alex Fuller, "Bar Chart" by Alfredo, and "Bear" (i.e., Abstracting Practices) by Musaplated.

structural relationships among data housed in the system; hierarchical databases adhere to tree-like logics, whereas network databases follow comparable branching but are more bush-like, allowing elements to splice from multiple higher-order elements. According to Paul, client/server databases support remote, distributed access, and object-oriented databases are usually built in anticipation of computational uses, such that the elements organized in them are readily assemblable, particularly for use with different object-oriented programming languages. Among the five types, however, relational databases have achieved the broadest contemporary favor for everyday uses because they are highly flexible, allowing content to be sorted, re-organized, and modeled with high degrees of flexibility. For a more general definition that reaches across these specific types, Lev Manovich (2007) wrote,

> In computer science, database is defined as a structured collection of data. The data stored in a database are organized for fast search and retrieval by a computer and therefore a database is anything but a simple collection of items. (p. 39)

Manovich's perspective on databases is worth noting because among his best-known scholarly assertions is the argument he advanced in his 2001 book, *The Language of New Media*, that narrative and database are "natural enemies." Arguing for databases as an emergent cultural form symptomatic of the computer age, he expressed the distinction and their rivalrousness as follows:

> As a cultural form, the database represents the world as a list of items, and it refuses to order this list. In contrast, a narrative creates a cause-and-effect trajectory of seemingly unordered items (events). Therefore, database and narrative are natural enemies. Competing for the same territory of human culture, each claims an exclusive right to make meaning out of the world. (p. 225)

Manovich's characterization of the relationship between databases and narratives as rivals responded in part to an exigency: It was a timely polemic set up to advance the status of databases, which became popular and gained cultural footing as a common computational form throughout the 1990s, in contexts of new media production. For Manovich, to create new media is to extend databases, to produce mediated handles on the data sets collected and organized in them.

In a 2007 symposium on databases published in *PMLA*, N. Katherine Hayles reframed Manovich's agonistic metaphor, casting as a more cooperative model narrative and database instead as *natural symbionts*. They depend upon one another, Hayles noted, recalling that "the great strength of database, of course, is the ability to order vast data arrays and make them available for different kinds of queries" (p. 1604). She accounted as well for the hyperflexibility of relational databases, pointing out many ways relational databases as media objects pluralize monolithic logics for expression. Database generally follows a paratactic logic (shuffling in any direction), whereas narrative generally follows a syntactic logic (linearly sequenced, progressive). If we can get beyond the high contrast in these primary logics, narrative and database have established undercurrents of complementarity and fortuitous interdependence (e.g., data-based narratives and narrativistic data sets).

Having staged this formulation of a mutualistic symbiosis between narrative and database, we can return to any of the discipliniographic accounts authored over the past three decades to inquire into the ratio between narrative and database, to call the question, in effect, of which logic led and which logic followed in any given snapshot of the field. That is, we can shift from the Manovich–Hayles frames and use them as an analytic, a basis for inquiring into tendencies long manifest in RCWS's accounts. With few exceptions, discipliniographies narrate, and when they have invoked data sets, those data sets have been small scale, situated within the narrative, and adapted as forms of evidence, local and temporary to serve as footings for the narrative arc of the account. Only with few exceptions have they drawn on data sets organized into databases, freely recirculating such that they might be reassembled relationally or influence follow-up accounts. This is not a problem to be solved, but an opportunity for us to acknowledge and pursue. As Grahame Weinbren (2007) has written, databases can treat narratives as their operationalized objects, and, to play this out further, we should be able to envision (if not fully develop) a database of localist, ethnographic, narrative-driven discipliniographies.

The Manovich–Hayles analytic is also useful for applying to major databases in the field. Consider the Digital Archive of Literacy Narratives (DALN), a robust collection of video- and audio-recorded narratives of literacy development housed at The Ohio State University. Certainly its contents accord with the definitions of databases presented earlier, and it is also in accord with Weinbren's (2007) two conditions for databases, that "1) it is composed of smaller elements . . . and 2) it can be traversed in a multiplicity of ways" (p. 66). Similar to the previous example, this analytic primes useful inquiries into the design of a disciplinary database, its narrativistic usefulness, but also its capacity for supplying data in tune with distant–thin methods. The scope of this study prohibits a full-blown analysis of this archive, yet the argument becomes more fully apparent through this addition: Disciplinary narratives and the visibility they seek depend vitally on open, searchable, circulable databases.

This limited discussion of databases invites new thinking about their importance to the work of thin and distant methods. That is, my hope is for this brief discussion to function as a catalyst for a second move, from the Manovich–Hayles debate as an analytic to the Manovich–Hayles debate as a heuristic to guide and influence future thinking about the interdependence of database and narrative for discipliniography. The visualizations modeled in the book's later chapters all rely upon datasets that, although they stem from seemingly ordinary disciplinary artifacts (e.g., full-text journal articles, citations, and geolocation), the data they abstract are not readily available, easy to locate, or pushed into wider circulation for expanded adaptations as a result of this work. Without venturing yet more deeply into the limitations of grand databases just as with grand narratives (Lyotard, 1984), and without teasing out distinctions between so-called big data and boutique data—useful and important though these are—the fundamental assumption of the importance of databases and data sets is adequate for the purposes of this book's primary goal: the advancement of distant/thin methods in service of network sense.

Two final points of value punctuate this case for revitalized considerations of disciplinary databases in RCWS. The first is David Weinberger's (2007) efforts to draw a correspondence between books and databases as each serves the *externalization of memory* (p. 170). Memory externalization is crucial to disciplinary visibility, and this quality of databases applies from robust efforts to establish records, such as with the Writing Studies Tree and the National Census of Writing, down to the seemingly innocuous but no less important record-keeping related to conference dates and locations, editorial rotations for journals, and geolocations of watershed events for the field—the sum of which are only sporadically, unevenly curated.

The second point of value arises out of speculation about possibilities for something like a disciplinary *database of intentions*, to use John Batelle's (2005) phrase. Database of intentions is an idea that has shifted considerably toward marketing in recent years, but the basic premise is that we can learn much about what people seek—as individuals or as collectives—by the terms they use when they search. To return to a marketing example, the person who searches for recliner chairs on Amazon is probably interested in recliner chairs. Online advertisers take great interest in this, presenting those who have entered "recliner chairs" as a search string with a deluge of leads—ads and images positioned to entice further pursuit of the recliner chair and possibly to culminate with a purchase.

But the database of intentions, taken to a disciplinary domain, opens onto the invaluable forms of knowledge that would become available if, for instance, we openly shared the search strings entered on CompPile, a collection of scholarly records for work published in RCWS. A high concentration of searches for "assessment," "archive," or "queer" would indicate piqued curiosities related to those terms. And the database of intentions also reports on omissions and silences. That is, if three or four years pass without a search for Kenneth Burke or Walter Ong (or any variation on their names), perhaps there is a corresponding insight into an ebb of influence, waning interest or displaced interest, or the relocation of searches to other niche databases altogether.

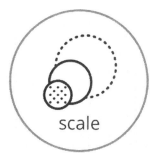

Having addressed the importance of disciplinary databases for the development of distant and thin methods toward a more fully realized network sense, scale is the next concept impacting these processes. Recalling the heuristic imperative of distant and thin methods, scale emphasizes that these treatments offer much more than measurement, quantification, and the presumed scientific force of data-backed assertions. Scale foregrounds as possible *traversals*, inquiry-movements that shift, whether purposefully or exploratorily, between isolated data-points and larger collectives. In an attempt to deepen the concept of scale for distant reading and thin description, here I account for the concept as it circulates commonly in geography and cartography, disciplinary domains located provisionally through Mark Monmonier's *How To Lie With Maps* (1996) and *Mapping It Out: Expository Cartography for the Humanities and Social Sciences* (1993). Read across these geographic approaches, I suggest that the concept of scale invests distant reading and thin descriptive methods as well as the visual models they generate with adaptive traversals, *scopic* change-ups that allow us—whether as makers (writers) or as interactors (readers)—to get at questions about anomaly and generalizability in the patterned phenomena such methods surface. Where distant reading and thin description methods scale, we elicit questions, as well, about comparison: How do the keyword concordances (or most frequently occurring *n*-grams) of any particular article relate to the keyword distillates of the issue or volume or year? Of the journal during a specific editor's tenure? Of the entire history of the journal? Across multiple journals in RCWS? Scale, in one sense, enables us to customize the aperture of the visual models, to move from a minute, local, and specific magnitude (*micro-*, *nano-*, and *idio-*) to high magnitudes and broadened orders (*mezo-*, *exo-*, and *macro-*) and back again, while exploring resemblances among phenomena at any other magnitude.

As commonly understood, the term scale relates both as a verb and a noun to accessibility across transcendable magnitudes. According to the *Oxford English Dictionary*, scale derives from the Old French *escaller*, which resembles staircase or ladder. Modern connotations for the verb include *climb, get over, ascend,* and *to get to or reach the top of.* Where the concept relates to metrology, or measurement, scale conjures associations with *proportion: To measure or represent (a quantity) in exact proportion to its absolute size or according to an arbitrary defined scale* ("Scale"). These selections offer a preliminary but adequate definitional perimeter—footing sufficient for capturing the most conventional attachments of meaning to the term where research methods are concerned. Scale applies to distant reading and thin description methods—and it is even underscored by this elaboration of the concept—because the abstract visual models demonstrated in the next three chapters, if they will be put to a wide range of rhetorical uses, must *do* what existing models have not done.

Consider indexes as another example of scale in relationship to distant reading and thin description. In most scholarly monographs, the index is inscribed at a fixed scale. The terms in the index are collected, arranged, and presented at the singular scale of the monograph. Following the conventions of print, indexes tend not to be scalable. That is, if we want to isolate the index for a particular chapter in the monograph, we are out of luck (or, as poor luck would have it, we have new work to do in manually sorting from the comprehensive index only the listed items whose page numbers fall in the specific chapter's range). The smaller-scale index is hidden, camouflaged among the pile of terms and phrases appearing elsewhere in the book. Distant reading and thin description methods set out to complicate this commonplace treatment, to alter it, and, with this tactical alteration, to generate new catalysts for inquiry. Animated indexes, citation distribution graphs, and maps plotting scholarly activity—each of which will be presented in chapters that follow—are designed with scalability as an imperative, a feature.

For mapmakers and geographers, scale is a basic convention and even a commonplace. John Campbell's (1991) *Introductory Cartography* defined scale as "the ratio between measurements taken between points [on the surface of a globe] and measurements taken between equivalent locations on the earth" (p. 24). In a strictly representationalist paradigm, scale initiates a referential correspondence between the map and that which it sets out, in more or less detail, to represent. Sticking to Modernist conventions for cartography, Campbell elaborated on the various ways in which scale is expressed on a map's surface—by word statement (i.e., one measure represents another measure), by numerical ratio statement (i.e., 1:10,000), and by graphic scale (i.e., a unit-specific graphical element). One advantage of a graphic scale is that once it has been defined, it adjusts with changes to the overall size of the map due to resizing or photographic reproduction. By contrast, the information graphic in the opening section of this chapter expresses scale by word statement: "Number of times words were used per 20,000 words spoken" (translated to a numerical ratio statement, this would appear as 1:20,000). Ericson's graphic also introduced an expression about the temporal scale with "20,000 words is about one day's worth of speeches."

Mark Monmonier (1996) began his book *How To Lie with Maps* with a discussion of scale that resembles Campbell's treatment. Monmonier refered to the three scale-types identified as verbal scales, ratio scales, and graphic scales, further emphasizing the adaptive aspects of graphic scales that make them the best choice for digital and photographic reproduction. Further, Monmonier distinguished between scales as *equivalent* (as in equivalency statements, a usage he discouraged) and as *representation*. *Representational scale* is an inclusive term to identify the common three-term typology (verbal, ratio, graphic) applied to conventional cartography. A counterpart to representational scale can be found in one of Monmonier's (1993) earlier books, *Mapping It Out*, which promoted the use of maps in tandem with expository writing in other disciplines while expressing concern at the limited uptake of mapping practices beyond geography.

While representational scales are primarily invested in establishing correspondences between real material spaces and cartographic representations of such spaces, conceptual scales apply to matters of symbolism, placement, labeling, and sizing of conceptual elements. Explaining a "scale of concepts," Monmonier (1993) noted, "the map author needs to identify features and relationships to be shown [as well as] their relative importance" (p. 102). Monmonier's main example is squarely in the domain of geography as he looked at the conceptual choices involved in a map developed by an anthropologist to show multiple routes between two towns. How much should the map depict the hazards impinging on any given route? This is a question of conceptual scale. A more conceptually inclusive map struggles under the burdens of excessive symbolism, which can become confusing. Conceptual inclusion and the principles of selection, reduction, and simplification pull in contrary directions. Their relationship, where distant reading and thin description is concerned, is in constant tension: a critical, or crisis, state. This is why we must engage in distant reading and thin description with an explicit, direct noticing of scale. Scalar choices have bearing on the visual models produced by these methods—particularly where they integrate cartography—as they do for any and all attempts to present spaces and concepts visually.

To convert scale from a technical specification to a practice, it may be useful to revisit Michel de Certeau's (1988) *flaneur*, the urban pedestrian who by footfall drifts in the city, practicing "ground level" operations and speaking in elective pathways of intensity, desire, and curiosity (p. 97). Elevated by maneuverability across scales, the flaneur's corollary in the context of distant and thin methods is the *planeur*, the gliding, aerial, drift-quester whose perspectival perch is configurable. Planeury—as an everyday practice—combines the capacity of screens as digital viewports to quickly switch between the zoomed-in and the zoomed-out, to explore by these variations the specific and the general as interdependent, and to foreground the synechdocal (or part–whole) quality of visualization methods, throughout which scale is a foundational consideration.

Pattern, a condition of comprehensible, repeated occurrence, is the third concept useful for establishing a groundwork for distant reading and thin description in service of network sense. Pattern is as common a reference in mathematics and computation as in art, music, and design. It is an encompassing concept whose wide gulf operates with great variation. For the purposes of supplying a third conceptual foothold for the methods demonstrated by this research, however, note that pattern—as a concept—tends to arise on a continuum between the latent mathesis of all observable phenomenon on one extreme and, at the other, the generative setup on an expanding horizon for switching between sensorial noticing (i.e., forms and rhythms) and predictive speculation: In consideration of some patterned phenomenon, what next?

The first chapter of Mark Taylor's (2003) *Moment of Complexity*, "From Grid to Network," is noteworthy for contrasting large-scale patterns and then generalizing those from the architectural urbanscapes where he located them to other phenomena, such as emerging media. This grid-network contrastive tension allows Taylor to account for the ways that network logics productively substitute distinctive patterns (often verging on chaotic, indistinguishable non-patterns) for the modernist constraints associated with grids. To explain this shift, a contemporary turn from one logic to another, Taylor drew on the work of postmodern architect Frank Gehry, whose buildings explored "new frontiers of complexity" without "simply negat[ing] modernism and the world it represents" (p. 41). According to Taylor, "The grid does not merely disappear but morphs into forms that are dynamic rather than rigid, organic rather than mechanical, complex rather than simple" (p. 41). Taylor noted several connections between Gehry's expansion of architectural principles that by extension create a clearing that would allow—methodologically—for more dynamic, organic, and complex structures and the data-driven, scalable models produced by distant reading and thin description. Such methods must be considered a response to the complex and maturing interdisciplinary domain of RCWS. Distant reading and thin description advance with the presumption that it is both possible and appropriate to seek, find, and express visually patterns that implicated an ever more complex conglomeration of disciplinary materials and activities—and, furthermore, that these pursuits do not simply negate existing reading practices and deeper–thicker ways of knowing.

Gehry's architectural response to complexity offered some precedent for thinking about models that integrate rigid, Euclidian shapes and more flexible network qualities. According to Taylor (2003), Gehry often relied on new media and digital interfaces to present his architectural plans: "With the moving images on these mobile surfaces, Gehry seems to achieve the impossible: he simultaneously sets forms in motion and gives movement form. Far from a static structure, Gehry's building is a *complex* ongoing event" (p. 42). It's a small but reasonable jump from Gehry's postmodern, hybrid architecture and the ongoing orchestration of events that constitute an academic discipline. Certainly we can find examples of the discipline as "a *complex* ongoing event." The ongoing, *live* quality of the discipline has for quite some time been a catalyst for new methods and methodologies. In 1987, Stephen North ended the introduction to *The Making of Knowledge in Composition*, noting "this was to be a new era, and it would demand new kinds of knowledge produced by new kinds of inquiry" (p. 17)—one of many statements about disciplinarity during the period of criticality from about 1986–1990 that came with new graduate programs, new tenure-track appointments, and the publication of theoretical monographs, like North's and Phelps's. As I have argued, the late 1980s marked a moment of criticality for RCWS—one that would demand the sharpening of methodological rigor and new devices for apprehending the vast materials of disciplinary interest. But I mention North here not only because his project is widely acknowledged as a turning point from the nascence of the discipline to an era marked by more widespread legitimacy and stability, but, as well, because his project was one that (a) attempted to demarcate the discipline as patterns of research activity and (b) clearly understood the abstract phenomena of disciplinarity as a "*complex* ongoing event." Twenty years later, this "complex ongoing event" continues to unfold. As such, "new kinds of inquiry" must keep stride.

I am not the first to suggest the complexity of disciplinarity (i.e., of coming to terms with the roiling amalgamation of activities and materials that constitute a field), nor do I hold that distant reading and thin description methods alone will absolve all the infrastructural challenges that accompany rising disciplinary complexity. Distant reading and thin description methods, however, aid attempts to understand this complexity differently by acknowledging that patterns emerge in a wide variety of data that have gone untreated historically. In this sense, the methods, where pattern is subject to deeper consideration, are additive rather than substitutive. However provisional they are, whether long-set or occurring only briefly before shifting again, the patterns germinated by distant reading and thin description methods should be considered in concert with other accounts of the discipline. Specifically, the next three chapters elaborate patterns based on the rising and falling of keywords, shifting citation practices, and mapping program and career path locations.

To assert the importance of pattern at the juncture of disciplinary complexity and architectural infrastructure yet further, recall Steve Johnson's *Emergence*, a 2001 book that examined "the connected lives of ants, brains, cities, and software." Writing about Manchester, England, in its industrial heyday, Johnson differentiated two varieties of complexity, one that resulted from sensory overload (the abundance of a frenzied scene) and another that yielded self-organizing systems (systems in which high-order phenomena are not explicitly decided by a central authority but rather where such rules rise tacitly from below). The discipline of RCWS, perhaps like many fields, coalesces as complex, following both of Johnson's types—as abundant with stimuli and as self-organizing. In response to complexities of both varieties, Johnson noted the degree to which pattern renders durable the emerging infrastructures:

> Understood in the most abstract sense, what Engels observed are *patterns* in the urban landscape, visible because they have a repeated structure that distinguishes them from the pure noise you might naturally associate with an unplanned city. They are patterns of human movement and decision-making that have been etched into the texture of city blocks, patterns that are then fed back to the Manchester residents themselves, altering their subsequent decisions. . . . A city is *a kind of pattern-amplifying machine*: its neighborhoods are a way of measuring and expressing the repeated behavior, and sharing that information with the group. Because those patterns are fed back to the community, small shifts in behavior can quickly escalate into larger movements . . . just a few repeating *patterns* of movement, amplified into larger

shapes that last for lifetimes: clusters, slums, neighborhoods. (pp. 40–41, emphasis added)

Johnson folded together dual connotations of pattern, and he read pattern through one densely populated cityscape known well for the industrial boom that accelerated it into a haphazardly planned urban center. Like Taylor, Johnson took an interest in the adequacy of architectural examples to illustrate concepts of complexity and pattern—concepts he elaborated in an effort to explain and explore the focal concept in his book, *Emergence.*

By analogy, many of Taylor and Johnson's assertions generalized favorably to the emergence and maturation of RCWS since 1987, particularly as pertain to the relationship between complexity and pattern. As the discipline has become more complex (some would say, in more derisive terms, *diffuse*), efforts to trace the outstretched lines of RCWS inquiry have been challenged by the depth, breadth, and rate of this expansion. Yet, pattern-amplifying devices are abundant:

- journals (not limited to the original nine studied by Maureen Daly Goggin [2000], but also those newer journals and others whose operations have slowed or halted altogether);
- graduate and undergraduate course descriptions and syllabi;
- monographs and edited collections;
- dissertations and theses;
- conference proceedings;
- textbooks (this one is the patterning device most often studied);
- conference keynote addresses;
- policy statements at all levels; and
- the writing circulated in social media and on listservs.

These constructs are things we have made: pattern-amplifying devices *constitutive of and constituted by* the field of RCWS. Their localizable spheres of circulation are neighborhood-like, offering "way[s] of measuring and expressing the repeated behavior, and sharing that information with the group" (Johnson, 2001, p. 41).

There are examples of studies designed to elicit patterns in some of these areas. We have pocketed studies that have surveyed and sampled nearly every one of these devices, and succeeded—by varied methods—in expressing patterns indicated by a set of materials (i.e., Richard Larson's well-known bibliographies [1988], Robert Connors's [1997] research on textbooks, and, more recently, Susan Peck MacDonald's survey of the Conference on College Composition and Communication [CCCC] program titles [2007]). Still, many of these samples and surveys work by the singular interval; they are anchored in time—temporally bracketed in a single moment of publication, often produced by an individual or small group as a one-time scholarly project. Distant reading and thin description must proceed more slowly and more inclusively; they must culminate in a series of built *things*—collections and assemblages that aid us in articulating the patterns woven through the field. Their greatest promise for success will depend on a long-term, painstakingly detailed treatment of the abundant materials that can be entered into this realm of consideration—where the *stuff* of the discipline is rendered for patterns that can be traced anew and where the tracing done by others is iterative, ongoing, and in full view. Although it is a modest starting point, this book features distant reading and thin description practices organized around keyword frequencies, citation trends, and locative projections. These are first steps, initial inquiries that, if effective, will prompt us to wonder what other patterns we can know.

abstracting
practices

Rustling beneath the radar of most conceptual debates about abstraction is the most commonplace example of academic abstracting practices: the one-paragraph summary of a journal article. Ordinarily positioned at the beginning of the article, such abstracts serve to reduce the article into a single paragraph whose purposes are many—efficiency, superficial assessments of relevance, the provocation of memory, and so on. Although individual article abstracts are neither systematically produced nor scalable, their functions are consistent with distant reading and thin description. Reading an abstract is not an exact substitution for reading an article, but, without motivating a storm of critical objection, abstracts are written and circulated to provide an alternative to the article—a double that is selective, reductive, and simpler than the full-length article. What is so satisfying about article abstracts—and perhaps the basic justification for their unquestioned proliferation—is that they do something the article itself cannot.

Abstracts started appearing in *College Composition and Communication* (*CCC*) in the February 2000 issue, during Marilyn Cooper's term as editor of the journal. Most would agree that abstracts make sense, no matter which of the uses they are put to, by readers, researchers, and those either prone to forgetting or too busy to read half of an article before deciding whether it might hold something of relevance. Abstracts, even though they are both magical (performing the article's temporary disappearance) and mundane (almost to the point of going unnoticed), set a precedent for the abstracting practices that are broadened through distant reading and thin description methods. With this in mind, the methods advanced here might be understood as a contemporary extension of *abstracting practices*—practices that, much like the speculative instruments they proliferate, make a difference in the ways the discipline is imagined.

In his brief introduction to *Graphs, Maps, Trees*, Moretti (2007) explained at different stages that his methods for visualizing text-based patterns are both abstract *and* concrete:

> Finally, these three models [graphs, maps, and trees] are indeed, as the subtitle intimates, abstract. But their consequences are on the other hand extremely concrete: graphs, maps, and trees place the literary field literally in front of our eyes—and show us how little we still know about it. . . . Here, the methodology of the book reveals its pragmatic ambition: for me, abstraction is not an end in itself, but a way to widen the domain of the literary historian, and enrich its internal problematic. (p. 2)

Models, on the one hand, are abstract; their consequences, on the other hand, are cast with an intensifier as "extremely concrete." Moretti's pairing of abstract and concrete as contrastive terms is to be expected considering that they are usually treated as dichotomies. The juxtaposition of these two concepts—abstract and concrete—hearkens back to a rationalistic tradition, in which the abstract is contrasted with an empirically verifiable reality and, as well, with the predominant epistemological realms of reason and logic. Moretti indicated that these terms operate together in distant reading and, as such, they are compatible and that they apply at different stages to the three types of datavisual models his book examines. Yet, because the quotation above is one of just four occasions in *Graphs, Maps, Trees* where "abstract" is mentioned, this passage invites a deeper inquiry into the concept of abstraction. Moretti's references to *abstract* and *concrete* could be viewed as a moment where he backslides from one of the key terms in the book's subtitle, *Abstract Models for a Literary Theory*. In effect, the passage quoted at length above serves to blunt the risk-taking pursuit of abstraction; abstraction in its potential drift away from strictly rationalistic epistemology is hereby attached to a scientistic agenda and tendered "as the unproblematic antithesis of the concrete" (Berthoff, 1986, p. 230). This is not a long-lasting problem for Moretti's project because he qualified the varied processual intervals at which these descriptors apply: "concrete" applies to consequences rather than to the visualizations themselves. However, as one of the few specific references to "abstract," the passage's discussion of distant reading as abstract prompts further consideration of distant reading and thin description as abstracting practices. Distant reading methods involve the selective arrangement of data sets in ways that allow us to apprehend patterns; where data sets are too large and unwieldy, often because such data span large corpora, geographic areas, or periods of time, distant reading supports an interest in the recognition of forms and patterns, which often involve translating data by selection and reduction from nonobvious assortments into observable, suggestive patterns. Considering that distant reading methods proceed in the interest of producing scalable, abstract visual models, what does the reference to "abstract" indicate about distant reading? And why should these visual models be thought abstract?

The abstractive qualities or capacities I want to emphasize in distant reading practices amplify patterns, interconnections, and relationships among selections of data. Recognizing forms and patterns in data fosters network sense; we begin to be able to see those distributed, circulating, and nonobvious formations previously compromised by a lack of field-wide record keeping. For the models presented in Chapters Three through Five, the forms relate to keyword concordances, citation trends, and geographic distributions of scholarly activity. Further, acknowledging a build-up from database, scale, and pattern toward abstracting practices suggests that we might encounter the models as extensions of the collections of discourse and metadata they are fashioned from, thereby regarding them as they produce a *wandering resourcefulness*, similar to a quality I.A. Richards (1994) attributed to words in his work on speculative instruments.

From this, two preliminary responses become clearer as to identifying what is gained from conceiving of distant reading and thin description as abstractive: (a) These practices are compatible with interests in the recognition of form and pattern, and in many cases such forms and patterns are obfuscated amidst complexity until they are presented with varying degrees of selectivity and abridgment; (b) these methods translate collections of disciplinary materials into patterned images, rendering forms recognizable through text mining, data mining, layering, visual design, and presentation. The disciplinary materials subject to distant reading and thin description consequently offer a plentitude of renderings; they are abundant, yielding a profoundly deep, complex resourcefulness that is only partly apprehended by conventional reading practices.

Having thus far deliberated on the abstractive dimension of these methods, briefly consider the quantitative, empirical dimension—the concrete. The reason for dealing with abstraction is that it supplies counterbalance to any presumption about these methods as aspiring to advance a pure science, that—because they deal with quantification, computational processes, and data visualization—they avoid rhetorical aspects of interpretation and meaning or that they are not especially appropriate for initiating a theoretical curiosity.

When Moretti (2007) contrasted the abstract quality of the models with "extremely concrete" consequences (p. 2), he referred to the potency of such models for the way they confront us with suggestive patterns that cannot be ignored—patterns that demand some judgment as to intelligibility, leaving us to judge them pragmatically "for how they concretely change the way we work" (p. 91). Just as Ericson's *New York Times* infographic materialized the word frequencies from the national conventions in 2004, so do distant reading and thin description typically feature concentrations of data that demand thinking through their implications. Ericson's graphic laid bare certain rhetorical strategies (e.g., Democrats didn't mention Bush as frequently as Republicans mentioned Kerry). These unearthed facts lend themselves to additional lines of inquiry and researchable questions. The models produced by these methods bear out some rhetorical force, especially where they materialize certain aspects of a large data set that have not been presented previously. For Moretti's (2007) work on literary histories, such models "enrich [the] internal problematic" of that field of study (p. 2). My aim is for this work to extend his assertion and to demonstrate that such methods, too, will enrich the internal problematic of disciplinarity for RCWS.

Distant reading and thin description methods and the scalable, abstract visual models developed by such methods integrate scientific and artistic aspects, abstract and concrete aspects, so much so that they are most appropriately described as hybrids. Hybridity, in this case, refers to the combinatory presence of these qualities, commonly argued to be at odds. But hybridity also addresses the inclusive attitude or disposition—the manner of distant reading pursuits—that embraces this combinatory quality while diminishing neither quantitative nor qualitative dimensions. David Foster, in a 1988 *JAC* essay, "What Are We Talking About When We Talk About Composition?" addressed this quandary, arguing for a receptivity to the hybrid epistemology that mutually values these seemingly incompatible methodological orientations in RCWS research:

> As informed readers and deliberately inclusive thinkers, we must be the measure of our discipline. Science cannot claim ascendancy in any area of human knowledge, particularly in that complex blend of knowledge-streams we call composition. We must be wary of those who, uncomfortable with the ambiguities of discourse and complacent with the quan-

titative, empirical perspective, would have us assume that perspective alone. As informed readers, we must juggle and juxtapose the claims of different modes of inquiry, recognizing what each contributes and what each lacks. To refuse this invitation to an intellectual pluralism, to settle in its place for a single perspective, is to invite the punishment we all hated in grade school: having to write the same sentence one hundred times. In this case, it would be "I will not know. I will not know. I will not know. . . ." (p. 38)

Distant reading and thin description methods operate as abstracting practices; their experimental pursuit is thoroughly rhetorical, even while it embraces the middle ground where science and art converge, ripe with both ambiguities and possibilities, where, as Foster said, "we must juggle and juxtapose the claims of different modes of inquiry" (p. 38).

In the section that follows, I extend the convergence of database, scale, and pattern beyond abstracting practices to examine just how it is these methods function by way of visual models.

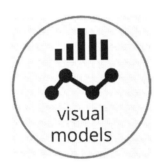

Michael Pemberton's 1993 *CCC* essay, "Modeling Theory and Composing Process Models" renewed basic definitional questions about models—asking and exploring just what models *are* and considering some of the points of terminological confusion and subsequent dismissals based on efforts to eschew models due to presumptions of their mere positivism. Beginning in 1914, with Pierre Duhem, who "criticized models for their failure to be positivistic *enough*" (qtd. in Pemberton, 1993, p. 40), Pemberton recounted the development of Linda Flower and John Hayes's cognitive process model and effectively summarized the series of strong reactions, including Marilyn Cooper and Michael Holzman's, that it provoked, many of which "suggest[ed] that the assumptions embraced by cognitivists are far *too* positivistic" (p. 41). The perception that models are too positivistic might persist, but Pemberton's work thoughtfully headed off this danger and provided a starting point toward understanding that such criticisms of simple models must not dissuade further development of abstract visual models.

By revisiting selected references to modeling where cognitive science and RCWS converged in the early 1980s, Pemberton (1993) highlighted the terminological ambiguity at play in references to "model." For instance, Pemberton explained that in their critique of protocol analysis, Cooper and Holzman used "model" and "theory" interchangeably; Flower and Hayes, too, were generous with the functional range of meanings they attributed to the term, as they claimed that their cognitive process model "is both a theory and a distillation of data" (p. 21; qtd. in Pemberton, p. 44). Pemberton deepened the concept of model by setting out from this conundrum—"this elusive and frequently shifting notion of what constitutes a 'model' in composition studies" (p. 44)—and by urging a more "careful" approach to models that would "guard against the urge to dismiss, preemptively, the value of a model merely because it contains imperfections" (p. 46). His article continued with an examination of the concept along two lines: models as simplifications, and models as misleading representations.

Pemberton effectively revisited the presumed-to-be clear epistemological weaknesses of models because they are simplifications and because they are (potentially) misleading representations. Where simplification is concerned, Pemberton brought aboard Michael Carter (1990) who wrote that the greatest strength of cognitive studies is that they are deliberately reductive (p. 47). This deliberate reduction occurs with distant reading, which is "not an obstacle, but a *specific form of knowledge*: fewer elements, hence a sharper sense of their overall interconnection" (Moretti, 2007, p. 1). Distant reading and thin description and the visual models produced by these methods are *deliberately reductive*. They reintroduce granularity where it had gone missing; as such, granularity of selected data sets materializes the nonobvious so that patterns might emerge, so that layers from large aggregates of data might be suggestively distinguished and so that connections and associations might be strengthened and amplified— if only temporarily or for the purposes of inquiry. How else might we work through such piles of data but by distant and thin methods and their deliberate reductions? In preparation for distant reading and thin description methods, then, still more work is due to break down the presumed epistemological weaknesses of models. Models, as the work in the next three chapters seeks to make clear, are crucial to distant reading and thin description because they function as an intermediary between dynamic data, which are too laborious to read in long form each time they are updated, and the insights generated from those data when they are presented differentially. Moreover, models help contextualize data; they establish relationships that bridge form and dynamism; and they are particularly effective at expressing such linkages succinctly and accessibly.

A secondary risk, according to Pemberton, involves misrepresentation. Pemberton (1993) explained this danger as follows: "This risk derives, principally, from the possibility that incidental properties of the illustrative model or preferred analogy may be mistakenly attributed to the process or phenomenon it is being used to explain" (p. 49). Again, models are limited and limiting, a truism that can be asserted about *all* research—whether examined at the scale of data, model, theory, or paradigm; Pemberton reiterated a related point: "incompleteness is an unavoidable epistemological weakness common to all models and all methods of data collection" (p. 53). Pemberton's work on models deserves such an extensive recap because his account offers a thorough and nuanced treatment of modeling theory stationed squarely in the wheelhouse of RCWS. Perhaps Pemberton's most pertinent contribution is in his identification of models as "*partial isomorphs* of their subjects" (p. 45). As partial isomorphs, models "will be similar in form to their subjects but embody fewer of their subjects' constituent properties," and, consequently, "it will always be possible to find certain properties in the subject that the model will not account for" (p. 45). His acknowledgement of this quality is consistent with the general principles grounding this entire section: Models simplify and reduce, and in so doing, they also amplify, granularize, and strengthen highly suggestive associations that become traceable.

The definitional depth Pemberton contributed to this discussion of models is not intended to curtail or reign in the array of models pertinent to this research project or to the field more generally; instead, it is offered in the spirit of honing the potential of models for materializing nonobvious patterns in the disciplinary data sets considered in the following chapters. Even though he focused on Flower and Hayes's cognitive process model, Pemberton (1993) accounted for models in general; he was not partial to visual models. In fact, he downplayed the presumption that models should be thought, by default, as visual when he wrote, in a parenthetical aside, that "although [Flower and Hayes's cognitive process model] has a graphic presentation, a diagram is not a requisite for something to be considered a model. A model may be presented, for example, in purely textual form" (p. 49). While this inclusive gesture is appropriate to his theorization of models, it leaves us with a momentary imbalance given that I am primarily concerned here with deepening the concept of visual models. We must now consider the adjectival term in the phrase by turning to theoretical expansion of the visual in visual models. For this, Johanna Drucker's work on graphesis will help us further align distant reading and thin description methods and visual epistemology.

Drucker's primary aim was to present graphesis as a hybridized middle domain that appropriates the felicitous influences of the sciences and the humanities on visual epistemology and that, in so doing, achieves a thoroughly rhetorical understanding of visual knowledge production. Drucker (2010) stated this case plainly: "graphical structures are rhetorical arguments" (p. 17). In itself, an assertion like this is not surprising to those who have been thinking about and writing about design, visuality, or the rhetorics of art, comics, computer interfaces, or photography for some time. Drucker acknowledged the extensive precedents for graphesis; she conceived graphesis to be "profoundly interdisciplinary" (p. 4) and she went on to account for some of the specific ways visual epistemology is produced and circulated. Drawing on scholars in the sciences as well as the humanities, Drucker also revisited commonplaces about visual epistemology held both by scientists and by humanists, with precedents that predate print technologies: "Even before the existence of print technology, visual images served varied epistemological functions—from the representation of information in condensed, legible form, to the expression of complex states of mind and experience" (p. 2). Her presentation of graphesis as a theoretical, rhetorical intervention into commonplace thinking about visual epistemology is conducive to distant reading and thin description methods and the visual models they produce. As you will see in the following chapters, abstract visual models produced by these methods, understood in accordance with graphesis, must "be conceived as procedural, generative, emergent, as a co-dependent dynamic in which subjectivity and objectivity are related" (Drucker, 2010, p. 4). Further, Drucker explained that graphesis depends upon opening up and expanding the concept of epistemology—of what knowing involves, of what can be known, and of what coalesces where knowledge is claimed:

> We have to go beyond thinking of knowledge in terms of mechanistic and static relations in which things known and things shown are assumed to be independent entities operating in an objective universe of phenomena existing in advance of their apperception. Visual epistemology is based on a more radical theory of knowledge. The radical concept of subjectivity, and of the co-dependent nature of knowledge and interpretation, have been integral to quantum physics for nearly a century and to cognitive studies for half that long. Graphesis takes these concepts as foundational and uses them to construct a theory of knowledge through attention to the graphical form of its many expressions. (p. 34)

To begin drawing distinctions between the "many expressions" of interest to graphesis, Drucker offered a loose typology: "They can work 1) through offering a visual analogy or morphological resemblance, 2) through providing a visual image of non-visible phenomena, or 3) by providing visual conventions to structure operations or procedures" (p. 5). Although these three types are most evident in the quantitative research found in the sciences, Drucker elaborated on each in such a way that makes the typology more broadly applicable for graphesis and its "profoundly interdisciplinary" reach. Drucker detailed these distinctions so that she could break down model-types, introducing an analytical scheme to more acutely historicize the precedents for graphesis before reuniting the three strands of model-types, as her discussion would "rest on an assertion that visual epistemology must be synthesized at the intersection of humanistic and scientific concepts of knowledge" (p. 10). This intersection, I argue, must be thought of as thoroughly rhetorical. For visual epistemology and the visual models proliferated to date in RCWS, we must reconsider not only how they have adapted and evolved, but we must also understand the models rhetorically—not as aging historical statements, but as performative figures perpetually animated and ongoing, as figures that *move*, compelling assent and changing the ways the discipline is conceptualized, imagined, and enacted, so that its *future* work can be carried out.

Visualizing a Discipline

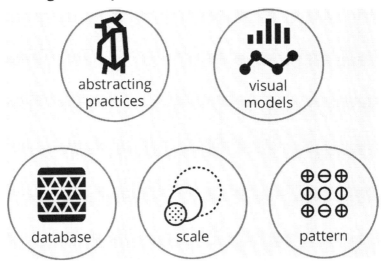

Up to this point, this chapter has reviewed selected concepts relevant to an emerging methodology designed to visualize patterns in the emergence and maturation of RCWS. Distant reading and thin description intervene into a disciplinary problematic—one grounded in matters of highly irregular data gathering, an abundance of reading materials piling up, and predominantly thick and narrativistic bases for claim-making about disciplinary formation—with datavisual models generated to bolster a sense of the field as an interconnected and ongoing phenomenon. Providing this conceptual ground-work, which emphasizes databases, scale, pattern, abstracting practices, and visual modeling, brings this methodology more fully into view as a generative epistemic technology whose thin, distant qualities offer handles for inquiring into complex, distributed disciplinary activities and materials: for developing a *network sense* of the field.

To recap, the chapter advances the following key principles for distant reading and thin description:

1. Distant reading and thin description *mediate* between collections of data and abstract phenomena that can be difficult to identify, such as disciplinarity.

2. Distant reading and thin description apply self-consciously at partic-ular *scales*. They are applied at various magnitudes of measurement (from the small to the large) but flatten out complex phenomena so that we can materialize traceable networks of associations. This asso-ciative capacity makes it possible to travel between the selections of data and the complex phenomenon under investigation.

3. These methods are *visually rhetorical* in that the visual models they produce articulate potentially patterned images that function as argu-ments, influencing ways of thinking, and widening the perspectives available as they relate to a phenomenon, such as disciplinary emer-gence and maturation.

4. The visual models produced by these methods stand as *partial iso-morphs* of the phenomena they depict. They induce a known degree of reduction and selection, though it is often temporary in the sense that the models are constantly reintegrated into the complexity that they are designed to help us apprehend. In this sense, the qualities of reduction and selection are, paradoxically, also expansive. By ren-dering a more granular, selected set of data, the selection is, by its reduction, amplified.

5. Distant reading and thin description are generative, convening a *heuretics*, in Ulmer's theorizing of the term. That is, they are above all *inventive* and highly *suggestive*. Resisting attachment to positivism or scientific proof, they function as *speculative instruments* that promote inquiry into *theoretical curiosities*; they are not wholly invested in interpretation of texts, nor are they constrained by a strictly represen-tationalist paradigm.

6. Distant reading methods involve *visual presentation* and almost al-ways pair the visual models with discursive accounts that advance the

matter under consideration by explanation and analysis. In this sense, the mode of presentation is *hybrid*.

This set of principles does not exhaust the full range concepts touched upon in this chapter, nor does it reduce to summary all the applications for distant reading and thin description imagined—and even enacted—by Moretti, Love, and also by Matthew Jockers (2013), whose monograph *Macroanalysis* applied distant reading and data visualization to large-scale analyses of literary texts. Certainly there remains still more conceptual groundwork to be refined if datavisual methods are to take hold and have a lasting impact on the ways we seek to understand such complex, abstract phenomena as an academic discipline. But the purpose of this chapter has remained to articulate salient concepts and to present them as a basis before proceeding with fuller demonstrations in Chapters Three through Five. It should be clear by now that visualizing a discipline involves a set of practices suited to a rapidly expanding range of applications—well beyond what have been, thus far, uses aligned with literary analysis and interpretive–hermeneutic ends. With the conceptual groundwork primed, we can now focus on the animated index, citation graphs, and maps of scholarly activity, thereby moving ahead with the development of patterned images of the discipline of rhetoric and composition/writing studies.

Chapter 3: Turn Spotting: The Discipline as a Confluence of Words

> What is the nature of this turn we are taking? (Corder, 1995, p. 114)

Declarations of turns, such as the global turn for rhetoric and composition/writing studies (RCWS) noted by Wendy Hesford (2006), run counter to Stephen North's (1987) lamenting a "chaotic and patternless" quality of disciplinary emergence in the late 1980s (p. 3). Because turns name temporarily stabilizing attention structures, it comes as little surprise that numerous additional turns have emerged and circulated in recent decades both for the field and for the broader domains of the social sciences and humanities. Turns seek to pinpoint cohering ideas, values, and focuses for intellectual activity, suggesting patterned thought as it fans out, expands, and accumulates salience and uptake. Some of these turns have expanded into wider-spread transformations in thought and action—what some would identify as *paradigm shifts*, recalling Thomas Kuhn's (1996) phrase for widespread, lasting diffusion and acceptance of new concepts in the sciences. Among the major turns of the past 50 years are the *linguistic turn*, which accepts language as significantly (though not exclusively) constitutive of epistemology; the *social turn*, which locates fundamental interdependencies between writing and the junctures of human sociality and materiality; and the *process turn*, which recognizes as situational and idiosyncratic the irregular unfolding of any document's development as fits with time-based activity. Each of these greater turns has been elaborated sufficiently in scholarship over the past several decades that their shorthand references, *x* turn, function as slogan-like, metonymically glossing the principle's complex, gradual development and reducing its history to something much quicker and sufficiently recognizable. Successful turns take hold. They grow and expand myth-like as they accrue assent. These epistemological formations might also be understood as widely held beliefs, or *doxa*. And this, to some degree, explains why contemporary scholars are posing more and more turns.

In addition to major, well-established turns, several lesser (or emergent, yet-becoming) turns have come to light—some blinkering in fleetingly, others circulating with acute sponsorship indicative of newness and recency. Consider these 13, which I have gathered from various publications and from searches in CompPile:

- Apocalyptic turn (Lynch, 2012)
- Archival turn (Brereton & Gannett, 2011; Clary-Lemon, 2014; Morris, 2006)
- Digital turn (University of Northern Iowa, Meryl Norton Hearst Lecture Series, n.d.)
- Ecological turn (Shepley, 2013; Tinnell, 2011)
- Ethical turn (Barton, 2008; Flynn, 2007)
- Multimodal turn (Sheridan, 2010)
- Public turn (Farmer, 2013; Mathieu, 2005)
- New material turn (Pilsch, 2016)
- Sociocultural turn (Johnson, 2006)
- Spatial turn in rhetorical genre studies (Reiff, 2011)
- Queer turn (Alexander & Wallace, 2009)
- Turn to design (Marback, 2009)
- Turn to social class (Zebroski, 2007)

The list is not at all meant to be comprehensive, but posing it nevertheless offers a suggestive point of departure for the portion of this book concerned with relationship between tracing vocabulary as particular terms rise and fall in a disciplinary corpus. After all (holding off temporarily several important and critical questions about turns, whether they are big or small, tentative or more deeply rooted), turns function as cohering, directional metaphors—*named* arrows of change that capture trends or shifts that at least some consider substantial enough to offset an otherwise "chaotic and patternless" development (North, 1987, p. 3). For the field of RCWS, articulations of turns respond to the concerns expressed by North. Turns are *discursive attention events*. Large-scale, well-established turns have gained footing as successful and long-lasting attention events, whereas small-scale and nascent turns may be primings for attention events that are perhaps localized among specialists or that are hoped by some to become more expansive and widely influential. Multiple, simultaneously developing turns are possible; a disciplinary domain, such as RCWS, can support many such attention events—as many as those who identify with the field can themselves entertain. Even so, with an influx of turns, we might inquire—as this chapter does—into how many turns a discipline can take while at once sustaining its coherence.

In his 1995 essay, "Turnings," Jim Corder explored from a personal perspective the disciplinary tension I've begun to set up here between anchored, coherent *doxa*, which turns admittedly acknowledge as open and adaptive, and patternless chaos as a tension between convergence and divergence. Corder wrote,

> When divergent, non-isomorphic rhetorics come together—
> that is to say, when any two rhetorics come together—the
> consequence is sometimes happy. Insight and learning occur,
> and sometimes love and marriage. Sometimes, however, the
> consequence is not happy; or habits of competition are too
> strong. Sometimes one rhetoric expands to fill all available
> space, prevailing as the other is compressed into submission.
> Sometimes two rhetorics compromise, to no one's complete
> satisfaction. Sometimes they are paralyzed, as practitioners
> are unable to choose. Sometimes they go to war. (pp. 105–106)

Corder's characterization of non-isomorphic rhetorics (sometimes they work together; sometimes they are incompatible) aids our focusing on the phenomenon of multiple co-occurring turns, some new and some old, some veering in compatible directions and others opposed, clashing, crossing paths. The point of Corder's essay is that rhetoric has helped him cope with seeming incommensurable positions, to celebrate paradoxes for their inventional possibility rather than to "call the whole thing off" (p. 106). And this is an insight appropriate for what follows in the remainder of this chapter—a chapter that regards words as a commanding ontological basis for disciplinarity. The field of RCWS is constituted to a large extent by its discourses. Setting out with this focal premise refreshed and reasserted, the chapter inquires into selected means of doing things with concentrations of keywords as they rise and fall in published scholarship. In pursuit of a network sense of the field rooted in its terminologies, the tracing of these rising and falling rates of usage carries out distant and thin methods that highlight the life cycles of turns, which can become threshold concepts, and that circumscribe turns and threshold concepts with semantic networks.

Word Watchers

The role of the word watcher is especially relevant in this context of continuing consideration of turn spotting, of turns as substantiated by patterns in disciplinary discourse. I first heard about word watchers from Tim Diggles, coordinator of the Federation of Worker Writers and Community Publishers in Staffordshire, England, who visited Syracuse University in Fall 2005 to lead a colloquium on working class writing and publishing. Diggles noted that in parliamentary governance, a designated word watcher would attend to terminological slippages, request etymological depth, and gather by way of real-time note-taking and tracing various usages as they inevitably fan out in any session's exchanges. Among the word watcher's purposes are to shift the focus with calm remove, especially when interchanges become heated (though perhaps this is no less valuable when exchanges become complacent, when words operate unchecked, unquestioned, or too coolly, underexamined). The point isn't to domesticate the meanings or to reduce usages merely to standard and official denotations, but to mediate. The word watcher seeks to make explicit the tacit and unexplored subtleties, admitting these intricacies to the discussion. To bring this back to rhetoric, think of the word watcher as loosing *stases*, as a wise and conceptually agile referee who aids the stream of discourse by adding perspective that hopes to unstick, ease, and differentiate. Word watchers are important not only in parliament and political debate. The word watcher's disposition is likewise valuable in other situations, such as where evolving cultural, professional, and disciplinary discourses play out, as well as in many contexts for teaching and learning, which I will address more fully in the concluding section of this chapter. Further, word watchers model practices suited to turn spotting—to noticing, differentiating among, and lending an evidentiary basis to so-called turns. After all, what does a turn require more than a narrow lexicon, or semantic network, to foster its circulation and uptake? A means of modeling that lexicon, making it directly accessible. Later sections of this chapter model an affirmative response to this question more formidably and with concrete examples.

In addition to the *real-time* performance of word watchers in parliamentary discussions, several books and articles have attempted to trace terms and inquire into vocabularies. Well-known among these attempts is Raymond Williams's (1985) *Keywords: A Vocabulary of Culture and Society*, a monograph that elaborated 127 terms, selected and explored by way of Williams's "starting point," which he characterized as a "cluster, a particular set of what came to seem interrelated words and references, from which my wider selection then developed" (p. 22). Williams's method is self-consciously idiosyncratic, directed largely by his own curiosity and sense of associative groupings. Choices include *country, ecology, hegemony, materialism, taste, science*, and *sex*—and each selection accompanies a brief definitional essay that sets out to orient readers by addressing what he distinguishes as "particular and relational" meanings (p. 23). His accounts established how these meanings combine antecedent (historical), highly situated (contextual), and intertextual usages through the use of boldfacing to an internal reference to other terms featured in the collection. Addressing the value of the project, Williams noted that "what can really be contributed is not resolution but perhaps, at times, just that extra edge of consciousness" (p. 24). He wrote,

> In practice many of these [word watching] processes begin
> with the complex and variable sense of particular words, and

the only way to show this, as examples of how networks of usage, reference and perspective are developed, is to concentrate, 'for the moment', on what can then properly be seen as internal structures. (p. 23)

Williams's meandering methods are only reproducible insofar as another could inquire into a vocabulary by similarly identifying a rich cluster and then tracing outwardly its associations and resemblances in pursuit of "particular and relational" meanings. But by bringing the "internal structures" of word watching to light, Williams's demonstrates a distant–thin methodology (p. 23).

Nearer to the disciplinary locus of RCWS, Paul Heilker and Peter Vandenberg's (2015) *Keywords in Writing Studies* (updated from a first edition in 1996, *Keywords in Composition Studies*) enacted an approach similar to Williams's, with the distinction that the set of terms they featured is much smaller and specialized—at just 36—and that the accounts were written by 31 different contributors. Here, too, entries include boldface to distinguish terms elaborated elsewhere in the collection, enhancing the impression of the set's interconnections. The editors' methods for selecting the terms were understated, like Williams's, perhaps because the set was built by a tacit process, assembled by the intuition of well-established scholars whose experience in the field has provided a felt sense of vocabulary that warranted definitional footing. Some of those keywords included *agency, design, ecology, network, queer,* and *silence.* But their qualifiers echoed the 1996 edition of their project, noting as "essential criteria for inclusion" each term's belonging to "general disciplinary parlance" and each being "highly contested, the focal point of significant debates about matters of power, identity, and values" (2015, p. xvii). These criteria extend the connection of this disciplinarily situated undertaking and thicken the collection's accordance with word watching for RCWS.

A more specialized example of a disciplinarily situated collection of terms, *A Handlist of Rhetorical Terms* by Richard Lanham (2012), has been in print and circulating since 1962, and was re-issued as a second edition in the early 1990s. In the preface to the first edition, which was republished as part of the second edition, Lanham (2012) imagined his primary audience as "students of English literature" (p. xiii), but in the preface to the second edition, nearly three decades later, he wrote that "the handlist has found both a more numerous audience . . . and a more varied one" (p. ix). Like the collections of keywords from Williams and from Heilker and Vandenberg, the methods underpinning Lanham's handlist are similarly focused on intertextual cross-referencing and qualified by spirits of additive exploration and openness: "No attempt has been made to single out terms that any one rhetorical or critical body of opinion might favor, or think important" (p. xiii). In his preface to the first edition, Lanham went on to account in some detail for the various sources he collected terms from, decisions he made about what to include and to exclude, and choices about synonyms and inconsistent spelling, amounting to a glossarist's rationale statement, and yet he also reasserted with humility the list's unavoidable incompleteness. Lanham's handlist contributes to this heaping up—*accumulatio*—of terminological collections that have endured into revised or second editions yet another variation on word watching, a decades-developed index of a highly specialized vocabulary whose bounds he expressed numerous challenges about locating and maintaining.

The words-focused collections I've described so far have emphasized openness, ongoingness, and fluidity while nevertheless building a reference suited to epistemological footing in narrower and narrower *loci* of specialization. Their methodological orientations are comparable: These are collections for the most part forged out of individual or tandem (in Heilker and Vandenberg's case) perspectives informed by lived professional experience within a definite scope—most broadly construed with Williams, most narrowly with Lanham. As variations in word watching, they model a range of approaches that will prove instructive as the remainder of this chapter builds toward a methodological framework for attending to turns and threshold concepts by tracing the families of terms mobilizing such turns and concepts.

Before we move to this methodology in action, I present one final example to illustrate word-watching projects at multiple scales: Claire Lauer's "Contending with Terms: 'Multimodal' and 'Multimedia' in the Academic and Public Spheres," a 2009 article that compared the uptake of just two keywords by looking closely at usage in academic and professional writing settings. Comparable to Williams's (1985) "particular and relational" rationale for *Keywords*, Lauer's (2009) study accounted for each term's *longue durée*, or historical and etymological accretions, as set up in relationship to contemporary, situated instances of usage. "Contending with Terms" also reflected the gains in watching words at a finer (i.e., zoomed-in) scale: intricacies of evolving usage, detailed examples, and hairline tracings that locate these terms in specific contexts all enter into the differentiating account, an account that generally finds multimedia as more common and familiar in industry and workplace contexts and multimodal as occurring predominantly in academic settings. For two terms supposed by many RCWS scholars to be interchangeable, this highly nuanced degree of word watching locates compelling consequences, particularly for rhetorical considerations of *ethos* and audience, and for the political and economic implications of adopting one term or the other to identify one's area of expertise or to name courses or academic programs. Among the salient points in extending word watching to such a refined granularity as this is that broad, general, and provisional inquiries into vocabulary catalyze potentially more refined distinctions with tangible, pragmatic consequences.

While these examples of deliberative word watching, glossary building, and usage comparison lend much to an emerging inquiry into the epistemological gravitas of words *qua* concepts, my purpose here includes inviting questions about how to foster disciplinary word watching for newcomers to the field and what is gained from it. In the following section, while continuing to regard as useful and even exemplary the keywords projects sketched in this section, I will consider contemporary word-watching gestures in digital environments (e.g., a preponderance of readymade word clouds) and thereby deepen an argument for the value in more systematic disciplinary word watching, particularly as it chances to advance insights into the nature of turns and the convergence and dissipation of threshold concepts.

Contemporary word watching practices in digital environments have gravitated toward readymade word clouds, which usually form as oval clusters, nebulous frames within which weighted lists of words or phrases are distinguished in frequency of occurrence using combinations of type size and hue. Word clouds operate according to thin and distant methods in that the text itself falls away and what stands in its place is an assortment of recurrent words and phrases. Precedents for this form might be traced to experimental visual poetics and concrete poetry, examples of which are discussed in Johanna Drucker's (1998) *Figuring the Word* and Craig Saper's (2001) *Networked Art*. The Wikipedia entry on "tag cloud," which includes as variations, "word cloud, or weighted list in visual design," attributes the earliest instances of this practice to "subconscious files" in Douglas Coupland's (2008) *Microserfs*, but there is also a passing attribution of similarity to Doug Lang's 1980 poem "Lester Leaps Out." And while there are nuanced distinctions between tag clouds and word clouds, when it comes to word watching, they function similarly, synechdochally presenting a lesser selection of parts as a stand-in for the whole.

Word clouds are by no means exclusive in the domain of word watching in digital environments. Word watching traces to wiki-based glossaries (e.g., the Threshold Concepts in Digital Rhetoric hub at the Digital Rhetoric Collaborative) and the participatory (if frequently not-safe-for-work) vernacular lexicon Urban Dictionary. But I am focusing on word clouds here because their presentational bases foreground an associative, network logic that corresponds to this chapter's concern for databased infrastructure related to disciplinary usages. Further, word clouds are distinctive as word watching because they display as visual models, and they leave behind from some of the essayistic depth that Williams, Heilker and Vandenberg, Lanham, and Lauer used. In fact, although word clouds lend themselves to exploratory definitional plumbing, they do not in themselves bother with definition, only with association and reduction, coalescing as a generative *gestalt* in combination.

The production and circulation of word clouds are a yet even thinner and potentially more distant attempt at word watching in that they are quickly and easily rendered by copying and pasting blocks of text into an input field at sites such as Wordle, Tagcrowd, or Tagxedo. These are visually compelling counterparts to prose text that offer a complimentary presentation: Words are weighted and arranged *paratactically* (or on all sides), lending contour and relief to the comparably unidimensional presentation of *syntactic* (or linearly ordered) prose. Further, word clouds reduce the text; much of it falls away and what remains is a temporary abstraction, though an abstraction both empirically verifiable and one that due to its metaphoric association with clouds imparts a roiling openness, an ongoing quality, incomplete and vaporous. Such clouds attract visual attention which is also among the reasons they have become popular as surface glosses on a variety of text sets, from curricular materials related to first-year writing (e.g., Eastern Michigan University's custom textbook uses curricularly based Wordles) to short-form writing in bounded timeframes (e.g., memes based on the 2015 "What Are Your Most Used Words on Facebook?" quiz). Comparable clouds have also appeared in media accounts of language comparisons, such as a 2016 analysis of Canadian and United States word usage on Twitter, which concluded that Canadians were more polite (Craggs, 2016).

Academic treatments of word clouds have appeared, as well, such as in a project I developed, "Views from a Distance: A Nephological Model of the CCCC Chairs' Addresses, 1977–2011," which uses a viewport and slider to present more than 30 chairs' addresses from the Conference on College Composition and Communication, introducing the series as "a string of word formations sized and weighted with meaningful visual cues, somewhat like a lexical heat map" (2012, para. 5). Numerous pedagogical applications have turned up also, including word clouds as an aid to interpretation for reading (i.e., rendering clouds as a preliminary inroads to gaining a sense of a complex text) and as an aid to invention and revision in writing (i.e., rendering clouds wrought from one's own writing at any stage of development).

As tempting as it is to level critique toward word clouds for their veneer, they nevertheless stand in as an evidentiary substitution for something else. Certainly there risks a triviality in the practice of creating word clouds; they are, after all, fun and easy readouts on something usually more elaborate and complex, and a site such as Wordle, which touts itself as a "toy," does not advance much more than cursory insights into the computational operations and semantic structures coursing through it. Contemporary word watching in many cases leads into a thicket of methodological limitations, but these limitations—the obscurity of how the clouds are rendered, for instance, or the withholding of the processes by which words are stemmed, combined, and counted, much less the actual counts—need not be a basis of criticism alone. Quite the opposite. These aspects of word watching via cloudmaking inform inquiries into (a) language processing methods and (b) tropology, which names a junction between rhetorical studies and theories of the feed-forward interdependencies of language on other language for meaning.

To expand upon these briefly, word watching in easy-to-render word clouds stands as a simple alternative to more rigorous and robust methods for processing and analyzing language. That is, the word cloud does not usually have the methodological sophistication one would find available with the Natural Language Toolkit, currently the go-to platform in computational linguistics for parsing and classifying corpora. Comparably, software such as NVivo, which supports quantitative data analysis, aids researchers who seek patterns in data collections usually associated with interviews, site observations, and manually coded text. For the purposes of the approach to language processing modeled in the following section, it is enough to acknowledge that the current research landscape includes numerous alternatives for in-depth computational language processing. While these approaches are important to regard as commensurable with the goals of word watching, simple word clouds are every bit as likely to elicit—for beginners—insights into the relationship between a readymade concordance and the comprehensive text(s) under analysis. We must be careful *not* to dismiss or downplay word clouds because they are also fun, playful, or methodologically casual.

Simply, word clouds are methodologically basic, but they function as powerful setups for the sort of word watching that helps us understand turns and threshold concepts so that we can more wittingly participate in the cultivation of them. Word clouds make possible what I describe as a nephological attitude toward the relationship between disciplinary language and epistemology—between the words we use and what we claim to know. Word clouds extend word watching to grasps of language that recognize it as billowing, vaporous, at the edges of signification, connotatively flexible, fluid-like, and ever-shifting in time. These qualities accord with theories of deconstruction, intertextuality, and heteroglossia that underscore more than four decades of poststructural thinking that has influenced the humanities and social sciences. And although it is beyond the scope of this chapter's focus to delve much more deeply than this, some acknowledgement of this relationship is warranted because it operates across the sequence that locates a relationship between word watching, word clouds, disciplinary turns, and threshold concepts. Practices of noticing and creating these formations position us—all of us, including newcomers to field—at the juncture between rhetoric, change, agency, and writing.

Thus positioned, and as a final point of emphasis before transitioning next to illustrations of word watching that are methodologically grounded in semantic fluctuations and that therefore lend insights into the emergence and formation of turns, I want to characterize this array of activity as venturing into the sort of tropospheric play mentioned in the previous chapter in relationship to the *planeur,* or glider whose perspective is incisively scalar, adjudicating between local, up-close ways of knowing and their distant, thin, and removed counterparts. In rhetorical studies, tropes are another name for words and phrases that turn or that signal turns, and thereby change concepts and introduce complementary schema. Not coincidentally, in meteorology, the troposphere names that layer of the atmosphere in which weather events happen. I don't mean to suggest that a discipline is astir with language precipitations only; rather I want to point out that looking toward a disciplinary troposphere anticipates further insights into articulation, assent, and diffusion as open, participatory, agentive processes. Gazing into these clouds—word watching—and bearing down on definitional etymologies, tracing terms as they shift and move through disciplinary resources—by these practices, we can begin to grasp more firmly an interrelationship between turns, threshold concepts, and the terminologies that mobilize them. Such an endeavor is advanced farther by the development of an animated index featuring terms mined from several hundred articles in one of the field's most prominent journals.

Turn Types in an Animated Index

In between the unsystematic selection processes behind the deep definition keywords collections by Williams and by Heilker and Vandenberg and the playful, exploratory enigmatics in web-based word-clouding platforms and practices, there arises an opportunity for developing more systematic and methodologically reproducible inquiries into an ongoing relationship between words and the emergence and maturation of RCWS. Word watching performs important work, especially for newcomers to disciplinary specializations and to stakeholders whose engagement is quick or circumspect, oftentimes lacking a nuanced handle on the field's discursive subtleties. In response to this opportunity, this section introduces what I call an animated index, a playable Google motion chart (Fig. 5) populated with data mined by computational processes from more than 500 articles published over 25 years in *College Composition and Communication* (*CCC*), one of the most prominent and long-established journals in the field.

The motion chart is animated in that it presents data points as part of a year-by-year time series whose elements change position with each passing increment. And it is an index due to its indexical relationship to the corpus under consideration; the words appearing in it come directly from the scholarship published in the journal—a set of 507 articles, or 3,943,528 words, published in *CCC* between 1989 and 2013. The changing positions of the bubble-shaped markers displayed in the motion chart correspond to rates of occurrence. Direct interaction with the animated index contributes greatly to the discussion through the second half of this chapter. That is, for the surest grasp on the arguments advanced here and for the details invoked as rationale for the connection between word watching and turn spotting, I encourage readers to spend time exploring the animated index, which is accessible online at http://www.derekmueller.net/turn.html.

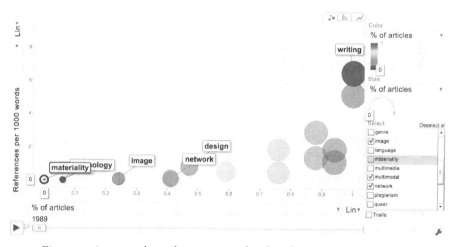

Figure 5. A screenshot of an animated index developed using Google Motion Charts. The interactive version of this screenshot can be viewed at https://wac.colostate.edu/docs/books/network/fig05-desc-video.mov.

This screenshot (Fig. 5) provides a cursory orientation to the animated index. Upon visiting the index online, clicking the playhead (grey) in the lower left-hand portion of the frame will begin its play process, as the bubbles rise and fall or shift right or left depending on the instances rate per 1,000 words (y- or vertical axis) and on the percentage of articles in which the term appeared that year (x- or horizontal axis). For example, in 1989, the word "network" appeared 10 times (.09 per 1,000 tokens) and in 7 of the 17 articles (41%) published in *CCC* that year. By comparison, "writing," which was also the most frequently occurring unigram (or one-word phrase) in *CCC* in 1989, appeared 699 times (6.48 per 1,000 tokens) and in all 17 articles (100% published that year). As the animated index plays, terms that shift up or to the right reflect an increasing presence in the journal, while terms that shift down or to the left reflect declining presence in the journal.

The 25 terms collected here are a modest representative sample whose rational for selection will become clearer before the end of the chapter. Note, as well, that while the animated index could feature myriad additional terms (e.g., several hundred unigrams or bi-grams [two-word phrases]), it operates here purposefully and as an indicator of possibilities yet underexplored at the crossroads of semantic networks and disciplinary emergence and stabilization. Further, the same data underpinning the animated index could be engaged through a textual account, comparable to the deep definition essays collected by Heilker and Vandenberg, or through a visual representation, such as a word cloud drifting freer from the concordance metrics (i.e., the quantitative basis for the chart). The motion chart, however, provides a fortuitous frame for exploring the data, rewinding it and playing it again to consider different dimensions and to notice coordinations that might initiate new questions.

Engaging directly with the motion chart, you will notice several customizable options. The play locator can be selected and dragged manually to exact locations in the series, which may aid in focusing on comparative moments. The playback speed is adjustable, as well, by moving the vertical indicator immediately adjacent to the play button. Individual words or clusters of words can be selected in the "Select" box on the right side of the playback frame, and just below users can turn on trails, which function as time series traces. Additionally, three tabs in the upper right-hand corner of the playback frame allow toggling between three different chart types: bubble, bar, and line.

The flexibility of the playback frame is among its most salient qualities for word watching, and for interacting with the semantic data set featured here. The platform, originally called Gapminder, was popularized by Hans Rosling, a world health researcher who in 2006 delivered a TED Talk based on an elaborate United Nations data set connected to birth rates, life expectancy, and distributions of income. Rosling's dance with data attracted widespread attention, not only to the correlations he so masterfully put on display between health and economics but also to the Gapminder playback frame. Rosling went on to craft and deliver presentations on a range of issues, including cancer statistics, swine flu, overpopulation, and child mortality—all of which expanded the impression of Gapminder's presentational intricacy for complex, multivariable data sets. Soon thereafter, Google acquired Gapminder and its availability widened when its coding infrastructure became a part of Google Charts. What this meant was that everyday users could easily build playback frames similar to Rosling's. It is now possible to create a Gapminder motion chart with a couple of clicks from any data set in Google Sheets—and this accessibility expands the possibilities for connecting the word-based animated

index linked above to pedagogical applications sketched in this chapter's concluding section.

As noted before, batch processes for creating concordances are numerous. By batch processes, I am referring to the use of a computer script to sift,
sort, and select designated words or phrases from a large collection of texts.
Concordances are alphabetical lists of words appearing in a text, much like an
index. The process involved here was run from the command line, a simple
interface where users initiate programming operations. For the *CCC* articles,
I executed a Perl script to render a collection of individual text files into individual concordances and a cumulative concordance for the set. To prepare for
running the Perl script, I converted each article into a text file—a process that
included manually removing abstracts, works cited, repeated details in head-
ers and footers, and pull quotes, as well as searching and replacing hyphenat-
ed line breaks that in some instances split words into two separate strings of
characters. Although some refer to this as cleaning the data, I have consistently referred to the process vernacularly as smoothing the text. I smoothed the
507 articles, organized them into year-based folders, and ran the Perl script
that converted each folder's contents into a two-column list, words in the first
column and frequency counts in the second.

Next I developed a simple spreadsheet in Excel for collecting and compiling lookup data. That is, after running several early, provisional operations on
more than 100 terms commonly appearing in the top 200 words in multiple
years, I gradually decided upon the set of 25 words to be featured in this iteration of the animated index. My rationale for choosing this list of 25 terms
was based on a manageable scope and on the relevance of specific clusters for
illustrating different turn types discussed next. I opened each year's cumulative
concordance, one by one, and searched on each of the 25 terms, transposing
the frequency count into the tallying spreadsheet. Second, I searched the contents of each year's folder for each word, which returned a list of the articles
containing the string (e.g., searching the 1989 folder for "assessment" yields
four files, indicating the word appeared in four different articles out of the 17
articles published in *CCC* that year). Together, these steps constituted 1,250
lookups (each word requiring two per year covered in the chart). Finally, I
counted words and articles (per article and cumulatively) for each year-based
folder and added those values to the spreadsheet. With these established, basic
Excel formulae calculated the two most prominent values used in the playback
frame: (a) the rate of appearances of x per 1,000 words published that year, and
(b) the percentage of articles in which x appeared that year. This dual variable
input contributes more nuanced insights into the circulation of a term. That is,
some terms appear infrequently but with great breadth (e.g., once per article
but in most articles); other terms appear thickly in just one article.

With the data assembled into the spreadsheet, matching it to the code specifications required by the Google Charts API involved precise sequencing and removal of blank spaces (using TextWrangler, a free text and code editor for Mac OS X). Following spacing and syntax guidelines, each data point in the animated index looked like this:

['assessment',(1989),4,0.04,4,0.24],

['audience',(1989),58,0.54,10,0.59],

['class',(1989),119,1.10,16,0.94],

['composition',(1989),313,2.90,15,0.88],

['computer',(1989),1,0.01,1,0.06],

Consider the last line of the code shown here in more detail. The first and second variables are clearly enough established as the word (computer) and the year (1989). Variables three and four are the raw word count (1) and ratio per 1,000 words in that year's articles (0.01). This means that the word "computer" appeared just 1 time out of 107,870 words published in the journal that year. The fifth and sixth variables are the raw article count (1) and the percentage of articles (0.06) in which the term appeared that year. This means that the single instance of "computer" appeared in just 1 of the 17 articles published in 1989, or 6%.

The unit of code is specified within the Google Motion Charts API, though it is flexible insofar as it can accommodate classes of data and additional elements within a single line. (It is entirely possible to develop a yet more elaborate set of variables to associate with each key data point.) In addition to a few lines of code to set defaults, name axes, and stylize the typefaces, the animated index required 625 lines of code like the ones shown above. Assembling the playback frame is in itself a function of word watching, yet by interacting with the animated index—looping its playback with different selections—patterns become clearer. This move, from word watching to noticing patterns, is akin to what I call *turn spotting*. The accretion and avulsion of selected terms and small clusters of terms constitute turns, and more than turns, they make possible a series of different turn types. In this case, distant and thin methods support inquiry into a vast data set (nearly 4 million words published in 507 articles over 25 years), aiding invaluable perspective on the discipline as a confluence of words. This perspective would be difficult to achieve by any other means.

Having freshly played and replayed the animated index, and with more granular, direct, and reproducable evidence of the ways terms rise and fall over 25 years in a prominent disciplinary corpus, an inquiry into turn spotting takes on greater nuance. The rise and fall of any keyword reports, to some extent, the magnitude of its operation in the thought and action of scholars in the field, and each individual term that appears in the animated index plots a possible turn. The words we use are thickly, inextricably linked with the ideas we sponsor (see, e.g., Bazerman, 1992; MacDonald, 2010; Prior, 1998), and some of those ideas have transitioned to *goddess*[7] turns, whose gulfs are so well carved and widely known as to circulate unquestioned (e.g., linguistic, social, process). The animated index proves generative for differentiating among turns and zeroing in on a series of different turn types, including goddess turns. Next, I consider four additional turns the animated index helps us see: non-turns, gradual turns, micro-turns, and amnesic turns.

Non-Turns: Students and Writing

Non-turns are associated with terms that appear stable or constant, having plateaued in the time series. Recalling the partiality of this data set's anchorage in but one journal, the non-turns reflected in *College Composition and Communication* from 1989 through 2013 emerge as *writing* and *students* (Fig. 6). Setting aside stop words—a collection of words the batch processing script ignores because of high rates of recurrence (e.g., parts of speech such as articles and prepositions)—writing and students stand out as the top two terms in every year but one. In 2012, the leading terms shift to *writing* and *research*, with *students* slipping to third, due in large part to a special issue of the journal dedicated to research methods. Based on this pattern, one could argue that *writing* and *students* operate for the field, or rather the field as read through the lens of *CCC* as a prominent locus for scholarship, attention, and discussion. Whatever else our words engage with, writing and students consistently reappear in that mix.

Extending this thin, distant methodology to other journals would broaden consideration of non-turns like these to include other terms. Cue the question: What in addition to writing and students do we never turn away from? If comparable word frequency data were available from even one additional journal in the field (e.g., *College English, JAC, Composition Studies, Rhetoric Society Quarterly, Rhetoric Review, Written Communication, Kairos, Composition Forum,* and *Research in the Teaching of English*), we could document these indexical stabilizers even better. Such work may eventually come to pass, and although it is beyond the scope of this study, my hope is for this work to pique extensions and continuations that dig further into the questions motivating

---

7   I've grown accustomed to feminizing god references, almost entirely as a tribute to my late mother, who taught me never to accept unquestioned the status quo gendering of abstract deities that serve patriarchal interests, and, as such, also as an acknowledgement that my daughter, who will never meet my mother, deserves to see this worldview gain traction in the world.

turn spotting—questions about the relationships between published scholar-ship, terminologies, and turns.

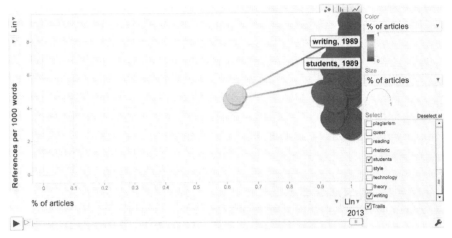

Figure 6. A screenshot of the animated index set to display non-turns as modeled by the frequencies of "students" and "writing" (trails on). The interactive version of this screenshot can be viewed at https:// wac.colostate.edu/docs/books/network/fig06-desc-video.mov.

Gradual Turns: Assessment

Gradual turns coalesce slowly, ascending into broader circulation, though perhaps without a defining moment of catalysis or without being declared explicitly as a turn. Consider *assessment* as an example. Assessment names a range of practices that seek specific alignment between goals and performanc-es. There is much more to assessment work than can be accounted fully here, although rising pressures to make teaching and learning activities accountable (reducibly so) have propelled assessment into common pedagogical practice. For instance, assessment has become a priority for writing program admin-istration, spawning new academic journals with assessment in the title and compelling academics to identify assessment at all scales, such as formative/ generative and evaluative, among their specializations. Even with a gradual increase of reference to assessment, what complicates this creeping tendency is that no one has, as of yet, declared an *assessment turn* in RCWS.

Nevertheless, assessment keeps turning up (Fig. 7). And so it is with this gradual turn—an assessment turn—that, even though it has not been declared a turn, the appearance of the word in *CCC* has increased across both variables reported in the animated index. More articles are using the word assessment more often. Its expanding circulation hints at questions that are posed all the more forcefully: How is assessment operating in the field? What are some of the narrower disciplinary domains—intellectual, curricular, programmatic, instructional, professionalizing, political, or economic—where assessment signals a shift? Distant and thin methods applied to the creation of concordances from disciplinary corpora provide equipment for varied turn spotting. And although the turns spotted are limited as answers in and of themselves, noticing a gradual turn initiates many more questions for yet further exploration. The animated index and the batch processed data set underpinning it combine as a compelling, suggestive question-generating technology: The index projects terms on arrows that lead into the future, what we might think of as ellipsing into a "possibility space" (Volk, 1995, p. 190). Word watching of this sort springs more promising questions about the continuing emergence and maturation of the field than it resolves.

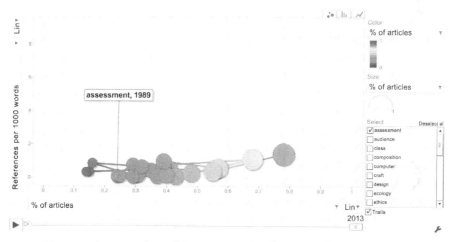

Figure 7. A screenshot of the animated index set to the frequency of "assessment" (trails on), which displays a gradual turn in this model. The interactive version of this screenshot can be viewed at https:// wac.colostate.edu/docs/books/network/fig07-desc-video.mov.

Micro-Turns: Multimodal

Following non-turns and gradual turns, micro-turns are those niche turns, small and not necessarily sustained over a long period of time. They blinker into disciplinary discourse, sometimes fleetingly, with a comparatively smaller circulation than their larger or longer-sustained counterparts, appearing only for a few years or boosted temporarily perhaps by a special issue or a watershed article. *Multimodal* is the first of the turn types plotted in the animated index to also appear in the list of 13 so-declared turns collected at the beginning of this chapter (see Sheridan, 2010). Multimodal—as was contrasted by Claire Lauer (2009) with multimedia—is a term more common in academic settings that accounts for the dimensions of composing to include much more than text. Multimodal refers to the rhetorical interdependency of material and other extratextual qualities of effective written communication, including visual, textural, olfactory, affective–somatic, and aural qualities. Notice that the animated index shows "multimodal" rustle only briefly, forward and back again, not quite ascending to prominence compared to turns noted previously (Fig. 8).

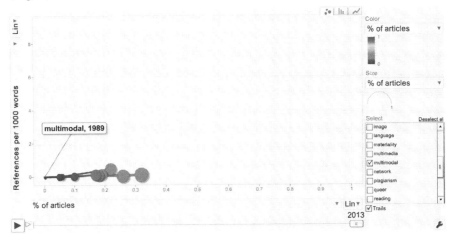

Figure 8. A screenshot of the animated index set to display the frequency of "multimodal" (trails on), which signals a micro-turn in the model. The interactive version of this screenshot can be viewed at https:// wac.colostate.edu/docs/books/network/fig08-desc-video.mov.

Micro-turns are *turn kernels* with the potential to germinate into flourishing disciplinary conversations. In the following section, I will return to multimodality—as a term, a turn, and a threshold concept—to introduce a series of visual models designed to illustrate how turns manifest not only as singular words and concepts. As you will see, they also travel in clusters—mobilized by semantic networks, or families of terms whose named concepts weave together and whose collective ascendance makes longer-lasting and more formidable status possible.

Turns Away: Style, Language, Rhetoric

Finally, the animated index (Fig. 9) provides an alternative perspective on what has elsewhere been framed as *turns away*: lacks, gaps, omissions, and left-behind ideas in particular venues or in the field more generally (see, e.g., Bernard-Donals, 2008, on rhetoric; Butler, 2008, 2009, on style; MacDonald, 2007, on language). I have grouped these as turns away because such claims are often framed as a critical call for more of whatever has gone missing, and the methods for noticing something has gone missing are not necessarily well suited to tracking it down elsewhere. In relation to the animated index, however, these three turns away—from language, rhetoric, and style—become more complicated when there surfaces parallel evidence that direct reference to each of these has continued, as is the case here. There is much, much more to explore with this matter of disciplinary turning away.[8] The animated index and the data set it presents intervene constructively into such claim-making, for turns away may very well be micro-turns elsewhere, and the locations of these elsewheres, if we can find them, not only deepen such claims, but they also project as dispersively connected the ever-shifting disciplinary landscape, which of course overlays a tapestry of inter- and transdisciplinary domains. This work sets up a needed practice akin to terminological ground-truthing, or continuously revisiting the critical, constitutive tension between a semi-stable disciplinary lexicon, published scholarship, and the discipline itself as it operates complexly across many different sites, locations, and publication venues.

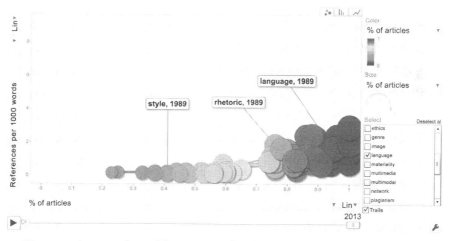

Figure 9. A screenshot of the animated index set to display the frequencies

8   This relates to what could be presented as *amnesic turns*, or forgettings. I don't develop the idea here, but it accords with linguistics research at University of Toronto on the declining range of unique tokens in Agatha Christie's late-career novels as a (possible) indicator of early onset Alzheimers (Lancashire & Hirst, 2009, pp. 8–10). The parallel between a field's turning away and an individual writer's declining lexical range is compelling though perhaps not quite relevant in the context of the animated index as applied to rethinking turns and threshold concepts.

of "style," "rhetoric," and "language" (trails on), which shows turns away in this model. The interactive version of this screenshot can be viewed at https://wac.colostate.edu/docs/books/network/fig09-desc-video.mov.

In addition to motivating the turn typology sketched here, the animated index proves useful for systematic and data-driven word watching, for tracing the paths of an ever-unfolding disciplinary discourse due to its density and rate of advancement (i.e., recall the *internal problematic of disciplinarity*, which includes data sets, a reading problem, and appropriate methods). The value in this for newcomers can hardly be overstated. In addition to demonstrating potential for further work on the constitutive relationship between corpus analytics and turn spotting, the typology recalls what I established previously as a need for surer and more accessible methods—and the forms of evidence they produce—as bases for turn declarations that shouldn't only be possible after spending a couple of decades in the field. Among the reasons these methods and visualization practices are important *now* is that they open the practices of turn spotting to newcomers who themselves, by virtue of their emerging commitments to teaching and research in RCWS, *are turn makers*, sponsors of the discipline's future.

To illustrate this more fully, I will revisit and extend the multimodal micro-turn, exploring it more carefully in relation to visual models that can help us locate its ascendance as more broad-based than the path a singular term suggests. Multimodality has been boosted by the ascendance of a family of terms, a small semantic network. The multimodal turn, as it happens, stabilized from a micro-turn into a threshold concept, and, in the next section, a series of visual models will extend word watching from isolatable term-paths to clusters with the purpose of theorizing how such a stabilization happens.

Turns Dream of Becoming Threshold Concepts

I risk framing the relationship between turns and threshold concepts too simply when I assert that turns want to become threshold concepts. Threshold concepts have gained influence since 2003 when educational psychologists Jan Meyer and Ray Land first proposed them as a way to name disciplinarily situated principles that function as gateways for newcomers: "In certain disciplines there are 'conceptual gateways' or 'portals' that lead to a previously inaccessible, and initially perhaps 'troublesome,' way of thinking about something" (p. 373). Meyer and Land extended and refined their work in a series of articles, and attempts to articulate threshold concepts have subsequently begun to surface in several academic disciplines, including RCWS.

In 2015, an edited collection by Linda Adler-Kassner and Elizabeth Wardle, *Naming What We Know: Threshold Concepts of Writing Studies*, appeared as RCWS's first formal, published attempt to list and introduce an expansive set of disciplinary threshold concepts. The development of the project is elaborated in detail in the collection's introduction. It entailed proposals made by 45 teacher–scholars, which ended up becoming a group of 29 contributors who worked individually and in pairs (5 entries were written collaboratively) to define 37 concepts in approximately 1,000-word essays.

In their introduction to the collection, Adler-Kassner and Wardle (2015) acknowledged that their approach was admittedly only a beginning that would no doubt be "contentious" and require continual development "in the coming decades" (p. 5). With an interest in the generative overlaps between articulations of disciplinary turns and the data-driven animated index *qua* word watching, I extend this chapter's inquiry into turn spotting in the spirit of engaging with threshold concepts in the coming decades. Motivations include an interest in the life's arc of a threshold concept (i.e., in a historical build-up that eventually tips the concept from conjectural to an epistemological cornerstone) and also in further opening the process of naming what we know—postulating threshold concepts—as more than the purview of experts, specialists, or those with long-standing status in the field. Put yet more simply, I seek here to adapt word watching as a collection of methods for examining the ascendance of concepts into threshold concept status and to extend the invitation to generate threshold concepts so it reaches beyond the senior-scholar establishment to include newcomers to the field, particularly graduate students.

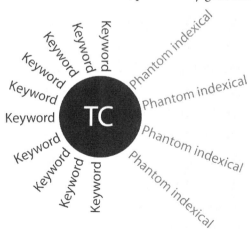

Figure 10. A simple radial model designed to illustrate the relationship between threshold concepts (TC) and keywords and phantom indexicals, as the terms that catalyze threshold concepts.

To more intricately describe threshold concepts as dynamic, morphing over time, and articulable not only on the basis of expert, experiential knowing but also on the basis of evidence-based word watching, I begin with a simple proposition: Threshold concepts are themselves mobilized by the ascendance of semantic networks constituted by interrelated terms. Many (though not all) such terms can be traced in published scholarship; additional terms participate in the ascendance, even though they cannot in some cases be traced directly. I refer to these untraceable terms as *phantom indexicals*. From this, a simple visual model takes form as follows (Fig. 10). It depicts a circular center for posing the threshold concept; 10 keywords and 4 phantom indexicals radiate, surrounding it as setae-like mobilizers for the focal concept. Related models could use more or fewer terms, add term types (i.e., go beyond keywords and phantom indexicals), and perhaps also pose more complex and compelling visual arrangements. What I offer here is but a simple model: a start.

Figure 11. A simple radial model designed to illustrate the relationship between a specific threshold concept, "All writing is multimodal," and selected keywords and phantom indexicals relevant to the threshold concept's emergence.

Adapted to the threshold concept, "All writing is multimodal," the model reflects explicit attunement to terms whose associations with multimodality stand as speculative openings (Fig. 11). On the left side of the radial model, the 10 keywords are *computer, craft, design, image, genre, materiality, multimodal, network, technology,* and *writing*. Determining which terms to include substantiates its own generative inquiry into semantic networks as they coalesce around concepts, and this should be recognized as a heuristic (i.e., a series of choices whose felicities are inventive, not overly restrictive or exclusive). I chose these terms for their illustrative efficacy, aware that such clustering is informed by supplemental reading, an understanding of the historical development of related concepts, and the respective fitting together of these terms as antecedents to multimodality. A related process of selection and differentiation goes into identifying the set of four phantom indexicals radiating on the right side of the circular model. Multimodality as an ascendant concept is boosted by *theory*, *media*, *method*, and *rhetoric*, although because these are looser, more expansive references, their operating on the ascendant concept is not necessarily explicit, direct, or traceable in the disciplinary corpus.

With the semantic networks provisionally though adequately sketched, we can return to the animated index to inquire into the network's rising circulation, thereby honing in on a hypothesis: "All writing is multimodal" rose to threshold concept status only since the early 2000s, and its ascendance corresponded to the increased circulation and influence of related keywords (Fig. 12). Selecting the 10 keywords in the animated index and clicking 'play,' this slight ascendance becomes visible in the rightward movement of the bubbles for many of these terms. The pattern hints at multimodality's recency as a disciplinarily influential concept. Threshold concepts are not forever; like stars, they come and go, intensify and fade. The combination of these simple visual models and the animated index fed with data mined from a disciplinarily salient corpus provides a methodology for inquiring into how a threshold concept emerges, matures, and perhaps also how it eventually quiets.

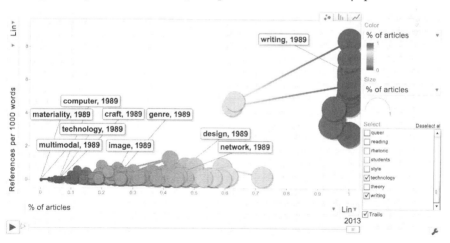

Figure 12. A screenshot of the animated index set to display the 10 keywords proposed in Figure 11 as catalysts for the ascendance of "All Writing is Multimodal" as a disciplinary threshold concept (trails on).

To emphasize yet broader possibilities for engaging with questions about threshold concepts mobilizing on the backs of relatively small semantic networks, consider the sparkline graph in Figure 13, which depicts the same data as the animated index screenshot in Figure 12. Here, the same 10 keywords are assigned line graphs representing year-by-year frequency scores. This alternative strengthens the impression made by the animated index: All but two terms—genre and design—show peak frequencies in the most recent two-thirds of the graph (approximately the most recent 15 years). The pattern suggests that mobilizing terminologies have gained steam, and, with their rising circulation, laid way for the ascendant status of multimodality as a threshold concept.

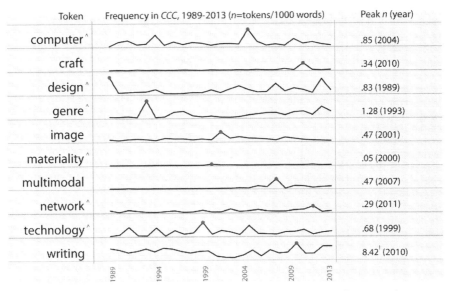

Figure 13. A comparative sparkline graph designed to illustrate the frequency patterns of keywords presented in Figure 11 as catalysts for the ascendance of "All Writing is Multimodal" as a disciplinary threshold concept. (Carots on certain words in Fig. 13 indicate keywords featured in Heilker and Vandenberg's [2015] Keywords in Writing Studies.)

These visual models underscore the temporal dynamism of keywords, turns, and threshold concepts and offer a thin and distant methodological intervention into contemporary word watching that directly serves inquiring into disciplinary emergence, stabilization, and maturation. In addition, the models also promote semantic network sense and reinforce many time-based rhetorical principles, such as *kairos* and *metanoia*, in the circulation of disciplinary discourses. As one more takeaway from this work, we might do well to revisit a 1926 lecture by Polish structural linguist and theorist Alfred Korzybski, "Time-Binding: The General Theory" (reprinted in 1962). Because Korzybski's work with the general semantics movement remains justifiably controversial (due primarily to its structurally normative overtures and incapacity to tolerate language diversity), invoking Korzybski presumes both patience and generosity. His theory of time-binding promoted an annotation system that assigned time-based superscript notes to words. A similar premise has bearing on the distinctions emphasized in this section. For example, design[1993] is not quite the same as design[2013]. Neither are network[1989] and network[2012] exact replicas. As we participate yet more robustly in declaring turns or in sponsoring threshold concepts—by discussing them or by attempting to create new ones—flagging their temporality (e.g., What year is multimodality?) will serve as a salient reminder of the constancy of disciplinary change for newcomers and long-timers alike.

Turn-Making in Rhetoric and Composition/Writing Studies

This chapter's emphases up to now have addressed ways word watching informs turn spotting and, by extension, how contemporary word-watching practices aid in the tracing of the emergence and formation of disciplinary threshold concepts. Beyond this analytical and methodological groundwork—an application of distant and thin methods to one disciplinary corpus—I want to reassert the heuristic value of these processes for newcomers to disciplinary discourses. Word watching and turn spotting demand a refined attentiveness to language patterns at differing scales, and these practices are anchored in language itself—a well of evidence that as contemporary readers and writers of the field, we must never deviate too far from as long as we consider our work to be threaded through and dependent upon its influence. Word watching and turn spotting offer more than epistemological footing; they open inventively onto the creation of turns and the possibilities for articulating the shape of the field to come.

Thus, to complement the analytical and methodological apertures of this project, in this concluding section I offer four practical and pedagogical derivatives useful for engaging newcomers as turn-makers. These are projects that extend the work of word watching and involve newcomers in forging connections between established epistemological domains and the contributions their work makes to the course of knowledge-making as influenced by their research and writing.

Glossaries

Conventionally, glossaries are specialized collections of words, usually presented alphabetically and with brief definitions. The definitions need not essentialize the term; in fact, in many encounters with new vocabularies it is useful for newcomers to pose their own understandings based on experience, association, and contextual clues from conversations and readings rather than to reduce glossary definitions to connotations pulled from dictionary look-ups alone. In nearly any course or program of study, glossaries operate as primers for provisional thinking about words that are curious, ambiguous, unfamiliar, or especially significant-seeming, important, and consequential. Glossaries may invite a great range of attempts to define, from formal to informal, constrained by length parameters (e.g., one-sentence or tweet-length definitions or much longer explorations). They also scale well, reducing in scope to a single reading or expanding to cover an array of texts, as well as adapting to individual or collaborative development.

For newcomers to a disciplinary discourse, glossaries can also shed light on known-unknowns, terms that are circulating without acute familiarity that are taken for granted as givens or commonplaces or that perhaps fall beneath notice as insignificant, outdated, or uninteresting. To illustrate the importance of engaging known-unknowns, consider the following ranking exercise. In Fall 2015, I taught Introduction to Graduate Studies in Written Communication using Heilker and Vandenberg's (2015) *Keywords in Writing Studies*. Students completed a brief survey to rate their interest in the 36 keywords included in the collection. Instead of reading the entire collection as flat or regarding all terms as essentially the same, we focused on the aggregate top five choices from the class based on the survey results and read and discussed the entries for each: silence, literacy, identity, discourse, and community. But we also took special notice of the five lowest-rated terms. For the following week, we shifted our attention to these, reading and discussing them as terms that, for reasons important for us to explore together, registered the lowest interest ratings: other, ecology, queer, civic/public, and contact zone. What is gained in attending to the popular terms among the class? What is lost in neglecting the unpopular terms? Informed by word-watching principles sketched in this chapter, such pedagogical activities can productively renew attention to terms and re-invest terministic awareness as an ongoing function of disciplinary wherewithal.

Deep Definition Inquiries

In relationship to glossaries, deep definition inquiries embark on word watching as a more fully developed, sustained, and substantive undertaking. A deep definition account, much like the keyword essays collected by Heilker and Vandenberg, examines a word or phrase by detailing its etymology, tracing it into specific contexts, and suggesting salient associations and distinctions. Such profiles of terms afford newcomers a highly focused research question that may deepen understanding of a referent's complexity while also generating new interests at the edges of the specified concept. Like glossaries, deep definition inquiries accord with word watching, and they also scale well whether attempted by individuals or small teams, or presented in various delivery and circulation methods (e.g., posters, presentations, or small-scale anthologies) that may gather together a class-wide set of terms.

Prompting deep definition inquiries can begin with self-selected curiosity or with class materials available in lists of keywords or in indexes. Consider the value in turning to a textbook's index, spending time with students discussing explicitly the usefulness of indexes, both for mapping the locations of these concepts in the text but also for providing a thin description of the conceptual domain it inhabits. Deep definition inquiries may be initiated from such lists, both for what the lists include and—this is one of my favorite pedagogical choices—for what it leaves out or ignores. Posing the exigence for deep definition inquiries as making a case for terms to be included orients the purpose to argumentation, to making a case for the consequences of an additional term surfacing in a particular context. Additionally, deep definition inquiries might also begin with scholarship that has carefully differentiated between vocabularies, such as Lauer's (2009) "Contending with Terms: 'Multimodal' and 'Multimedia' in the Academic and Public Spheres." Such work proves a rich precursor for deep definition inquiries, and yet, as the preface to the updated Heilker and Vandenberg (2015) *Keywords* collection notes, such accounts are always due for updates due to the ongoing dynamism of these words as they age and as usage shifts. In light of this, turning to past treatments of keywords to ask "what has become of this term?" for specific entries indicates a regenerative capacity of word watching where it informs this suggested project framework.

Semantic Worknets

Whereas glossaries and deep definition inquiries take a predominantly textual approach to word watching, semantic worknets introduce a visual component to the gathering and tracing of a family of salient terms in the context of a scholarly article. The word *worknets* is a playful inversion of networks; I have elaborated the idea elsewhere in terms of a pedagogy that involves readers in creating a series of visual models (spokes emanating from a hub or center that stands in for the germinal article) that tease out aspects of sources (Mueller, 2015).

Semantic worknets aid readers in attending to a sample of phrases whose meanings—both as established internal to the source material and as extensible, connecting to experiences, situations, and references elsewhere—are regarded to be important, insightful, or thickly set to the article's focus. Noticing published articles as concentrations of specialized vocabulary and inventorying the ways those vocabularies are linked and traceable produces a localized (here, in this one article) and immediate (now, in the time I am reading it) conductor of network sense that primes further inquiries into the interrelationship between disciplinary knowledges and the words we use. Along with the visual representation of the small cluster of salient words or phrases (Fig. 14), the semantic worknet accompanies a textual account that recognizes the situated significances of the terms and their relationships and that gestures speculatively to further possibilities for these terms as prompts for an emerging research question.

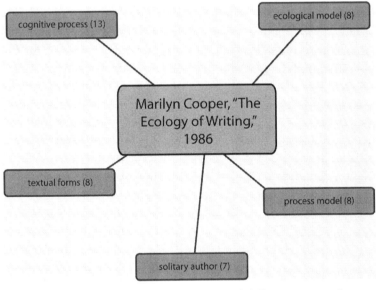

Figure 14. A semantic worknet, or radial model illustrating a selection of bi-grams derived from Marilyn Cooper's (1986) "The Ecology of Writing."

Semantic worknets offer but one phase of a more expansive framework for engaging sources. The other phases are complementary insofar as they attend to sources cited (bibliographic worknet), authorship and influences (affinity worknet), and world events or popular culture coincident in time and place to the source's production (choric worknet). The hub and spoke visual model offers a simple formulation of a connection between the article and salient words and phrases recurring therein. It would do well, however, to include a further extended periphery beyond the prominent terms that pose as possible keyword-led inquiries. To suppose dotted lines that extend orbits, and orbits removed from the core article is, in effect, to realize intertextuality and its traceability as generative for priming researchable questions and for articulating connections.

Animated Indexes of Tomorrow

One more pedagogical possibility comes in the form of prompting students to create what I consider animated indexes of tomorrow—futurecast, playable motion charts populated with sets of terms they believe their research will promote and mobilize over the next decade. Compared to glossaries, deep definition inquiries, and semantic worknets, which favor an interpretive–hermeneutic relationship to existing texts, animated indexes of tomorrow are positioned as the most experimental of the four pedagogical adaptations sketched here. These are especially promising for advanced undergraduates and for graduate students working on major projects or dissertations because students can locate in these more substantive projects a family of terms that are particularly load-bearing, whether due to frequency or distinctiveness.

Because animated indexes of tomorrow are speculative, the numerical values assigned to the keyword positions are conjectural. Even so, they are also suggestive, as they set up a hypothetical tomorrow that newcomers to the field—especially when they think of their work as mattering, as they should—may find generative and useful for focusing on what precisely they think their work will do, what ideas it will advance, and what difference it will make when it is taken up. An animated index of tomorrow sets up quickly in Google Sheets, with columns set aside for keyword, year, references count, number of articles, and percentage of articles in the given year. Simply, the purpose of the animated index of tomorrow is to recognize as explicit and foreseeable a relationship between one's own writing and the creation of future-oriented disciplinary focuses. Long-timers to the field already recognize this relationship in ways newcomers are still discovering: The discipline is written by us; its future shape is ours, by the force of language, to articulate.

Finally, across these four practical and pedagogical derivations lingers a deeply political question about the nature of disciplinary invitation—whether it should gravitate toward paying homage to established, pre-existing conversations (as is the emphasis of the well-known if highbrow Burkean parlor) or whether it ought to instead introduce change, even transgressively so. Extended word watching to speculative projections of a discipline opens onto the inevitably transgressive quality of invitation, a notion developed in Jacques Derrida's (2000) *Of Hospitality*. At its simplest, this means that upon accepting an invitation, upon entering the parlor, the order is transgressed, altered, and reconstituted. The degree of transgression has much to do with the entrant's heeding established practices *or not*. Every rhetorical choice is inflected with a tension between continuity and change. As such, I end this chapter on turn spotting with its impact on turn making as a priority. Within the conditions for change in a discipline lingers a paradox much like that which motivated Jim Corder's (1995) concern for "Turnings," about how to honor divergent rhetorics, how to bridge separations that do not seem to compromise, to participate in the field's coherent maturation with the fullest possible command of its responsibilities, and at the same time advance change insistent on radical eclecticism.

Chapter 4: The Thin, Long
Tail of Citation Frequency

> Newcomers to this dialogue are sometimes unfamiliar with the heteroglossia of our heritage, with the voices that have created the conversation upon which we continue to build. For example, as composition and rhetoric matures, who was speaking? (Phillips, Greenberg & Gibson, 1993, p. 443)

Inventorying an Epistemic Court

Nearly two decades ago, Donna Burns Phillips, Ruth Greenberg, and Sharon Gibson (1993) inquired into rhetoric and composition/writing studies' (RCWS) maturation using methods of counting and sorting to distinguish various subsets of aggregate data drawn from *College Composition and Communication* (*CCC*). Phillips, Greenberg, and Gibson's project provided an early snapshot of what Janice Lauer (1984) described 10 years before in a *Rhetoric Review* essay titled "Composition Studies: Dappled Discipline" as an *epistemic court*, or a locus through which disciplinary knowledge circulates, attracts attention, and gains its status. Although the Phillips, Greenberg, and Gibson (1993) study was limited to a single journal, their compilation stands as an early investigation into broad-scope data from *CCC*, which included the most frequently cited authors and works, the journal's material forms, and the journal's editors since March 1950. Their report cannot be considered a comprehensive, evidence-based Zeitgeist of the disciplinary activity spanning more than 40 years into the early 1990s; however, the inventory provided a data-driven statement against which competing perspectives on disciplinary activity could be compared. For how it was cast as both exploratory and data-driven—much like the work that follows—it must be regarded as an early instance of post-positivistic data science (Kitchin, 2014) and an agent of new and emerging big data epistemology that distinguished itself from the proof-oriented noetic trappings of a purer empiricism.

In an effort to update and contribute further to the ongoing inventorying of RCWS' epistemic court, this chapter adopts a similar exigency to that heeded by Phillips, Greenberg, and Gibson (1993) as it relies upon quantitative data, bibliometrics, and graphing as a means of thinly describing the changing nature of "who [has been] speaking" over the past 25 years, according to citation frequencies in *CCC*. Essentially, I contend that graphs, as a form of distant reading (Moretti, 2007, 2013) and an instantiation of thin description (Love, 2010, 2013), help us to know continually unfolding tensions among specialization, the interdisciplinary reach of RCWS, and the challenges these present to newcomers to the scholarly conversation.

Suspending judgment from the outset about the consequences of specialization and interdisciplinary borrowing as generally positive or negative, this chapter seeks to demonstrate how graphs can function as a productive, suasive abstracting practice that will allow us to look more carefully at what has happened to citation practices in *CCC* from 1987 to 2011. Toward this end, first I will say more about the studies using graphs and relevant quantitative methods to understand journals and the fields sponsoring them. Doing so highlights the three basic principles of distant reading and thin description elaborated in Chapter Two. Graphs operate as data-driven visual models; their visual force is in translating a collection of data into a comprehensible figure. Graphs deliberately alter scale, and as such, they aggregate patterns linking details and nonobvious phenomena otherwise at risk of passing unobserved. As a function of their systematic compilation of replicable data, graphed patterns may empirically corroborate local, tacitly felt impressions about changing disciplinary conditions. In the second half of this chapter, I adopt as an exploratory framework Chris Anderson's (2004, 2008) work on long tails (Pareto distributions) and present graphs based on a compilation of 16,726 citations in 491 journal articles[9] published in *CCC* over 25 years. Departing from studies of citation that have focused exclusively on the most frequently referenced figures, I argue that graphing the relationship between the most frequently cited figures and the changing distribution of infrequently referenced figures produces a unique perspective on a changing disciplinary density of great relevance to specialists, generalists, and initiates alike.

Precedents for Graphing and Quantification: Accounting for Scholarly Activity

Graphing and the methods of quantification at their foundation have precedents in RCWS. For example, Maureen Daly Goggin's (2000) well-known history of the field, *Authoring A Discipline: Scholarly Journals and the Post-World War II Emergence of Rhetoric and Composition*, presented eight graphs, each designed to render apprehensible some data set aggregated manually

---

9   To reduce anomalies, two issues of the journal—61.1 and 61.2—were restricted only to the articles catalogued in JSTOR. In each of those issues, 19 additional articles were published online, but those articles (38 in all) have been omitted from this study because the unusual publishing cycle skews comparisons across the 25-year collection. In effect, an extra year's worth of articles were published online with these two issues.

from the nine journals at the center of her study.[10] Goggin's study is one notable example where graphs have been applied similarly to the way Moretti has used them to study literary genres in historical contexts: to deliberately alter the level of detail at which texts are customarily read with the aim of connecting overlooked minutiae and broader phenomena. Five of Goggin's eight graphs accounted for some criterion applied to all contributing authors for nine major journals from 1950 to 1990: a pair of line graphs showing affiliations of authors to two- and four-year institutions, an area graph showing institutional affiliation (public or private, college or university), a horizontal bar graph presenting the number of contributors from departments other than English, and a two-line graph drawn according to the (assumed binary) gender of contributors to the journals. Goggin also used a vertical bar graph to show MLA membership by geographic region and a pair of line graphs for the percentages of conference papers published in *CCC* and *College English*. Although *Authoring A Discipline* is unreflective about its reliance on graphs, Goggin's disciplinarily innovative work provided strong examples of graphing methods that, because they translated a collection of data to a visual figure, thereby established a new scale of engagement, rendering recognizable patterns of disciplinary activity that would otherwise be difficult to discern, particularly for newcomers to the field.

This use of graphing to engage with data at a new scale deliberately adjusts the level of detail at which we ordinarily experience texts, and as such it reaffirms database, scale, and pattern as key motives for exploring disciplinarity this way. Experientially, reading tends to be a local, direct encounter, typically involving (or demanding) an identifiable, focal text. While there are sure to be exceptions (e.g., a bibliographic essay pursues a similar purpose: synthesis by reduction, the full text falls away and in its place stands a proxy, a textual double), there exists a default level of detail commonly associated with reading. For traditional scholarly journals, the default scale is the article, and more specifically its words, sentences, and paragraphs. Print journals already include numerous features designed to help readers assess smaller-scale units, such as the issue and article, before reading more thoroughly. A simple table of contents, for example, supports a glancing sort of distant reading at one scale, and article abstracts operate as thin descriptions at a scale only slightly closer to the content of the article than the title and author alone (for more on article abstracts, see Chapter Two). Readers rely on these devices to make quick decisions about whether to read a particular article or not, but reading the journal through these devices alone is

---

10   Goggin gathered data from *College Composition and Communication, College English, Research in the Teaching of English, Rhetoric Society Quarterly, Freshman English News (Composition Studies), JAC, Rhetoric Review, Pre/Text,* and *Written Communication.*

not quite the same as reading a scholarly journal in the common sense of the activity.[11]

Reading across a series of journal articles gathered around a specific research question, one might or might not notice variations in the lengths of the articles or patterns in the number of sources cited in each. And yet, article lengths have changed significantly over 25 years, as have the number of sources referenced in a given article, issue, or volume on average. Readers might notice trends related to these mundane details across a collection of research (whether it is random or more purposefully gathered), but these details are, nevertheless, transparent and easily tabulated. Graphs allow us to zoom out, to see patterns in length and citation count across a selection of articles. This illustrative exercise in distant reading renders tangible those patterns that almost certainly go unrecognized (except intuitively) when we read at the default scale, picking up a few articles at a time.

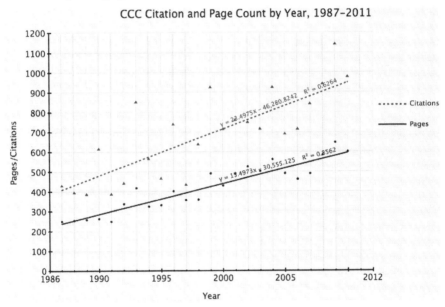

Figure 15. A plot graph indicative of page count and citation count by year in CCC, between 1987 and 2011. Trend lines for page count (solid) and citation count (dotted) indicate the gradual but steady increase in these basic features of the journal.

Figure 15 employs graphing to present growth patterns in the number of citations and the number of pages in CCC over 25 years. This graph illustrates

11 Malcolm Gladwell's (2007) Blink is suggestive here. Gladwell's work relates numerous examples of rapid cognition, the quick, subconscious judgments that tacitly shape our impressions of the world.

just one form of knowledge available to us in exploratory quantification, in the distant reading and thin description that comes of counting, recording tallies, and plotting coordinate points. The figure overlays two sets of data: The lower area accounts for page counts by year; the upper area accounts for citation counts by year. Indeed, over the 25 years sampled, articles published in *CCC* have grown longer and they have also have come to draw more extensively on source material appropriate to include in a references list.

Besides suggesting a gradual inflation in the page count and number of sources in scholarly articles published in *CCC* over the 25 years sampled, Figure 15 also elicits questions. This inventive and generative capacity constitutes a heuristic with unmistakable bearing on questions about the field's formation as well as the material and discursive bases for disciplinary maturation. Why have page counts and citation counts nearly doubled in 25 years? Do other journals exhibit similar trends over the 25 years sampled? What about journals in other fields? How have alternative length publishing models emerged as an implicit response? For instance, *Present Tense* publishes medium-form scholarship online and *Intermezzo* (2016) is a series that corrects in the other direction, inviting "essays that are too long for journal publication but too short to be a monograph." How high might page counts and citation counts ascend before leveling off? Or before significantly altering the work entailed in reading or writing a scholarly article? What culpability in this trend do a journal's stakeholders bear, from publishers, editors, editorial board members, to reviewers, writers, and readers? Absent distant reading and thin description methods these questions would warrant hunches and speculation, but we would be unable to present the pattern as compellingly. The graphed pattern refreshes the questions with vivid presentational force.

Related quantitative studies foreground the promise of graphing techniques informed by distant reading and thin description for RCWS scholars as depends upon the systematic archivization of reusable, interoperable, field-wide data sets. Phillips, Greenberg, and Gibson (1993) presented a history of similar scope and quantified basis (i.e., the counting of citations, the listing of editors, etc.) to Goggin's book-length project. There is a high degree of overlap between Goggin's (2000) interest in elucidating patterns and the aims that justify their pursuit: chronicling the discipline's genesis. Phillips, Greenberg, and Gibson (1993) relied on tables and historical narrative rather than graphs to deliver their findings; however, even by simple quantification they were able to distinguish patterns related to who has published most frequently, how citation counts have steadily (perhaps quietly) risen, and who, at 15-year intervals, has been cited most frequently. They speculated, from these tallies, about the causes for the rising rates of citation:

There is a dramatic contrast in the number of citations between early and recent *CCC* issues, attributable to the developing body of composition scholarship, the maturing of the field, the increasing demand for theoretical grounding of pedagogical practice, and the political necessity for supporting the professionalism of the discipline. (p. 451)

Whether or not this speculation holds as an enduring theory is less important than is the way these methods catalyze questions heuristically and begin to provide a means of addressing such questions more systematically than has been established to date. The demonstrable force of graphs renews the points Phillips, Greenberg, and Gibson raised concerning the field's development and maturation, the growing demand for theoretically and methodologically sophisticated scholarship, and the complicated politics of citation, as well as related matters, such as pressures to publish, the competitive nature of traditional publishing, and citation as a function of *ethos* insofar as it represents the sources one has taken into consideration. Graphs reinvigorate these questions and give us different ways to grasp nonobvious trends.

Bibliometric Methods and Techniques

With a few key distinctions, the methods and techniques I used to compile the frequency of citations appearing in *CCC* from 1987–2011 are similar to those applied by Phillips, Greenberg, and Gibson. Phillips, Greenberg, and Gibson (1993) recorded references appearing in any piece of work published in *CCC* between 1950 and 1993, including reviews, interchanges, and features unique to an editor (e.g., Ken Macrorie's "Miscellany"). I have focused exclusively on articles—items likely to have been anonymously peer reviewed following that change to the publishing process in 1987 and that adhered to the roster-like listing of works cited appearing in alphabetical order at the end of the article (a convention that was introduced to the journal at nearly the same time as anonymous peer review; for more on this change, see Chapter One). Thus, this study includes every citation listed in association with the 491 articles published in *CCC* from 1987 to 2011, amounting to a comprehensive record of 16,726 works cited entries.[12]

I prepared the list by gathering all the works cited for each article in a single spreadsheet.[13] Because individual works cited entries often include

---

12   Thirty of the articles do not use any formal citations whatsoever.

13   *CCC Online Archive*, an online resource sponsored jointly by NCTE and Syracuse University from 2005–2009, was one laboratory for the development of this data. The works cited available at this site were transferred from dynamic text PDF files and through optical character recognition (OCR) processing for articles available only as static PDFs.

multiple authors (or clipped lists of authors denoted with *et alia*), the citation list required extensive smoothing, which I handled manually. I coded each bibliographic entry in the list so that listings with editors, *et alia*, hyphens (repeated reference to a single author), and nonstandard authorship could be sorted apart from author listings.[14] I removed the citation entries for editors, replaced the hyphen placeholders with the full names of the appropriate author(s), and replaced the "et al." with the names of all authors collaborating on a given work. Finally, using text-matching algorithms and manual proofreading, I double-checked the list to ensure correct spelling and name formatting. These alterations to the comprehensive works cited list resulted in an expanded roster of authors whose names appeared with every instance of a publication associated with their names.[15]

The labor involved in coding a collection of several thousand citations is due for acknowledgement. This was slow, detail-oriented work, carried out over several months and later updated to extend the data set into another half decade. And yet, the methods scale, as is demonstrated in Eric Detweiler's (2015) "'/' and '-'?: An Empirical Consideration of the Relationship Between 'Rhetoric' and 'Composition,'" which sampled two years (2001–2002 to 2011–2012) a decade apart to inform an analysis of shifting citation practices in *College Composition and Communication* and *Rhetoric Society Quarterly*. In another example, Joe Torok's (2013) "Visualizing *Present Tense*: Graphing and Mapping a Corner of the Discipline" studied citations in the first three years of articles published in *Present Tense* to investigate whether and to what extent medium-form scholarship (i.e., shorter articles) reflected distinctive patterns related to the scope of sources cited therein. While both were rigorous and substantial projects concerned with citation, the scope of these studies attests to the scalability of distant reading and thin description—and to the usefulness of projects inquiring into network sense at different scales.

With each name-reference assigned to a single slot in the comprehensive listing, various tabulations were possible; the 16,726 works cited entries

---

14   Nonstandard authorship citations included anonymous, corporate, organizational, institutional, username, listserv, and other varieties where human authors were not explicitly named.

15   In their 2006 study of three decades of footnotes in *Critical Inquiry*, Anne Stevens and Jay Williams began with a selective (rather than organic or comprehensive) list. Explaining their methods, they noted, "To begin our investigation, the staff of *Critical Inquiry* devised a list of theorists whose work we knew had been frequently cited. (To have tabulated every author cited in every article would have required more resources than we had at hand)" (p. 212). With their preliminary list, they then worked page by page through the 30-year archive of the journal, counting each appearance of a name on the list.

became a list of 19,477 name-references.[16] This also means that 2,751 name references surfaced from secondary, tertiary, and *n*-ary authors. Developed out of this expanded data set, Table 1 shows the top 103 scholars sorted in descending order by the number of references made to them in *CCC* articles between 1987 and 2011.

Table 1. The 103 most frequently cited authors in *CCC* from 1987–2011.

	# out of 19,477 references	Name (461 articles)
1	145	Linda Flower (66 articles)
2	133	Peter Elbow (85 articles)
3	118	Patricia Bizzell (82 articles)
4	112	David Bartholomae (93 articles)
5	111	James A. Berlin (90 articles)
6	110	Robert Connors (78 articles)
7	102	Andrea Lunsford (74 articles)
8	101	Lester Faigley (79 articles)
9	96	Mike Rose (64 articles)
10	77	John Trimbur (57 articles)
11	73	Kenneth Burke
12	68	Sharon Crowley
13	67	Mikhail Bakhtin
14	65	Cynthia Selfe
15	62	John Hayes
16	58	Anne Ruggles Gere, Joseph Harris
18	57	Charles Bazerman, Lisa Ede
20	55	Ellen Cushman, bell hooks, Kathleen Yancey
23	52	CCCC, Maxine Hairston, Stephen North
26	51	Shirley Brice Heath, Mina Shaughnessy
28	50	John Dewey, Min-Zhan Lu
30	48	Susan Miller
31	46	Marilyn Cooper, Donald Murray
33	45	Edward White
34	44	Jacqueline Jones Royster

16   Each author listed in association with multi-authored works was credited with one reference tally. That is, where Linda Flower and John Hayes (and others in certain cases) appear as authors, each of them recorded one reference tally in the overall listing. This explains why the reference count (19,477) is higher than the original number of works cited entries (16,726).

	# out of 19,477 references	Name (461 articles)
35	43	Janet Emig, Michel Foucault, Henry Giroux, Gesa Kirsch, Geneva Smitherman
40	42	Kenneth Bruffee, David Russell
42	40	Deborah Brandt, Paulo Freire, Richard Haswell
45	39	Lil Brannon
46	38	Bruce Horner, Charles Knoblauch
48	37	Nancy Sommers, United States
50	35	James Britton, Glynda Hull, Mary Louise Pratt
53	34	Linda Brodkey, Elizabeth Flynn, Gail Hawisher, Ira Shor
57	33	Thomas Newkirk
58	32	Ann Berthoff
59	31	Susan Jarratt, Walter Ong, James Porter, Patricia A. Sullivan
63	30	Carol Berkenkotter, Pierre Bourdieu, Victor Villanueva
66	29	Sarah Freedman, Lucille McCarthy, Louise Wetherbee Phelps
69	28	Albert Kitzhaber, Carolyn Miller
71	27	Aristotle, James Paul Gee, Diana George, Gerald Graff, George Hillocks, Jr., Brian Huot
77	26	Janice Lauer, Richard Ohmann, Susan Wells
80	25	Judith Butler, Peter Mortensen, Stephen Witte
83	24	Pat Belanoff, Robert Brooke, Keith Gilyard, Anne Herrington, Bruce Herzberg, Gunther Kress, Ken Macrorie, Greg Myers, Adrienne Rich, Joseph Williams
93	23	John Ackerman, Chris Anson, Arthur Applebee, Ellen Barton, Jacques Derrida, Michael Halloran, Susan McLeod, Richard Miller, Kurt Spellmeyer, Brian Street

The simple tabulation evokes many questions worthy of exploring more deeply in the contexts of disciplinary formation, scholarly influence, professional development, and graduate education: What is at stake in knowing or not knowing any of the figures shown here? What presences and absences are most striking? To what degree do well-established scholars overshadow new scholars in such a listing as this? What are some of the intriguing juxtapositions where positions in the list are shared? This latter question is a tangential one, but one worth considering for its inventive richness in a course that introduces graduate students to the field. Wondering about coincidental pairings is germane to a practice I think of as *heuretic discipliniography*, or writing and re-writing the field by exploring the enigmatic intersections across different scholars' work as well as the associated pedagogical, theoretical, and methodological approaches advanced thereby.

The single, comprehensive list in Table 1 is suggestive in its own right, but it tends to occlude temporal variation: the changing tide of citation practices at lesser increments within this 25-year period. In the interest of beginning to see into this variation, consider an alternative table (Table 2) developed out of the same data set.

Table 2. Top 10 most frequently cited authors in *CCC* from 1987 to 2011, by five-year interval.

1987–1991	C	A	1992–1996	C	A	1997–2001	C	A
Total references: 2,755			Total references: 3,595			Total references: 3,881		
Total articles: 79			Total articles: 102			Total articles: 93		
Flower, Linda	56	22	Bizzell, Patricia	43	29	^Berlin, James A.	37	29
Hayes, John	41	16	^Elbow, Peter	43	30	Bartholomae, David	35	25
Lunsford, Andrea	27	18	Rose, Mike	37	22	Bizzell, Patricia	31	19
Connors, Robert	25	14	^Dewey, John	32	4	Faigley, Lester	30	22
Bizzell, Patricia	23	16	Flower, Linda	32	17	Elbow, Peter	28	18
Rose, Mike	23	14	Bartholomae, David	30	24	Connors, Robert	26	18
Faigley, Lester	22	14	Lunsford, Andrea	26	19	^Crowley, Sharon	25	15
Bartholomae, David	20	19	^Shaughnessy, Mina	25	15	^Miller, Susan	24	19
Berlin, James A.	20	14	Faigley, Lester	24	21	Lunsford, Andrea	22	15
Britton, James	20	9	Connors, Robert	23	18	Rose, Mike	20	14
			Out of top 10 from previous five years			**Out of top 10 from previous five years**		
			Britton, James			Dewey, John		
			Hayes, John			Shaughnessy, Mina		
			Berlin, James A.			Flower, Linda		

2002–2006			2007–2011			Totals, 1987–2011		
Total references: 4,289	C	A	Total references: 4,957	C	A	Total references: 19,477	C	A
Total articles: 93			Total articles: 94			Total articles: 461		
^Burke, Kenneth	31	9	^Yancey, Kathleen Blake	26	19	Flower, Linda	145	66
^Flower, Linda	28	12	Cushman, Ellen	25	13	Elbow, Peter	133	85
^Smitherman, Geneva	28	10	Elbow, Peter	23	13	Bizzell, Patricia	118	82
^Trimbur, John	28	17	^Russell, David	23	13	Bartholomae, David	112	93
^Bakhtin, Mikhail	23	10	^Bazerman, Charles	22	17	Berlin, James A.	111	90
^Cushman, Ellen	22	12	^Gere, Anne Ruggles	21	19	Connors, Robert	110	78
Bartholomae, David	20	18	Selfe, Cynthia	21	10	Lunsford, Andrea	102	74
Elbow, Peter	20	11	^Haswell, Richard	20	12	Faigley, Lester	101	79
^hooks, bell	20	16	Burke, Kenneth	19	11	Rose, Mike	96	64
^Hopkins, Edwin	20	2	^United States	18	8	Trimbur, John	77	57
^Selfe, Cynthia	20	7						

Out of top 10 from previous five years	**Out of top 10 from previous five years**	
Crowley, Sharon	Flower, Linda	
Berlin, James A.	Smitherman, Geneva	
Bizzell, Patricia	Trimbur, John	
Faigley, Lester	Bakhtin, Mikhail	
Connors, Robert	Bartholomae, David	
Lunsford, Andrea	hooks, bell	
Rose, Mike	Hopkins, Edwin	
Miller, Susan		

Notes: C: Citation count (total number of name references). A: Article count (total number of articles in which citations appear). ^ Indicates a scholar not ranked in the Top 10 for the previous five-year period. This table bears direct correspondence to similar tables appearing in Stevens and Williams's (2006) work with *Critical Inquiry* and in Phillips, Greenberg, and Gibson's (1993) work with *CCC* from 1950–1993.

What does Table 2 *do*? Certainly, it provides compelling quantitative evidence for trends and patterns in citation practices, and it foregrounds the temporal subsets within the 25-year sample by adjusting the timescale. In it, we encounter a form of knowledge unavailable at the usual and customary scale at which journals are read—the individual article. The data as presented also lends itself to potential analysis of the centrality of a given figure in a given period of time as well as the waning centrality of even the most frequently cited authors in the most recent five-year period. In other words, we can see that Linda Flower was cited in 22 of the 79 articles (i.e., 27.8%) published between 1987 and 1991; Kenneth Burke, the leading figure between 2002 and 2006, was referenced in just 9 out of 93 articles (i.e., 9.7%). Further lines of inquiry include examining the lists with attention to gender, sexuality, class, race, ethnicity, and disability; theorizing what constitutes career longevity; and exploring the relationships between bibliographic prominence and other criteria, such as national leadership roles, institutional affiliation, and areas of research. Granting all of the known limitations in what we can extrapolate about the field at large from this sample, this also suggests a change within *CCC*: the prominence of the top-most cited authors is gradually and relatively steadily declining. Admittedly, there are clear dangers in leaping from patterns in *CCC* to patterns applicable to the field at large. Yet, this work with citation frequency in *CCC* should suggest the value in extending these methods to other journals in RCWS and, perhaps, other fields where such work has not yet been done.

Based on the approach modeled so far, we can begin to see how quantitative studies of citations spark insights and advance questions concerning the ways citation practices change.[17] Yet these methods are not without qualification. A conventional listing of citations does little to reflect the scope of the reference as it is taken up or the framing language used to introduce the source within an article itself.[18] The list simply affirms one fairly narrow kind of presence. In other words, citation listings lack volume; they do not report whether a single source greatly influenced (and appeared repeatedly, throughout) in, say, more than 10 (or more) pages of an article or whether,

17   For a critical discussion of citation practices, see Howard Tinberg's (2006) "In the Land of the Cited," which addresses a concern that two-year college faculty tend to be obscured in such work. Tinberg made a case for more and more diverse citation practices.

18   Assessing these limitations may generate further research projects. For example, although the study featured in this chapter provides a cursory introduction to what graphing can offer, researchers in rhetoric and composition, computational rhetorics, natural language processing (NLP), and computational linguistics could begin to examine the in-text locations where citations are brought in. Doing so would allow us to know more fully which references are subject to elaborate framing and which are subject to less. Sentiment analysis would also help us rethink the positive and negative evaluations made about sources where they appear in scholarly corpora.

on the other extreme, it was hardly mentioned at all. When aggregating a long list of references, these dimensions fall away. We are left with a basic list, a reduced, concentrated record. Also, the gathering of name-references into a single list downplays aspects of production, reception, and circulation of a source, as well as the career of the author. In their own acknowledgement of related limitations, Phillips, Greenberg, and Gibson (1993) wrote that we will find sharp differences between the popularity of a particular source (like Mina Shaughnessy's *Errors and Expectations*) and a particular author (like Andrea Lunsford, who is cited frequently but for a wide array of different articles): "One explanation for this circumstance may be focus: Shaughnessy, for example, generally restricted her work to a single area, while Lunsford published on a variety of issues" (p. 454). Across a given career, one author might remain highly specialized while another might shift from one area of inquiry to another, thus producing a record of scholarship more reflective of a generalist's wanderlust.[19] Further, a bibliometric methodology privileges presence as a function of publication, although there are many other kinds of professional and interpersonal presence essential to disciplinary stabilization, including mentorship, conversation, and the writing and circulation of what Louise Wetherbee Phelps (2016) has called *humble genres.*

In their discussion of methods used to study the journal's authors and works cited quantitatively, Phillips, Greenberg, and Gibson (1993) wrote,

> Such quantitative measures help determine what can be considered within the community as common knowledge, and common knowledge is the power base. Writers will construct their discourse around what their audiences can be assumed to know and accept. Researchers will see the investigative techniques as models. Initiates will ingest this core as part of the membership rite. CCCC members will rely on name recognition in the elections shaping the organization that molds the field. In sum, work associated with these names becomes the traditional paradigm, and all subsequent work moves toward its support, its enlargement, or its overthrow. (p. 454)

---

19   An alternative approach could use specific titles of sources rather than author names as its primary sorting key. With tracing sources, however, comes a greater challenge due to republishing. Sources commonly appear in iterations, such as electronic texts that exist in many copies whose precise differentiations become muddled like email threads. Consequently, I have preferred to sort by author name. Consider, as an example, Franco Moretti's (2007) *Graphs, Maps, Trees,* which appeared as a series of articles in the *New Left Review* before it became a monograph. Using source titles as a primary sorting key would, in this case, reflect a differently skewed number of citations.

So while quantitative studies of authors cited in a well-known journal may offer a reasonable indication of the common knowledge of the field, this approach must not appear to produce a definitive roster of influences on the discipline. Compilations drawn from lists of citations might prompt us to wonder about the kind of knowledge formal references demand of a reader, and a wide variety of contextualizing techniques within the articles themselves are sure to help familiarize readers with those voices brought into the piece, whatever the motive. The lists presented in Tables 1 and 2 indicate frequency—a convergence, possibly, of popularity, notoriety, and influence. Lists like these are powerful indications of the "hits" in composition studies. Who, identifying themselves with the field of RCWS, would claim to know *none* of these figures or the impact of their work? And yet, the top 103 authors cited over the 25 years sampled in *CCC* or the top 10 authors by five-year increment—even though they are indicative of certain currents in a disciplinary conversation—do not tell us enough about what has happened across the entire sample of name-references in the set of citations.

Turning to graphs based on the entire data set, there is more we can know from this quantitative approach. The well-known influences, after all, are likely to rank relatively high in a comparable sample of citations drawn from other journals in the discipline—although this research, like so much work with large data sets significant to the field's formation, is only beginning to take shape (Chamberlain, 2016; Detweiler, 2015; Miller, 2014; Miller et al., 2016). To make sense of the comprehensive record of citation within *CCC* in this 25-year period, to corroborate the degree of dappledness, we must look not only at what has changed among the top-most cited figures. We must also come to terms with what has happened among those sources invoked infrequently in a 25-year period—those who, by the record of citation frequency, registered a singular appearance. For this question, another series of graphs proves insightful, enabling inquiry into just how cacophonous the epistemic court has become.

Too Dappled a Discipline? Graphing the Long Tail of Author Citation

> In our fixation on star power, we cheer the salary inflation of A-listers and follow their absurd public lives with an attention that far exceeds our interest in their work. From the superstar athletes to celebrity CEOs, we ascribe disproportionate attention to the very top of the heap. We have been trained, in other words, to see the world through a hit-colored lens. (Anderson, 2008 p. 40)

In October 2004, Chris Anderson, an editor at *Wired Magazine*, reached out to a popular audience in his article "The Long Tail" with arguments about how economic notions of scarcity and abundance have been transformed with the rise of digital commerce. The article distinguished between spatially constrained traditional retailers and their comparably abundant online counterparts. According to Anderson, the typical Borders[20] bookstore, for example, carried 100,000 titles, but its leading online competitor, Amazon.com, offered a vastly deeper (i.e., longer) selection to consumers: more than 3.7 million titles. Anderson's research, which he expanded into a monograph, centered on the idea of the long tail: the uncommon products and specialized interests that online markets can support. *The Long Tail* (2008) is an extended inquiry into the phenomenon of these market niches—how they work, how digital circulation stimulates them, and how they have fundamentally challenged more conventional storefront economics.

Anderson didn't come up with the idea for the long tail himself. In his work, he cited many influences on his thinking from economics and technology studies. But his timely insights and striking examples certainly have done much to popularize the concept in recent years. Conceptually, the long tail comes from statistics and graphing and is also known as a power law called the Pareto distribution[21], which uses graphed patterns to show the distribution of power in an activity or phenomenon. In his article-length work on the long tail, Anderson (2004) provided a version of the infographic in Figure 16 to illustrate.

Here, music is the focal premise. Walmart, like Borders, offers a limited selection; even while the discount retail giant provides a large selection of hits, it simply cannot match what an online competitor, such as Rhapsody, makes available, which includes less popular titles that continue to sell actively, despite ranking well beneath the threshold of popularity that justifies the entirety of Walmart's stock. From left to right, the graphed distribution accounts first for the high-ranking hits commonly available on store shelves; gradually it gives way to the long tail—the rich expanse of less-popular albums and tracks that continue to sell at markedly lower rates than their counterparts at the head of the curve. The long tail's recurrent niches are thin but extensive; thus, it represents a formidable base for economic activity untouched by conventional store-shelf retailers and what Anderson (2004) called the "tyranny of geography" (p. 17).

---

20   The Ann Arbor, Michigan-based company filed Chapter 11 bankruptcy and closed in 2011.
21   These laws of distribution go by many different names in economic theory. Vilfredo Pareto, a 19th-century Italian economist, is generally credited for coming up with the law of distribution, better known as the 80:20 Rule, which generally poses that a small percentage of a population will hold disproportionately high measures of wealth and power relative to the large percentage of a population (Ball, 2006, p. 247).

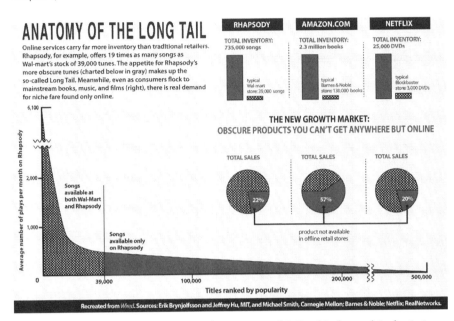

Figure 16. Anatomy of the long tail. A recreated Wired infographic depicting the distribution of songs available in traditional retail spaces, such as Walmart, as compared with online retail sites, such as Rhapsody.

Anderson's early work on long tails focused explicitly on these market trends; he later adapted the premise to look into patterns in media and entertainment sales. Yet, Anderson (2008) also acknowledged that his research has opened up to even broader possibilities for the long tail as an apparatus for exploratory and descriptive statistics:

> Seen broadly, it's clear that the story of the Long Tail is really about the economics of abundance—what happens when the bottlenecks that stand between supply and demand in our culture start to disappear and everything becomes available to everyone. (p. 11)

He arrived at an expanded view of the long tail, one that recognized that its application reaches beyond economics to other cultural phenomena. Assuming a similarly broad view of the long tail, I contend that it serves generatively as a basis for graphing the citation-frequency data introduced earlier so that we can make sense not only of what has happened in *CCC* to those names mentioned most often (i.e., the hits), but also what has happened to the long tail of author citation over the 25-year sample. The top-ranking author-citations in *CCC* between 2007–2011 are less than they were for the same period of time

20 years earlier. The frequency of the citation set's highest circulating figures is more spare in later years than in earlier ones in this data set. But graphing all the author-citations does more than confirm what we already know about those few at the top. The graphed citation frequency distribution sheds light on what has happened to the long tail of author-citation—those names appearing just once or twice in the journal's works cited during the same periods. The long tail accounts for how citations have scattered and dispersed. Once more, graphing functions as a form of distant reading and thin description—a means of engaging with large-scale data at multiple scales to notice nonobvious patterns. The long tail shows how an abstract visual model potentially elicits new insights and, with its descriptive acuity, raises new questions, some of which might help explore the continuing genesis and maturation of RCWS.

Following the Long Tail's Thinness: The Names Invoked Just Once

> It is too easy to overlook elements of our history that reinforce and enrich our current work. We are too prone to let superficial differences blind us to significant connections between past and present. (Odell, 2006, p. 149)

What do Maya Angelou, Andy Rooney, Bill Gates, Queen Hatshepsut, Roger Ebert, and Elvis Presley have in common? Despite being well-known figures, each of them was cited in *CCC* just once between 1987 and 2011, thus inhabiting the long tail of *CCC* citations. These six figures share this distinction with 5,761 other names referenced just once (out of 8,035 unique name references in the 25-year period in question). Another 986 names appear in the cited works just twice, which leaves 1,287 names (i.e., 16.0%) that appear in *CCC* citations three or more times within the 25-year sample. By assigning these figures to a simple graph, we can see that they follow a power law, meaning relatively few names rank highly in citation frequency (see Tables 1 and 2 above for specific references) while more than 80% of the names register a momentary appearance, usually appearing in a single article. Translated into a graph, the 25-year data sample appears visually, converting quantitative measures into an abstract model with qualitative effects.

As a model, the long tail helps us recognize just how thin a sliver of citations are captured in the list of the top 103 author-citations shown in Figure 17. Attending to the immense shelf of the less-frequent citations in the data set demands a more comprehensive view—a more *distant* view, that is. We must step back even farther than did Phillips, Greenberg, and Gibson (1993) to realize, on the one hand, the limits of a hit-driven view of citation activity and, on the other hand, the ever-fuller breadth of activity that manifests in the long tail. Certainly the figures at the top tell us *something* about citation practices and centrality in the journal's scholarly conversation; however, the larger number of figures at the bottom indicates something *more*. It is, after all, in this long, flat expanse of unduplicated references that we can begin to assess just how broad-based the conversations (in a given journal) have grown—and just how much the centered, coherent, and familiar locus of conversation, based on citation practices, has slid.

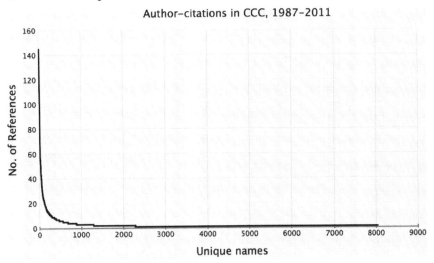

Figure 17. References to unique names in CCC works cited from 1987–2011.

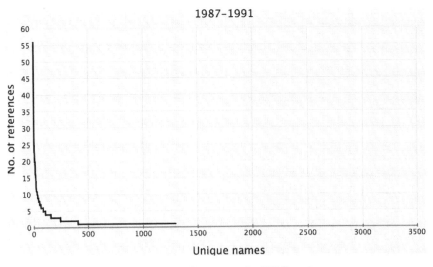

Figure 18. Citation frequency in CCC, 1987–1991.

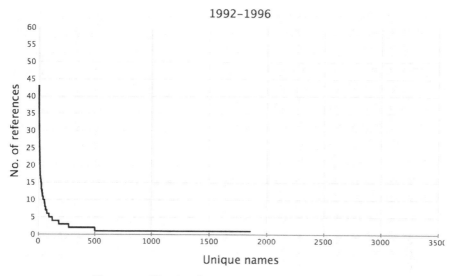

Figure 19. Citation frequency in CCC, 1992–1996.

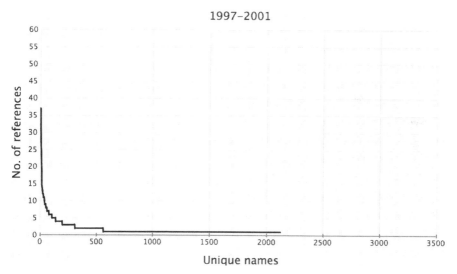

Figure 20. Citation frequency in CCC, 1997–2001.

Keeping in mind this more general thread of inquiry into the maturation of the field foregrounds the incremental development seen in Figure 17: How and at what rates did unique references grow? When did the vertical portion at the left first spike sharply from the horizontal axis? Has the tail always been as proportionately long? Have the two *ends* grown at relatively consistent paces since 1987? To answer these questions, consider a more nuanced series of graphs, each displaying a five-year data sub-set (much as Table 2 did). Figures

18–22 are also available online at https://wac.colostate.edu/docs/books/net work/citationfrequency.gif as an animated GIF that loops to show the declin- ing head of the curve (left) as contrasted with the elongation of the tail (right).

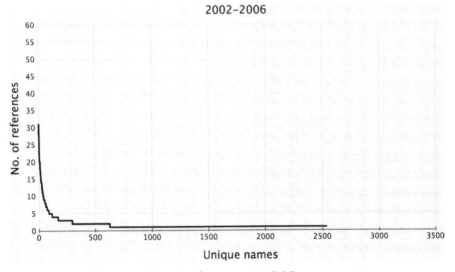

Figure 21. Citation frequency in CCC, 2002–2006.

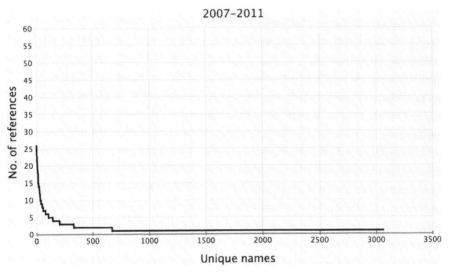

Figure 22. Citation frequency in CCC, 2007–2011.

The series of graphed distributions at five-year increments highlights a gradual transformation while also confirming that since 1987, even as the to- tal number of citations climbed higher in each subsequent five-year period, the once-steep grade has flattened out considerably. As the scholarly record grows, authors have a more complex array of sources to draw upon. Across 25 years of citation activity in *CCC*, the long tail has grown longer, indeed, while the head has dwindled over time.

Figures 18–22 present a chronographic report on the evolution of one sample from the field's scholarly record, and this evolution would be easy to overlook if we fixated only on the most frequently cited figures or if we relied on experiential impressions of the journal. Approaching the full record in this way allows us to perceive these gradual transformations—shifts so subtle that it is easy, at the scale of a career, to disregard. The methods featured here are also amenable to sorting by other criteria, as well. It would be possible, for example, to determine the changing rate of reference to different forms of publication (e.g., chapters in edited collections, single-author monographs, peer-reviewed articles, online resources, etc.). Thus, we can use distant reading and thin description methods to understand with more granularity factors affecting citation distribution. Furthermore, although the graphs I have produced reflect the full data set, it is possible to use these methods to isolate and compare smaller segments of the data. Separating sub-sets of the citation data would allow us to search for patterns according to many different criteria, exploring, for instance, the frequency of citation made to work by scholars within the first 5 or 10 years of their careers, to work by alums of specific graduate programs, or by scholars whose research focuses on a specialized area. The methodology is considerably more dynamic and robust than what this necessarily limited introduction of it can feature.[22]

A changing citation frequency also affects the depth and variety in what one reads. The reading problem—a problem of "keeping up with new work" acknowledged by Richard Lloyd-Jones (2006) in his 1977 CCCC chair's address (p. 50)—remains a contemporary challenge not only for newcomers to the discipline but also for those who have spent many years actively practicing and participating in the field themselves. Even self-described generalists, in those moments when they are again reminded of the Sisyphean demands of the field's ongoing quality, inevitably experience (if indirectly, by felt sense) the lengthening of the long tail as a burdensome certainty: the unyielding march of time coupled with the burgeoning material resources piling up in

---

22 By applying a classification scheme similar to the 14 cluster areas used by the Conference on College Composition and Communication to categorize conference presentations, the full data set could be subdivided into corresponding groupings for "Language," "Creative Writing," "Basic Writing," and so on. Graphs produced by this technique could suggest distinctions in the scholarship associated with these respective areas as well as the values embraced and promoted therein. These would not necessarily reflect widespread disciplinary values, but they would make accessible a view of area-specific citation patterns within *CCC* since 1987.

the disciplinary commons. In economics, the long tail is sometimes called the *heavy tail*. The tail is, in this sense, paradoxical: an abundant, weighty expanse consisting of a highly uneven mix of sources, from the new, to the forgotten, to the idiosyncratic (viz., Elvis Presley, as well as disciplinary figures, like Mary P. Hiatt, who won the 1978 Braddock Award). Burke's parlor is nowadays full and teeming, more crowded than ever before. Even while the head of the distribution stands tall—an indication of the recurrence of fairly regular, recognizable names (e.g., Linda Flower, Patricia Bizzell, Peter Elbow, etc.)—the long tail tests the limits of comprehension and memory. Although we do not at this time have data from all of the major journals to investigate this fully, the changing shape of the graphed distribution reiterates more emphatically a question only hinted at in Tables 1–2, but one nevertheless crucial to the idea of a common disciplinary domain: How flat can the citation distribution become before it is no longer plausible to speak of a discipline?[23]

To clearly and responsibly engage with this complicated, shifting expanse, we need the full spectrum of data, not only the list of the most frequent appearing names. The full distribution is required if we are to examine the relationship between what has happened at the head of the distribution and what has happened furthest from it, in the long tail. From graphs, from one exercise in visual epistemology, then, come new insights, new provocations, and new questions: What has changed, over time, in the relationship between the head of the curve and the long tail? Switching to a simple bar graph (Fig. 23), the patterns become still more vivid; the visual model more concisely conveys a shift in citation practices. In the first period, from 1987 to 1991, there were 2,755 citations. Using two criteria, (a) the number of citations made to figures at the head of the curve and (b) the number of citations to unduplicated figures in the long tail, we can create the percentage-based bar graph shown in Figure 23. In the first five-year period, then, 16% of the citations referred to figures in the top 20 and just more than 32% of the citations were in the long tail. Over the next five years, we find a slight decrease in the percentage of citations occupied by the head; one-time references in the long tail reached slightly higher. Over the next five years, again the same shift appears: the head shrunk, the tail grew. And between 2002 and 2006, the number of citations climbs to 4,289, and the trend continues: The head fell below 10%, and the tail approached 50%. The trend continues into the last five-year period sampled. The most frequently cited figure—Kathleen Blake Yancey—was invoked in scholarly articles roughly half as often (26 references) as Linda Flower was in the comparable period of time 20 years earlier (56 references).

23   This is not only a question for RCWS to consider; this method for graphing citation rates ought to generalize, suggesting its usefulness for other journals and in other fields, as well.

Head and Tail by Percentage

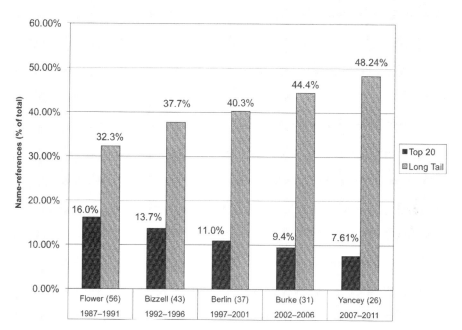

Figure 23. Percentage-based comparisons of the number of citations in a given five-year period at the head of the curve (i.e., citations by the top 20 figures) and in the long tail (i.e., those figures cited just once).

Thus, graphs underpinned with citation data assert themselves as a suggestive form of knowledge. As graphs condense, reduce, and render distant and thin the default level of detail, they make possible a more comprehensive engagement with patterns and trends. Power law distributions apply to citation practices in all journals and all academic disciplines; with graphs, we can see how those distributions change over time. Rather than proving, confirming, or validating claims about disciplinary fragmentation or, more positively, eclecticism, I prefer to cast these graphs in terms of what they allow us to *corroborate*. Corroboration is a term that, in its connotations of contingency and flexibility, suggests we might suspend judgment while simply granting credence to new forms of evidence (i.e., these models and abstracting practices), using this credence to flex and strengthen ("corroborate," n.d.). Corroborate, with its Latin root *robur*, a root shared by "robust," places an emphasis on the mobilizing, inventive capacity of these graphs as visual models that can do much to shape our insights into disciplinary patterns. This emphasis on corroboration also foregrounds our individual and collective agency in shaping the field rather than resorting too quickly to endist speculation, pre-diction-making, or discourses of disciplinary crisis.

The Heads and Tails of Disciplinary Density

Long live the dappled discipline. (Miles et al., 2008, p. 511)

Scholarly publishing has entered a time of tremendous flux, which is precise-ly why we must be more systematic than we have been about inventorying an evolving epistemic court. Susan Peck MacDonald's (2010) study of dis-ciplinary patterns is particularly helpful as one interpretive framework for these inventorying efforts. Drawing on David Kolb's research, MacDonald (2010) emphasized the importance of examining disciplinary materials to understand a field's general approach to problems, which she distinguishes as compact or diffuse (p. 22). Fields with compact problem orientations tend to align with the sciences as they enroll "assimilators" (p. 26) who synthesize divergent theories and methods and bring them to bear on common prob-lems, whereas fields with diffuse problem orientations tend to align with the humanities as they enroll "divergers" (p. 26) whose attention to problems may be more singularly and discretely focused. Tabulating and graphing one jour-nal's citation distribution over 25 years may help us be more fully aware of the field's evolution *while it is happening* and, furthermore, realize how different scholarly outlets, such as *CCC*, are situated and re-situated in relation to a shifting compact–diffuse orientation.

Graphing provides a limited, partial read-out of the field's pulse with re-spect to compactness and diffuseness, which complicates speculation about where the field stands at any given moment and where it is headed. Implicit in recent claims about disciplinary disunity and fragmentation, such as those by David Smit (2004) and Richard Fulkerson (2005), is an assumption about an idealized state—a relatively contained, balanced ecosystem within which disciplinary conversations about the most pressing concerns, the most via-ble methods, and the most promising theoretical grounding lend stability to the notion of disciplinarity. These normative visions of RCWS are not easy for us to pin down and examine because they operate tacitly, informed by one's institutional and departmental location, the time period one's career has spanned, and a large number of other factors (training, publishing activity, leadership roles, etc.). But we should, nevertheless, remain fully cognizant of subtle references to what Jack Selzer once characterized as the *golden age* of composition studies wherever it lurks as a backdrop to this or that observa-tion about the field's uncertain—and some have argued tenuous—future (qtd. in Odell, 2006). Lee Odell (2006) mentioned Selzer's golden-age reference in an afterword to Odell's 1986 CCCC Chairs' Address, which was republished in 2006. In this afterword, Odell recounted the optimism that resonated in his keynote; he remembered that Richard Larson argued back, answering Odell's optimism with a warning of fragmentation. Reflecting on the moment, Odell acknowledged that his optimism may have been premature, that "it was a mistake to disregard what Dick Larson said" (p. 152). Twenty years following the delivery of his upbeat keynote address on the then-maturing discipline, Odell admitted a far more cautious, reserved attitude. By the end of the afterword, however, he turned again toward optimism:

> Change will continue to be rapid, and progress will always be slow. But at the center of the process of change and progress we find ourselves and our students continually growing— testing, reflecting, refining our assumptions about teaching and learning. So are we there yet? Are we mature as a profession? Probably not, especially if maturity means a time of stasis, a time without change. Are we maturing as a profession? Quite possibly—at least as long as we continue to grow as professionals. And that's cause enough for optimism. (2006, pp. 154–155)

Disciplinary terrain is constantly shifting, perhaps at what appears to be a faster rate than in many fields due to the adaptive, dappled spirit of much of the work in RCWS. Depending largely on one's vantage point—that is, on whether one looks at the head or the tail of a citation frequency distribution, the field can appear to be highly focused, with a recognizable set of shared, dedicated principles and motives, or it can appear as a loose amalgamation of pocketed clusters and enclaves, each holding fast to a relatively unique set of interests while neglecting (mindfully or not) an agreed upon concept of disciplinarity *in general*.[24] The full spectrum of citation data brings to light how both vantage points—generalist and specialist—are simultaneously implicated. As specialized enclaves negotiate a shared disciplinary frame, they simultaneously contribute to the shaping of the field at higher orders of magnitude. Though they are significant for us to evaluate regularly, the divergent factors motivating compositionists to specialize, even as they risk of turning

---

24   Anderson (2008) acknowledged that long tail distributions adhere to a fractal pattern, according to which the curve and the tail incorporate smaller sub-distributions within the larger one. These small niches help us account for the ways specialization perpetuates micro-patterns that are locally consistent with the larger patterns in the field. Many special interest groups articulate distinctive perspectives on the field and their relations to it. The methods introduced here might help us understand how larger-scale conceptions of disciplinarity can be negotiated with the perspectives promoted by smaller groups whose identifications with the field at-large require qualification.

away from shared disciplinary perspectives (individually or in groups, as divergers or as assimilators), are beyond the scope of this study. Yet, with the graphing methods demonstrated here, we might better understand the ways specializations and those invested in them negotiate and cohabit disciplinary scenes, such as scholarly journals. We may prefer to be upbeat or recalcitrant about the patterns suggested above, but by noticing—whether by graphing or other distant reading and thin description methods—we are better able to have a sense of the dynamic networks that continuously proliferate across our disciplinary materials and practices.

A changing disciplinary density is not a condition for us to solve; nonetheless, it demands a certain reckoning, particularly for visibility initiatives, graduate education, and professional development. For instance, the questions listed earlier in the chapter regarding how citations change and impact the making of the discipline remain unanswered. But, even though we cannot muster answers to those questions, we can with renewed conviction accept what David Foster described in 1988 as an "invitation to an intellectual pluralism" (p. 39), within which we can embrace these abstracting practices and the insights and questions they might productively open up for us.

Chapter 5: Emplaced Disciplinary Networks: Toward an Atlas of Rhetoric and Composition/Writing Studies

> Locating, positioning, individuating, identifying and bounding are operations that play a key role in the formation of personal and political subjectivities. Who we consider ourselves to be (both individually and collectively) is broadly defined by our position in society and in the world. This positioning occurs with or without any formal map of the generally understood sort. There are mental or cognitive maps (perhaps even whole cartographic systems) embedded in our consciousness that defy easy representation on some Cartesian grid or graticule. (Harvey, 2001, p. 221)

Consider carefully this litany of orienting verbs from the epigraph: "Locating, positioning, individuating, identifying and bounding." Those in the field of rhetoric and composition/writing studies (RCWS), from students and initiates to instructors and established scholars engage in these activities routinely. Ordinarily, activities such as these take place among divergent acts of composing; listed together, the orienting actions constitute fairly generic but indispensable designations for aspects of thinking, acting, and writing familiar to many, in this field and in others.

The handful of verbs appeared in a lecture by David Harvey (2001), an influential and well-known critical–cultural geographer, who went on in his discussion of "cartographic identities" to note that everyday orienteering—routinely making sense of emplacement—commonly "occurs with or without any formal map of the generally understood sort" (p. 221). In other words, even though tacit, cognitive maps may be highly idiosyncratic and uneven, most of us make do with mental models and locative senses informed by immediate sensory verification, signage, mobile devices, memory, imagination, direct inquiry, and nuanced noticings, as all of these give bearing to course. The point here is that people rely upon myriad orientational resources to position themselves in relationship to what is near and far, known and unknown; they often make good (or make *good enough*) with degree of locative aptitude, even when wayfaring without a conventional map in hand.

Setting out with an interest in geographic knowledges, cartographic projections, and disciplinary wherewithal, I begin this chapter by entertaining more deeply the implications of Harvey's (2001) "with or without" comment about maps and use his proposition as a segue to the case I will make for the invaluable forms of disciplinary knowledge that rely upon maps—maps that aggregate disciplinary data sets to showcase geolocative patterns across layers and scales and that operate as an additional illustration of distant reading and thin description methods in service of network sense. In effect, this work models the role map projections can have in oscillating between general, widespread disciplinary phenomena and highly specific, local, situated cases. This is a cartographic endeavor toward a provisional atlas of RCWS that articulates a multiscopic view of disciplinary activities and complements and fortifies appraisals of the intellectual landscape that have, perhaps too often, gotten by "without any formal map" whatsoever.

The following chapter advances a demonstrative argument for the value of formal maps, their layers, markers, and scalable viewports, as these wield formidable relief when set against the field's informally circulating geographic knowledges. The chapter proceeds first by surveying some of the ways geographic and cartographic knowledges have circulated in RCWS scholarship. Revisiting several examples of ways spatial considerations have entered into RCWS scholarship reinforces precedents for speculative openings such as *why maps? why now?*, while also forwarding recommendations for the importance of understanding disciplinary maps and the data they project as fluid and contingent depictions of the "moving terrain" Stephen North described in 1987. In this context, and as an echo of the concern expressed in Chapter One about the field's favor of thick description and ethnographic methodologies, I also relate the privileging of hyperlocal perspectives in existing scholarship concerned with space, taking stock of current mapping projects suited to a provisional atlas of the field and calling attention to six examples of models and maps that range among spatial-conceptual inquiry and cartographic representations.

Finally, in the second half of the chapter, I introduce three original maps I developed using distant and thin methods. The first is a chrono-cartographic projection of historical conference locations for the Conference on College Composition and Communication, Rhetoric Society of America, and Computers & Writing, each on a selectable layer. The second is a locative–aggregative projection that layers three consortia in RCWS—Doctoral Consortium, Master's Consortium, and Consortium of Undergraduate Programs—allowing users to switch among and combine views of them in a single map. The third is a traversive projection, indicating movement and pathways throughout a career as it relates to institutions where selected scholars have studied and worked. To conclude, the chapter acknowledges the limitations of a strictly representationalist paradigm for mapping along-side a discussion of the variety of data suited to cartographic distant reading and thin description on multiple scales, including as a way of inquiring into schools of thought as well as the theoretical and methodological priorities of individual programs based on where their faculty are from. With the marked rise of readily accessible mapping applications, we are now more than ever able to engage in mapping practices that can have transformative effects on our sense of the patterns, and networks, proliferating in the field.

Where is the Making of Geographic Knowledge In Composition?

One need not travel for many miles into the scholarship in RCWS to find that there has long been an emphasis on local scales in analyses of and reflections upon space—what I will refer to as a *localist impulse*. The causes for this per-sistent small-scope interest in space at local, material scales are not singular or simple. In part, the localist impulse stems from postmodern theoretical influences in geography that resist universal and generalizable cartographies, such as Michel de Certeau's (1988), which privileges the up-close intimacy of the sidewalk over the bird's eye view of Manhattan and sense of detachment he recounted after gazing out at the "wave of verticals" from the observation deck of the World Trade Center (p. 91), or Henri Lefebvre's (1992) destabilizing *trialectics of spatiality* in *The Production of Space*, which challenges absolute or purely representationalist reductions of complex spatio-perceptive con-tours and variables. These works provide theoretically justified movements toward subjectivity and situatedness in space that has been taken up in RCWS scholarship focused on the local. It is also tremendously practical to focus on the local: the here and now is *here* and *now*. The local scene offers defen-sible methodological choices and *de facto* boundaries, especially in research that has adopted ethnographic methods, the discipline's favored approaches. Reckoning with everyday sites and activities lends itself to understanding di-rect encounters through sensory experience grounded in one's immediate, material surroundings. Contextualism (Pepper, 1942; Phelps, 1991) reigns this tangible treatment of space, and the localist impulse is apparent in many re-cent articles and books that stand as moments when RCWS scholars studied space or inquired rigorously into geographic knowledges without explicit or sustained reliance on cartographic projections.

Consider Nedra Reynolds's (2004) *Geographies of Writing: Inhabiting Places and Encountering Difference*, a monograph influenced explicitly by the think-ing of de Certeau, Lefebvre, Edward Soja (1989), and others, and a work that remains the single-most notable book-length project on space and place in

RCWS in the last 15 years. Reynolds focused on engagement with local scenes and walking rhetorics (a premise forwarded by de Certeau in *The Practice of Everyday Life*) as she expanded upon the discipline's captivation with geographic metaphors. By developing accounts of students' explorations of the imagined geographies of Leeds, including their powerful misperceptions of no-go zones in Hyde Park, Reynolds effectively demonstrated the ways writing through spatial encounters can re-route lingering (mis)perceptions of space as well as intractable forms of spatially enforced exclusion. Another project, "Mapping URI," urged students to explore the University of Rhode Island campus to account for their felt senses of belonging and exclusion: "Students began with maps of the campus and, working in groups, marked the areas of campus with which they were completely unfamiliar, places where they'd never been" (p. 158). Reynolds was interested in maps and the complicated role they play in shaping perceptions of place; her pedagogical program held that many such perceptions must be deepened through on-foot, *flaneur*-like encounters "with difference at street level, complete with visuals, smells, sounds, and the tools that make both movement and dwelling possible" (p. 176). Given this recognition of the power of maps, however, Reynolds's work mentioned them but included only a few visuals. With a clear emphasis on subjecting local sites to spatial exploration and critique, the accounts of space are almost entirely textual.

The same can be said of Jonathan Mauk's 2003 *College English* essay, "Location, Location, Location: The 'Real' (E)states of Being, Writing, and Thinking in Composition," a compelling argument about the bland institutional geography students experience on the community college campus where he taught in northern lower Michigan. Mauk contended that *where*—a mix of spatial imagination and material environs—matters greatly to the viability of the courses he teaches. The presumed *wherelessness*, or sense of detachment that students feel within the institutional spaces they inhabit, plays a great part in configuring their attitudes toward acts of writing. Given Mauk's interest in space, the absence of maps is again conspicuous (though not necessarily any cause for discredit). The emphasis on the local is again pronounced: Quoting Reynolds, Mauk wrote "Because the vast imagined geographies of composition studies do not necessarily serve students (like those at Gordon Community College) or their teachers, 'it is time to think smaller and more locally'" (p. 375). Mauk ultimately set out to "practic[e] third space" to recast the "particular academic space that contextualizes their own writing and thinking" so that students who don't want to be there can reclaim a cartographic identity within which they can not only locate themselves but realize their roles in shaping such spaces (p. 379).

Short of providing a comprehensive review of scholarship on space in RCWS, I have highlighted these projects by Reynolds and Mauk because they undertook thorough, theoretically grounded studies at the intersection of space and writing invested unmistakably at local scales of activity. I will return to this matter of working at a local scale in a moment. Further, they presented their research without traditional maps—absent visual cartographic projections of the spaces concerning them and their students. This notes the viability of research-based inquiry into geographic knowledge that attends to imagined space and textual accounts of orientation and that demonstrates the functions of writing in negotiating cartographic identities. Further, noting this quality—the scarcity of maps in these influential works—primes the proposition I am leading up to, in which disciplinary geographic knowledges make full use of textual explorations of space and place in addition to the ways visual maps may play a more focal role in documenting disciplinary activity operating at a distance and across scales. Thus, I am interested in the matter of compositionists engaging in considerations of space while *doing without* maps because it lays the groundwork for a key question: How do our sensibilities about space and place change when we revisit spatial imaginaries *with* maps in hand? Moreover, what if RCWS scholars created those maps themselves?[25]

Karen Kopelson's 2008 essay in *College Composition and Communication* (*CCC*), "Sp(l)itting Images; or, Back to the Future of (Rhetoric and?) Composition" offers two arguments to clarify and reinforce the contemporary exigencies of scalable maps invested with disciplinary interests. To open the article, Kopelson recounted narratives of "coming to composition" (p. 751). She dealt turn-by-turn with Joseph Harris, Stephen North, Ross Winterowd, and Robert Connors, noting how each experienced or characterized their own intellectual migration from something that was not initially familiar with RCWS to something that, eventually, was. Such narratives are commonplace, and, of course, they typically invoke some variation of *here* and *there*: markers of movement, whether epistemological, spatial, or both. Read separately, these narratives bear out certain familiar resonances with our individual experiences, but what would happen if we read them, or mapped them, more collectively, perhaps accounting for the ways people have found RCWS through a wide variety of intellectual and institutional inroads? Such a project would be fruitful for newcomers to the field, whose "coming to composition" narratives are very much works in progress. But I also suspect that such a chart—an aggregate of widespread activity—would prove to be valuable for

---

25   One difficulty here comes from the large number of maps of the field that are more conceptual or philosophical, such as taxonomies that have offered descriptive matrices for how people think. There is a lot about so-called mapping that I do not introduce here. But I have tried to focus on space; it feels like a necessary limitation to keep this chapter within a reasonable length and scope.

discipliniography, for writing the field. More to the point: We don't all come to the field in the same way, but perhaps the worth of sharing journey narratives would increase if newcomers had ready access to a far-reaching collection of data that visually presents migrations such as those Kopelson briefly recounted. The traversive projection presented in this chapter's fourth section models such maps and offers a framework for considering the value of pairing textual accounts of "coming to composition" with mapping career paths as a way to grasp the simultaneity of emplaced and distributed identifications.

A second point from Kopelson's (2008) piece is elicited in a sub-heading: "Philosophical Foraging: Where *Is* the Making of Knowledge in Composition?" Kopelson answered this query with skepticism, implying in effect that if there has been much knowledge made over the last two decades, we won't find it in circulation outside the discipline: "Though we have long foraged about in other bodies of knowledge [. . .] we are still primarily importers only, consumers, an 'interdisciplinary' field, if it can be said that we are one, with little to no interdisciplinary influence" (p. 768). Clearly Kopelson was working with metaphors of space; the *where* is conceptual, not physical or material. By the end of the essay, however, Kopelson argued for less self-reflexivity over the matter of disciplinarity. "A living rhetoric and composition," she contended, relies upon a collective refusal to continue "the pattern, which is perhaps our rhetorical inheritance, of attempting to determine what our current and future intellectual work *is* as a primary facet of *our intellectual work*" (p. 775). In effect, Kopelson suggested that we should dwell less on disciplinary self-reflexivity and instead produce more "innovative and far-reaching forms of knowledge." With this in mind, the corrective she called for aligns with the project advanced in what follows: The problem has not been with self-reflexivity per se, but with the hasty extrapolation from local, immediate experience to the field at large without building up through the intermediary scales of activity. As I have sought to demonstrate all along, network sense wrought by watching words, charting citation frequencies, and, finally, plotting scholarly activity onto maps condenses, granularizes, and amplifies that "rhetorical inheritance," and thus these practices enrich, deepen, and complicate existing claims about the maturation of the discipline while contributing alternative forms of evidence to ongoing discipliniographic practices, wherever they may be headed in decades to come.

So: Why maps? Why now? New and emerging mapping platforms have become both easier to use and more rhetorically elaborate over the past decade. We should not expect that the localist impulse in RCWS is in any way less valuable for advancing a more collectivized and disciplinary cartographic identity, nor should we insist that the localist impulse ought to undergo a radical shift any time soon. After all, scenes of professional activity are primarily local, our narratives of coming to the field tend to be individual and idiosyncratic, and we conduct our most obvious, tangible deeds from the institutional scale on down—in programs, classrooms, meeting rooms, offices, desks, and hallways. Furthermore, interests in embodiment and materiality have flourished in recent years, and these are undoubtedly valid, vital matters. My framing of the localist impulse is not meant to suggest that there should be less of this local, situated, and material-oriented work but rather that there are gains to be made by complementing such interests with distant reading and thin descriptive methodologies that support insights at other scales of activity. Engaging other scales is necessary if we are to grasp such an abstraction as the discipline. Moving beyond local knowledge and aggregating local events and sites into a presentational form (a series of maps) where widespread phenomena can be grasped at a glance, this practice has a potential for generating insights into meaningful, ground-changing patterns. Tools are currently available for furthering the development of a series of contingent, provisional map projections that address the intellectual landscapes of the field. And there should not be much doubt that the modern development of RCWS yields much that would be appropriate to map.

Before turning to a presentation of such maps, however, the next section inventories selected forerunners to an atlas of the field—a small collection of existing engagements with geographic knowledge that involve visual models, graphs, and maps—that move beyond the local scale and resonate with disciplinary and cartographic identities.

Compiling an Atlas of Rhetoric and Composition

> Ultimately, the map presents us with the reality we *know* as differentiated from the reality we see and hear and feel. The map doesn't let us *see* anything, but it does let us know what *others have seen* or found out or discovered, others often living but more often dead, the things they learned piled up in layer on top of layer so that to study even the simplest-looking image is to peer back through ages of cultural acquisition. (Wood, 1992, pp. 6–7)

There are a few exceptions to the localist impulse where geographic inquiries and RCWS converge. Examples occur throughout predominantly textual scholarly accounts interested in the geographically distributed phenomenon of disciplinary formations and patterns (see Fitzgerald, 2001; Masters, 2004; Muchiri et al., 1995). These broad-scale studies are most commonly regional or multi-institution histories of writing programs, or they take stock of the Midwestern or North American orientation of the field's modern emergence. Further, such studies are not directly concerned with advancing geographic knowledge, except to the extent that geography constitutes an implicit dimension of the research because it aids in reconciling distributed activities with locations, and it provides place-references to identify and locate the events being historicized. Certain qualities of studies like these correspond to distant reading and thin description methods, but the studies have tended to be highly selective and do not, in most cases, include formal maps or other visual models.

In addition to these regional and multi-institution accounts, a growing number of projects have taken up more direct and explicit interests in mapping to the field beyond the local scale. My aim in this section is to gather together some of these to establish past engagements with geographic knowledge and to note the degree to which there are precedents for similar explorations in the field to the ones undertaken in this book. The interests underlying these maps are much like my own: a desire to aggregate locations, collect them onto a map projection, and notice in them identifiable patterns that may inform the field's maturation. In this section, I introduce six projects that have used graphical models pursuant to geographical knowledge: Peter Cramer's (2007) "Archipelago Rhetorica," James Porter et al.'s (2000) diagram of a site for institutional change, Maureen Daly Goggin's (2000) graph of the geographic distribution of journal authorship, John Ackerman's (2007; Phelps & Ackerman, 2010) map of the Rhetoric and Composition Doctoral Consortium, Jim Ridolfo's (n.d.) *Rhet Map*, and Tarez Samra Graban's (n.d.) *Metadata Mapping Project* before finally calling attention to Denis Wood's (1992) perspective on the rhetoricity of maps.

Peter Cramer's (2007) "Archipelago Rhetorica" presents a formation of islands labeled with place-names to accord with disciplinary domains or areas. The land and sea layer consists of a raised relief projection of the Philippines. By strategically locating the major labels of Speech Communication, English, and Linguistics, Cramer developed a series of implicit claims about the expansive field of English studies and the relationships between sub-specializations and niche interests. The Sea of Hermeneutics, for example, occupies the lower-left portion of the experimental map, while the Sea of Rhetoric appears in the opposite corner. To an extent, this design choice proposes, but does not explain, a diametric relationship between rhetorics and hermeneutics. The map provides a canvas onto which Cramer projected his own disciplinary insights; the map's meaning is both made possible by and constrained by its linguistic codes and conventions of geography (e.g., seas are typically assigned different names on opposite sides of a land mass). Like any conceptual map of the fields of English studies, "Archipelago Rhetorica" is not authoritative but propositional—it constructs, suggests, and instigates rather than proves. The viability of the map is, in some sense, determined by its uptake, by the degrees of circulation and influence that ripple out in delayed succession following its production.

Archipelago Rhetorica ca. 1999

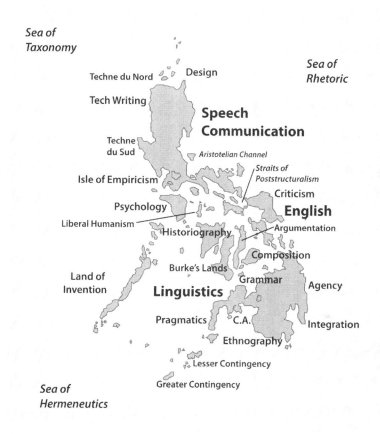

Sea of Taxonomy

Sea of Rhetoric

Techne du Nord   Design

Tech Writing

Speech Communication

Techne du Sud

Aristotelian Channel

Straits of Poststructuralism

Isle of Empiricism

Criticism

Psychology

English

Liberal Humanism

Argumentation

Historiography

Composition

Land of Invention

Burke's Lands

Grammar

Agency

Linguistics

Pragmatics   C.A.

Integration

Ethnography

Lesser Contingency

Sea of Hermeneutics

Greater Contingency

Figure 24. Peter Cramer's "Archipelago Rhetorica."

Cramer developed "Archipelago Rhetorica" as a humorous provocation while he was a doctoral student at Carnegie Mellon University, and he presented the map in a talk—"Archipelago Rhetorica: The Ambivalent Discourse of Anti-Disciplinarity in Rhetorical Studies"—in 2007. Apart from his explanation of the significance of the locations he chose, the locations of the place names raised more questions than they directly answer. But this is often the case for conceptual mapping of the field, like those collected in the "Alternative Maps" section of Mark Wiley, Barbara Gleason, and Louise Wetherbee Phelps's (1995) *Composition in Four Keys*. There, Mark Wiley explained that the map, like myth, "articulates what isn't real, but nevertheless finds intelligible patterns that make sense of certain human experiences" (p. 543). As indicated in the collection's opening chapter, conceptual mapping practices offer a "method of structured inquiry" (p. 2):

> We offer a map to organize what you read by means of four categories, or keys. This map is intended to be heuristic— an exploratory tool rather than a definitive claim—that can serve as a provisional framework for reading with immediate, if partial understanding. By means of your own experiments in applying and testing the limits of this scheme, you will gradually make it more complex and qualified; complement it with other ways of reading and interpreting texts and arguments, define its strengths and limitations; maybe abandon it and invent your own maps. It is this probing, critical, reflective process of mapping, not the categories of the map itself, should enable users of this book to learn how to make their own sense of composition and rhetoric. (p. 2)

The do-it-yourself ethic stands out distinctly, as *Composition in Four Keys* anthologizes four map-like pieces—by Richard Fulkerson, James Berlin, C. H. Knoblauch, and Stephen North—selected for the ways they propose useful categorizations, "exploratory tools" that might assist wayfarers "to a desired destination" (p. 544). Even though these conceptual maps raise questions as much as they answer them, they remain invaluable devices for coming to more deeply understand one's relationship to existing theoretical, methodological, and pedagogical orientations in the field.

Another conceptual map appears in James Porter et al.'s (2000) "Institutional Critique: A Rhetorical Methodology for Change." The methodology advocated used spatial analysis from postmodern geography for *boundary interrogation*—the examination of institutional dynamics that, even while they may seem unchanging, are shaped from within. Institutions, even when they seem inertial and slow-to-change, adapt from the inside, from the activities and practices of internal agents. The authors noted a concern with too narrow a focus on traditional scenes—at scales too abstract, on the one hand, or too local, on the other—as the commonplaces for initiating change and the critique that fuels it. They wrote that disciplinary critique and institutional action "usually focused on a limited set of organizational spaces: the composition classroom, the first-year composition curriculum, the English Department. . . . We are frustrated by the nearly exclusive focus on these organizational units to the neglect of others" (p. 625). Key among their solutions is a spatial model attendant to and conductive across scales between the localist impulse and, at the other extreme, accounts of the comprehensive discipline.

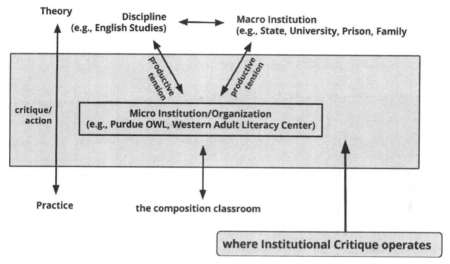

Figure 25. A redrawn version of Porter et al.'s "Site for Institutional Critique." Originally published in "Institutional Critique: A Rhetorical Methodology for Change" by James E. Porter, Patricia Sullivan, Stuart Blythe, Jeffrey T. Grabill, and Libby Miles. College Composition and Communication *51.4, June 2000, pp. 610–642. Copyright 2000 by the National Council of Teachers of English. Used with permission.*

More pronounced than their interest in mapping as a visual practice, however, is their theoretical turn to postmodern geography for the ways it lends traction to the "zones of ambiguity within institutions" that have tangible, physical bearing on the other scales commonly critiqued (e.g., classrooms, curricula, the discipline at-large, etc.) (Porter et al., 2000, p. 625). The authors acknowledge that "there is not one, holy map that captures the relationship inherent to the understanding of an institution, and all of these relationships [between administration, the classroom, and the discipline] exist simultaneously in the lived—actual, material—space of an institution" (p. 623). This allowance for multiple, overlapping maps is similar to North's (1987) characterization of the "shifting terrain" of disciplinary knowledge. Institutional critique ties into the concept of scale addressed in Chapter Two: Even while we are acting locally when we engage any scale of activity, spatial models (including maps) make it possible for us to articulate relationships that have bearing at multiple orders of magnitude. Mapping supports efforts to examine and critique local conditions in relation to broader conditions. When these maps are rendered visually and when they reflect aggregations of data too large or too small to apprehend by conventional devices, they not only ascribe to the principle motives for distant reading and thin description methods (and the exigencies and interests behind them), but they can also help us see how we are, in whatever situations we find ourselves, *constitutive* of the field. Spatial interrogations, like those in the Porter et al. model, help us shift perspectives and action across scales, especially when they are reintroduced into an emerging atlas of RCWS as one distant and thin mapping practice among many.

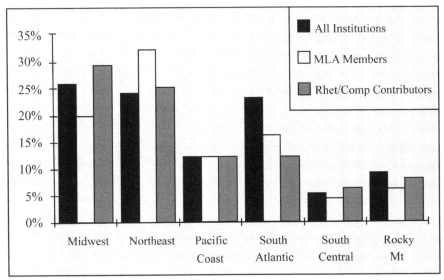

Figure 26. Maureen Daly Goggin's Graph of "geographical distribution across academic institutions, MLA members, and rhetoric/composition contributors" (p. 158).

In this third example, Maureen Daly Goggin's (2000) presentational choice fits more with graphing than with mapping; nevertheless, the data set behind Figure 26 clearly invokes a geographic bearing and advances geographic knowledge. In *Authoring a Discipline*, in which Goggin extensively studied scholarly production over four decades, she presented the graph shown above—a regional breakdown of institutions, Modern Language Association (MLA) members, and RCWS contributors to the nine journals grounding her study. The six regional designations correspond with the regions established by the MLA. Across each of the three data types, the graph affords certain comparisons on the basis of region. For example, with the aid of the graph Goggin identified the disproportionately low level of scholarly production in RCWS from South Atlantic institutions—low considering the number of institutions in the region. Goggin went on to account for several specific examples of editors throughout the first two decades of *CCC* who commented on the problem of uneven geographic distribution of contributing authors. The editors were interested in achieving an even and balanced reach, thereby publishing scholarship representative of the greatest possible geographic range of contributors. As the journal matured, Goggin explained, direct expression of those concerns abated, but this, in turn, raises further questions: Did the journal's longevity and presumed stability gradually satiate questions about geographic distribution? Has balanced geographic distribution been achieved, and is this balance established exclusively within the contiguous United States? With the rising internationalization of the teaching of English, how much longer will a North American survey of RCWS be sufficient for grasping at patterns, geographic or otherwise, in the scholarship of the field?

The three visual models introduced by Cramer (2007), Porter et al. (2000), and Goggin (2000) exercise geographic knowledges relevant to disciplinary wherewithal, relying upon aspects of scale, pattern, relational bearing, and comparative proportion. And they contribute to disciplinary–geographic knowledge despite circumventing the locative specificity commonly associated with grid-based cartography. Similarly, the next three examples document disciplinary geographies by layering geolocations for disciplinary activity onto map projections. As such, their genesis has in common a pursuit of disciplinary cartography, and they make important contributions to a gradually forming atlas of RCWS.

John Ackerman's map depicted members of the Rhetoric and Composition Doctoral Consortium—a map he shared during his talk, "Plotting the Growth of Rhetoric and Composition," at the 2007 CCCC and which is reprinted in a 2010 *CCC* article with Phelps. Ackerman's map layered doctoral program locations and startup data (designated by the color-coding of place markers) onto a Mercator projection of the contiguous United States. The map is coded with spatial and temporal information that sheds light on dimensions of the emergence and maturation of RCWS since 1965. According to the data presented with the map, six doctoral programs were founded from 1965 to 1975, 16 in each of the 10-year periods after that, and 11 between 1996 and 2010. Compared to the idiosyncratic conceptual maps and the middle-scale institutional boundary interrogations discussed in earlier examples, Ackerman's map of the Rhetoric and Composition Doctoral Consortium is one of the most conventional, pragmatic cartographic representations of the field to date. Yet, for all that this projection accomplishes in terms of mapping a layer of disciplinarily pertinent data, it relies on a limited, partial data set—one of the internal problematics identified in Chapter One. Ackerman used survey data to produce the map, a survey to which only 51 out of more than 70 members of the Consortium are included. So, on the one hand, the map satisfies an interest in establishing a cartographic projection of the field, but on the other hand, inadequate field-wide data remains a minor, correctible obstacle to the effort.

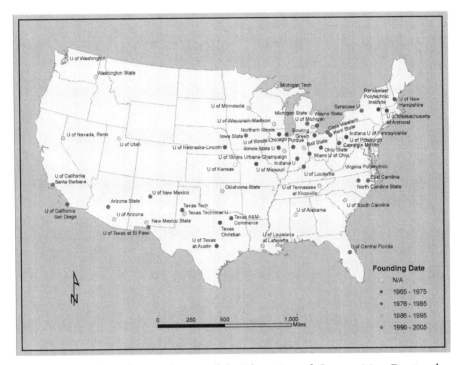

Figure 27. John Ackerman's map of the Rhetoric and Composition Doctoral Consortium. Originally published in "Making the Case for Disciplinarity in Rhetoric, Composition, and Writing Studies: The Visibility Project" by Louise Wetherbee Phelps and John M. Ackerman. College Composition and Communication *62.1, September 2010, pp. 180–215. Copyright 2010 by the National Council of Teachers of English. Used with permission.*

Since 2012–2013, Jim Ridolfo (n.d.) has data-mined job postings in RCWS from the MLA's Job Information List (JIL), collecting institutional locations, using a script to geocode the locations, and outputting the geolocations to a scalable, digital map. The series of Rhet Maps stand as an invaluable real-time report on the hiring climate in any particular year, and they accumulate to form an archive of employment activity useful for gauging not only the geographic distribution of positions, but also the temporal circulation within any year (i.e., the rate of postings to comparable dates in past years) and across the set. Ridolfo's maps are cast alongside other invaluable analyses of trends in the job market for RCWS. The maps provide one geographical vantage point from which to view jobs in RCWS—called a *viewshed* in cartographic terms— for considering the market. Placed alongside other data, such as tallies of the number of postings each year, these maps serve as an entry in the provisional atlas I am suggesting and function as a growing database that can be used to examine patterns in ad language. While the data favors ads for tenure-track faculty lines at four-year universities and graduate programs in RCWS, the maps can be read as a year-by-year report on the change (or constancy) of the field's locations, taking hiring to be one indicator of program renewal and sustainability.

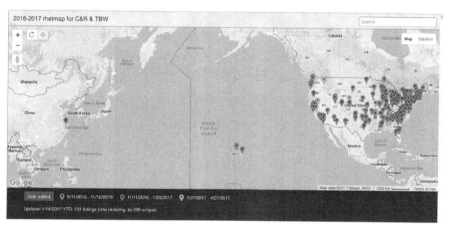

Figure 28. Jim Ridolfo's Rhet Map, "2015–2016 JIL for R/C & TBW."

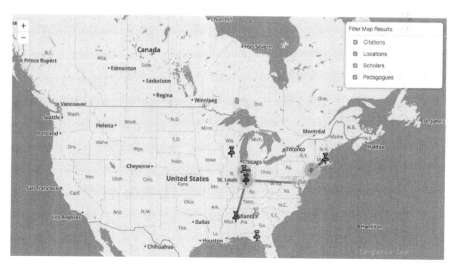

Figure 29. Tarez Samra Graban's MetaData Mapping Project (MDMP).

Finally, in the *MetaData Mapping Project* (MDMP), Tarez Samra Graban (2015) used maps to visualize women's intellectual work in RCWS. On the MDMP website, she explained the exigence and subsequent critical, locative tracings in this project:

> In the absence of women's published or publicly circulating texts, how else can rhetorical historians recover the reach of their pedagogical activity, and what can that recovery teach us about our disciplinary history? The MetaData Mapping Project (MDMP) answers that question by tracing women's intellectual influence through the migration of people, motives, texts, curriculum, and ephemera. (index.html)

For example, one map plots points related to rhetoric and composition primers that were used by women to teach writing and that are no longer in circulation. These traces of women's intellectual work in RCWS proceed cartographically and historiographically, turning maps toward investigations of the field's unevenly documented history and showcasing the value of maps whose data sets reach well beyond demonstrable institutional locations and urban centers, showing a deeply interconnected history. And although the MDMP reinforces the prominence of the United States as epicenter for disciplinary formation, it calls our attention to what remains: the need for much more mapping that will make visible the important, often invisible work of writing and rhetoric teachers, literacy sponsors, and the nonobvious interdependencies among them. These have been and remain still today a formidable part of what constitutes the discipline. Mapping can help us gain perspective, to discover afresh whose work is implicated in ongoing disciplinary formation and where that work is happening. Still other mapping projects, such as Jeremy Tirrell's (2012) examination of online journals and their geographic histories, and Christopher Thaiss and Tara Porter's (2010) mapping of Writing Across the Curriculum/Writing in the Disciplines (WAC/WID) programs internationally are important to note as belonging to the expanding work that constitutes an atlas of RCWS.

Having examined these mapping forerunners, such a compilation hints at the contingent, shifting terrain of the field because it indicates a degree of interplay across these six approaches suited to an emerging atlas of RCWS—visualized concept maps and taxonomies, mid-scale models designed to aid in boundary interrogations toward institutional change, geographic analyses of scholarly authorship, program-location maps reflective of Rhetoric and Composition Doctoral Consortium membership, and maps whose data is mined both from contemporary job ads and from historical ephemera. This small collection of geography-focused discipliniographies suggests that there already exists a fair amount of interest in mapping—as well as in distant reading and thin description, implicitly—in the deliberate intervention of scalable visual models to apprehend patterns not observable at conventional scales of engagement.

Before turning to the chapter's remaining three maps in the following section, I want to reiterate that all mapping projects are thoroughly rhetorical, and, as Denis Wood (1992) argued, constructed by authors. Maps, that is, are interest-serving articulations between some territory—conceptual or physical—and anything else relative to it. Addressing the uses of maps, Wood explained,

> The *uses* [e.g., navigation, planning, etc.] are less different than the *livings* that incorporate into their present the endless labor all maps embody. This is what it means to use a map. It may look like wayfinding or a legal action over property or an analysis of the causes of cancer, but always it is this incorporation into the here and now of actions carried out in the past. This is no less true when those actions are carried out . . . *entirely in our heads*: the maps we make in our minds embody experience exactly as paper maps do, accumulated as we have made our way through the world in the activity of our living. (p. 14)

Moreover, what makes mapping such a felicitous fit with distant reading and thin description is how it allows us to engage visually with widely distributed patterns across multiple scales, within and beyond our own lived experience. Through the use of maps, we can begin to grapple with dimensions of time and space that might elude us otherwise but that are nevertheless constitutive of some valuable knowledge or insight and within which, by an often-unarticulated proxy, we have ourselves set foot.

The Making of Maps in Rhetoric and Composition/Writing Studies

> Fold up the maps and put away the globe. If someone else has charted it, let them. Start another drawing with whales at the bottom and cormorants at the top, and in between identify, if you can, the places you have not found yet on those other maps, the connections obvious only to you. Round and flat, only a very little has been discovered. (Winterson, 1998, p. 88)

Jeanette Winterson's provocation hints at eschewing established mapping practices as an invitation to make our own maps, to articulate our own connections. The six examples showcased in the previous section honor a similar credo, as Cramer (2007), Goggin (2000), and Porter et al. (2000) fostered geographic knowledge by developing visual models to initiate a curiosity-motivated folding up of the maps and putting away the globe, and as Ackerman (2007), Ridolfo (n.d.), and Graban (n.d.) collected and plotted "the places . . . not yet found on other maps." Early in this era of digital mapping, an era signaled most pointedly by the release of Google Maps in the summer of 2005, geography scholars such as D. R. Fraser Taylor (2005) termed the flourishing of digital mapping as *cybercartography*. Cybercartography included the release of application program interfaces, or APIs, for mapping platforms provided by Google, Yahoo, and Mapquest and capitalized on the rapid proliferation of what were at the time heralded as Web applications that supported participatory map-making, which included location awareness for mobile devices and geotagging of images.

The map-it-yourself ethic that coalesced around these practices has been reiterated since 2005 such that, by now, it seems almost commonplace. Globes and foldable maps are increasingly anachronistic in the domain of wayfaring; they are artifacts of a former time swiftly left behind. But the notion of participatory cartography, such as digital mapping-it-yourself, has caught on and redoubled, ascending into an everyday practice despite the sloughing off of more traditional geolocative technologies (e.g., globes, compasses, paper maps, even dedicated GPS devices). In *The Wiley-Blackwell Companion to Cultural Geography*, for instance, geographers Andrew Boulton and Matthew Zook (2013) wrote of an "increasingly ubiquitous phenomenon of locative media technologies," calling particular attention to "the smartphones, online maps, and proliferating layers of geographically referenced content that are fundamentally imbricated with contemporary experiences in and representations of place" (p. 438). The question remains unsettled whether this "fundamental imbrication" generalizes as a collective wherewithal about geolocations. Yet, the fact remains that the available means of mapping have flourished, and the occasions for mapping have reached both into and across everyday life.

However, map-it-yourself technologies are not quite adequate for capturing the exigency for the disciplinary maps introduced in this section. Certainly, the conditions are right for accepting an invitation like Winterson's and for exercising cartographic discovery work, as examples listed in the previous section have done. But I would append to Winterson's invitational occasion a second compelling cause for mapping: Nobody else is going to create or curate our maps for us.

To add to the geographic knowledges initiated by prior RCWS mapping examples, and with the aim of adding to a more comprehensive atlas of RCWS,

I developed three layered maps that grant a viewshed to distributed institutions and events constitutive of disciplinary activity. Each map type will be featured in the three sections that follow. The first map shows the historical locations of three major conferences—Conference on College Composition and Communication, Rhetoric Society of America, and Computers & Writing—from the first meeting until present. This *chrono-cartographic projection* aggregates historical activity and presents it flatly, as if to suggest that all past instances of these conferences persist with a lingering degree of *now*-ness. The second plots the geolocations of institutions affiliated with the Doctoral Consortium in Rhetoric and Composition, the Master's Degree Consortium of Writing Studies Specialists, and the Consortium of Undergraduate Majors in Writing and Rhetoric. This projection is a *locative–aggregative* map insofar as it incorporates all three consortia into a single viewport with selectable layers. The third map documents career paths by blending two distinctive logics for comprehending the ways individual scholars move through a career, first as a segmented pathway (diachronic) and second as a host whose every institutional waypoint laminates and carries forward (synchronic). Thus, this is a *traversive projection* for calling attention to its movement. This movement, I contend, applies not only to individuals, but also to programs and disciplinary activities, such as conferences. Engaging these three maps offers insight into disciplinary formation and solidity, and the circulation of such maps stands to compel initiates and various stakeholders alike that the field continues to expand and thrive. Additionally, this expanded atlas demonstrates distant and thin methods as well as their emphases on data, scale, and pattern.

These maps serve at least two purposes (possibly many more, but for the aim and scope of this chapter, it is sufficient to elaborate upon just two): (a) a pragmatic end of boosting and continuing to promote visibility as an integral and ongoing dimension of disciplinary maturation, never to be taken for granted, and (b) a theoretical distinction that accepts the simultaneously emplaced and distributed quality of both individuals and institutions and events (manifestations of disciplinary activity). After introducing the maps and accounting for how I created them, I will return to these points to outline more thoroughly the contemporary exigency for continuing to expand and refine an atlas of RCWS.

Conferences: A Chrono-Cartographic Projection

The chrono-cartographic projection foregrounds selected disciplinary conferences, assigning time and location to indicate an accumulating time–place build-up, accounting for the field's gradual but continuous contemporary tour across the North American landscape. Figure 30 presents three major conferences—the Conference on College Composition and Communication (CCCC), Rhetoric Society of America (RSA), and Computers & Writing (C&W). The map's admittedly banal, everyday return to these conference locations describes this tour thinly. There is little here beyond the theme of the conference to immerse in; that is, compared to attending a conference or leafing through a program, the map captures only the thinnest slice of activity. What else, though, can be said of such a map? It conveys an interplay among conferences, a locative relationship among organizations that is nowhere articulated by these respective organizations. Collecting together and mapping this data poses a graphically verifiable locus, reminding us of CCCC's upper-midwestern orientation (i.e., twice as many conventions in Chicago [10] as in the next most frequent hosting sites). Similarly, the map's memory function recalls, as geographical originations, Minneapolis for C&W and Arlington, Texas, for RSA. As the field matures, these place and time accumulations risk surrendering to memory's inevitable dissipation, and yet such a map stands in as a statement on durability, expressing that-has-been as an aspect of recall but also of foretelling disciplinary expansion and circulation, visibility and reach.

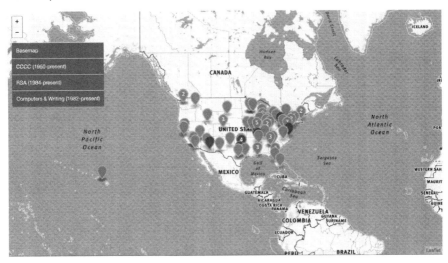

Figure 30. Conferences: A Chrono-cartographic Projection. The map depicts the geolocations of three major conferences in rhetoric and composition/ writing studies since each conference's inception. An interactive version of the map is available at https://wac.colostate.edu/docs/books/network /conferences.html. A video describing the map is available at https:// wac.colostate.edu/docs/books/network/fig30-desc-video.mov.

Consortia: A Locative–Aggregative Projection

Maps reflecting member programs in the Consortium of Doctoral Programs in Rhetoric and Composition have surfaced and circulated more frequently in recent years with demonstrable gains that attest to disciplinary solidity and visibility. Ackerman's (2007) map (Fig. 27) figured into an early effort to combine location with the roster of doctoral programs and to render them into a visual projection that would lay plain the locations and spatial relationships among programs, in effect, indexing the set geolocatively (Phelps & Ackerman, 2010). The map was tremendously important for disciplinary visibility, which it aided in catalyzing as a set of Classification of Instructional Program (CIP) codes and designation by the National Research Council (NRC) as an "emerging field" (Phelps & Ackerman, 2010, p. 184). It also for provided prospective doctoral students an invitational viewshed—an at-a-glance *gestalt* view—to the textual directory of the 89 member programs. In other words, the map performs a considerable advisory function, lending senses of location and regional proximity to the field's doctoral programs.

Figure 31. Consortia: A Locative–Aggregative Projection. The map brings together in selectable layers the locations of 338 programs associated with the Undergraduate Majors Consortium (60 programs), the Master's Degree Consortium of Writing Studies Specialists (189 programs), and the Doctoral Consortium in Rhetoric and Composition (89 programs). An interactive version of the map is available at https://wac.colostate.edu/docs /books/network/consortia.html. A video describing the map is available at https://wac.colostate.edu/docs/books/network/fig31-desc-video.mov.

Recognizing the viability and advisory benefits of the doctoral consortium, in 2012 the Master's Degree Consortium of Writing Studies Specialists set about generating a comprehensive list of 179 programs "offering master's level training specifically in writing studies and related fields" (Dunn & Mueller, 2013, p. 1). The comprehensive listing was a priority for this initiative, since it had not been established previously for MA-granting programs in RCWS, and throughout the process, planning included developing the roster into a map, which circulated informally via listservs and on the MA consortium website in 2013, where it remains available.

However, there doesn't appear to be any previous attempt to map the affiliated programs listed by the National Council of Teachers of English (NCTE) Committee on the Major in Writing and Rhetoric. The committee provided a report in 2008 on their website, which lists 60 programs—a substantial roster that would serve as an adequate data set for a map. The date stamp on this roster brings to light a key complication among the rosters for the three consortia: They are difficult to keep current in that they require annual tending, but there is not any organization nor formal charge to keep such lists up to date. Arguably the doctoral consortium leveraged visibility and was translated most readily into a map because of its relatively small and stable core of programs, and largely due to the efforts of Ackerman. The roster of MA programs, because it was new, was a substantial undertaking with many details, and the means of maintaining the roster remain to be established. Finally, the undergraduate programs roster, while it is due for an update, also spotlights the challenge of undergraduate programs being a scene of great change, especially with the emergence of new programs as a consequence of continuing disciplinary maturation. Most of the field's national organizations do well to maintain individual memberships, but there is, as of yet, insufficient regard for the vital importance of annually maintained program directories at all levels of disciplinary viability. The three consortia marked on this map have made great gains, and yet their coordination remains nascent and underdeveloped. I would argue (hardly a risky assertion!) that the relatively simplistic and admittedly thin combination of the three consortia into a single, layer-selectable map renders the field's breadth and solidity more formidably than do separate, isolated maps of each consortium unto itself.

Career Activity: A Traversive Projection

Finally, the third set of maps reflects iterations of a collaborative study of Canada–U.S. cross-border interdependencies in RCWS. The maps also appear in the second chapter of *Cross-Border Networks in Writing Studies* (Mueller, Williams, Phelps & Clary-Lemon, 2017), which features the results of a survey of writing studies scholars from or who have lived and worked in Canada. In the process of developing maps to document the career paths of 55 respondents to the survey, two distinctive patterns emerged. The first pattern indicates diachronic career paths, or paths that function as a series of segments. Consider as an illustration the way a person moves sequentially from place to place, relocating from a hometown to a college or university for first degree program, then to another, and so on. Diachronic career activity is linear, sequenced, and segmented. Synchronic career paths offer a contrasting logic in that these are understood from the current time and place to be an accumulation of emplacements. In the case of the synchronic career activity, a scholar who has moved from place to place is simultaneously inflected with every place she has ever lived or studied. Figure 32 models these distinctive, complementary logics, foregrounding discernible differences in career traversals of individuals.

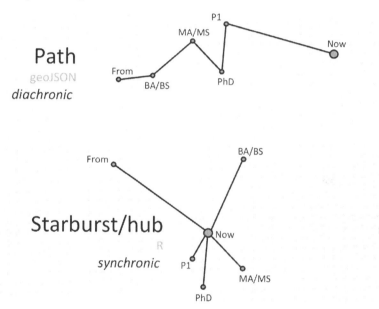

Figure 32. Contrastive logics for charting career activity.

The following two iterations became possible by applying institutional geolocations (markers) and line segments (connectors) to data gathered from the survey, which included a collection of CVs. Figure 33 follows the diachronic model, whereas Figure 34 applies the synchronic model to the same data: one data-set, two visual articulations of career activity as it manifests traversal-like in that scholars really move from place to place, but they are also inflected with every place they have ever been. Careers are simultaneously emplaced and distributed. The two maps also introduced a wicked visual problem. With so much data and with so many lines, they became congested and noisy. Even when zooming in, it remained difficult to distinguish one series from another. Slight variations in color-coding of each individual line and layer selectors distinguished by stage of career mitigate the map's overcrowding somewhat, but the maps remain too snarled a cat's cradle—albeit differently snarled according to the synchronic and diachronic logics defining the lines. Even so, the maps contributed to a gestalt impression, which confirmed a pattern: Many Canadian scholars in the field are from Canada, took BAs and MAs in Canada, then came to the US for a PhD before returning to work in Canada. The pattern was especially significant for the study on U.S.–Canada interdependencies; here, the point I wish to emphasize is that, despite data crowding and the initial impression of visual inelegances, a pattern is nevertheless corroborated. The aggregate elicits a pattern with great impact for disciplinary visibility in Canada.

The final iteration of traversals shown in Figure 35 indicates the value in smaller samples of map data for rethinking the interplay of the career-path models. This map suggests a distinction between mentors and mentees, calling attention to the ways mentors, such as Dale Jacobs at the University of Windsor, tend to be positioned synchronically, while those they mentor are in many cases positioned diachronically because they are usually only stopping through before moving to another institution and location. In spite of the thinness of such maps, they contribute a formidable conceptual apparatus useful for reconsidering disciplinary activities essential to the proliferation of the field.

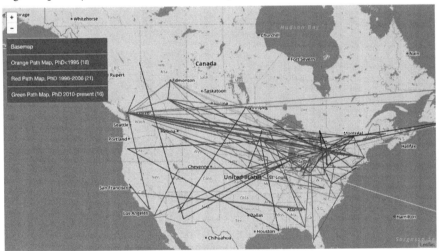

Figure 33. Survey respondents' diachronic career paths, following a series of segments from a point of initiation to a current location. An interactive version of the map is available at https://wac.colostate.edu/ docs/books/network/path.html. A video describing the map is available at https://wac.colostate.edu/docs/books/network/fig33-desc-video.mov.

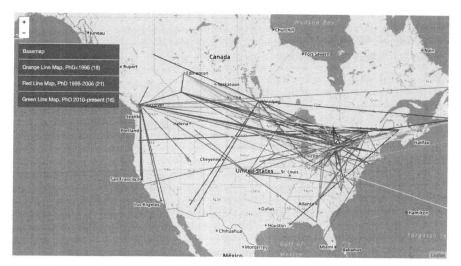

Figure 34. Survey respondents' synchronic career paths, showing line segments connecting a current location to every place previously occupied. An interactive version of the map is available at https://wac.colostate.edu /docs/books/network/lines.html. A video describing the map is available at https://wac.colostate.edu/docs/books/network/fig34-desc-video.mov.

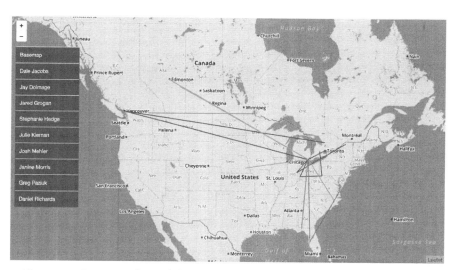

Figure 35. Career path models combined and applied to a smaller sample of map data. An interactive version of the map is available at https://wac .colostate.edu/docs/books/network/network.html. A video describing the map is available at https://wac.colostate.edu/docs/books /network/fig35-desc-video.mov.

With this in mind, we might extend these traversal maps to include the conference location data shown in Figure 30. Beyond accounting for career paths as a series of long layovers affiliated with hometowns and institutions where we have studied, a traversal map focused on conference activity would lend perspective to the role conferences play in professional identification. Scholars often identify home conferences, or conferences they return to repeatedly, but many also negotiate conferences variously associated with subfields and adjacent disciplines. Upon being mapped using both synchronic and diachronic logics, these, too, would produce an account of career paths as constituted by short stops, or conference-length experiences. I offer this as a thought experiment for others to map, theorize, and develop, anchored in the idea that conferences serve as an important scene of disciplinary activity. Mapped in the way I am suggesting, such projections would render visually these vital loci of collective activity that are both emplaced and distributed across many institutions and in time. Upon consulting such maps, initiates and other stakeholders may begin to know *here and now* as inflected with and set in constant relief against the *elsewhere and at other times*.

Making the Maps

The series of maps offered in the previous section primes numerous other issues that are up to this point addressed thinly—a thinness appropriate to the scope of this chapter and the case it makes for the importance of actively curating a disciplinary atlas as a contribution to disciplinary visibility. But in order to make this visibility *visible*, I offer a brief look into the making of these maps. They rely on a combination of GeoJSON, a coding specification amenable to several contemporary mapping platforms, and MapBox, a robust infrastructure for creating and hosting custom cartography projects. To begin, I gathered locations into a list, then geocoded them, translating the locations to latitude and longitude coordinates. Numerous free geocoding tools are available online. Finally, the coordinates and descriptive details together constitute the GeoJSON markup, which, at its simplest and for a single point on a map, looks like this:

```
{
"type": "FeatureCollection",
"features":
[
{
"type": "Feature",
```

```
"geometry": {
"type": "Point",
"coordinates":[-95.3438263, 29.7216396]},
"properties": {
"title": "Doctoral Consortium, University
of Houston",
"description": "University of Houston",
"marker-size": "medium",
"marker-color": "#26ADE4"}
}
]
}
```

Once compiled, the GeoJSON file, with all the locations for a given map layer encoded, can then be dragged and dropped onto the MapBox editor pane, and all the mapped elements adjusted for color, size, position, and updates to descriptive text, as desired. Although a comprehensive account of GeoJSON is beyond the reach of this chapter, it is a standardized coding specification designed for geographic data. As with comparable coding endeavors, assuming a tinkerer's disposition, searching for and spending time with online tutorials and visiting code hubs, such as http://geojson.org/, are requisite to executing this process.

The Contingency of Map Data

> By this time, we hope that you've become subversives, not only fine-tuning this map, but also imagining and arguing for entirely new schemes. Follow the trail of your own reading: Look to see where you have been and where you might go next. (Wiley et al., 1995, p. 549)

One peril lurking among these three map projections—chrono-cartographic, locative–aggregative, and traversive—is that their basic dependence on place markers and timestamps plays into the limited view of maps as universal reports on geospatial phenomenon. With this precarity in mind, in this concluding section I want to reassert that—extending from Harvey's (2001) litany of everyday orienting operations to include "locating, positioning, individuating, identifying and bounding" and Winterson's (1998) map-it-yourself imperative—now is the occasion to apply cartographic practices to disciplinarily relevant geolocations and "become subversives," imparting personal geographic knowledge (Harmon, 2004) and advancing counter-cartographies

(Wood, 2010a, 2010b, 2013). This might queue any number of off-beat mapping projects similar to those featured in Wood's (2010b) *Everything Sings: Maps for a Narrative Atlas*, which includes maps of "squirrel highways" (p. 42), or the utility wire infrastructure of one suburban neighborhood, and "families" (p. 84), which shows the number of divisions area houses had been broken up into. What are the yet-unplotted disciplinary cartographies that would illuminate tacit infrastructure or that would report on clustering and division among the field's schools of thought, its latent intellectual families?

Mauk (2003) and Reynolds (2004), in their respective accounts of location and geographies of writing, acknowledged the inseparability of subject and scene, arguing in effect that student subjectivities and campus spatialities (including importantly, campus surroundings) are inextricably linked, with vital bearing on the overall experience students have when they enroll at a university. Adapting this as a point of explicit emphasis in a first-semester, first-year writing class, I have in the past asked students on the first day of class to draw a "campus map of the imagination," inviting drawings that sketch senses of location, proximity, direction, and course. What results is a mix of projections, many documenting confidently the dormitories or commuter lots, the student center, and the classroom building where we meet. As an early indication of one's impression of campus, this is not especially surprising, and yet it indicates that upon initiation to any domain— whether epistemological or spatial or both—there is a drawn-out period of exploration and adaptation, of learning, *really* learning, what is where. Such activities are easy to revisit and, whether applied to our own campuses or the field of RCWS more broadly, quickly sketched maps of the imagination remind us of the continuing wayfinding that stands between reconciliations of others' maps and our own.

Where the maps in the previous section stick to conventional, practical questions of program, conference, and career locations, perhaps they do not make their contingency explicit enough. Developing and presenting these and other distant–thin models demands a constant assertion of their dynamism as well as their implicit assumptions about what warrants inclusion. The maps are dynamic objects, all the more rhetorically and theoretically responsible when we recognize the situations in which they are produced, the evolving nature of the data encoded in them, and the delicate ideological balance between historical proof and future-oriented speculation. For visual maps, territorial transiency, much like North's (1987) metaphoric characterization of composition's domains of knowledge as a "shifting terrain," tends to become more tangible when maps are displayed using new and emerging mapping platforms available online and increasingly amenable to dynamic, even animated or sequenced, digital presentation.

In a 2008 *Rhetoric Society Quarterly* article, "Urban Mappings: A Rhetoric of the Network," Jeff Rice went one step further, identifying what he called a *database rhetoric*, which combines "new media expectations as well as rhetorical concerns regarding arrangement, delivery, and space" (p. 200). For Rice, the relational database exists not only in a detached virtual space, but it also activates a network of spatial relationships by rendering ties between the material world and the "quirky data" assigned by novice map-makers (p. 216). Rice continued,

> What I am calling a database-rhetoric is not only what may allow a speaker, writer, or rhetor to change or evoke different notions of self through various arrangements; it is also a way for a composition (and I use that word broadly) to be "stylized" in a "myriad" number of ways as well. (p. 205)

The maps shown above make use of this database rhetoric; with them, we can find ways to grapple with the disciplinary problematic of sketchy and uneven data while presenting a chosen few "stylized" projections from a "myriad" of possibilities. Mapping, like the production of animated indexes and citation graphs, render more tangible and traceable patterns latent in the field's activities at varying scales.

I maintain that at the intersection of newly available mapping practices and interests in geolocative data bearing on disciplinary activity, we have an unprecedented opportunity to pursue, by collective effort, an expanded set of map projects of the field. Such maps follow suit with visual engagements of disciplinary geographies developed by others that have preceded us. However, the methodological and technological conditions are improving for an even greater assembly of maps: an atlas of rhetoric and composition, properly theorized to account for the contingency of mapping data, the rhetoricity of the projections, and the interests served by such work. But the maps introduced here, viable though they are despite their thinness, offer beginning points for yet further developments toward an atlas of RCWS. Many other disciplinary activities can be rendered apprehensible by processes of data mining, aggregating, and locating large collections of texts.

To conclude, I will outline some possible initiatives—hypothetical maps that would build upon these openings and expand an atlas of RCWS using distant reading and thin description methods. First, we might develop program-level maps of faculty or graduate students by associating them with their former institutions—places they have worked, places from which they have taken degrees, or both. Using faculty profiles and CVs, a single map could display the many career paths taken *en route* to a given institution. The map could improve internal understandings of the nature of the faculty's institutional experiences, and it could also be used for attracting new students and leading to deeper insights about the make-up of a group. Such a map would have been instructive in my MA program at the University of Missouri–Kansas City, where faculty in the late 1990s who influenced my program of study held PhDs from SUNY–Albany, Ohio State, and Rutgers and, as such, enacted inflections of training and influence they carried with them from relationships at each of those institutions. These are points of programmatic definition in a given moment. A map like this and the data it expresses would be contingent, changing according to faculty hiring. Inflections of institutional and mentor relationships carry over into scholarly focuses, the ways faculty members imagine curricula, and the pedagogies they sponsor in their classes and in administering the composition program. Many of these influences operate tacitly, but with mapping, such linkages can become more transparent, focal, and insightful into assumptions and hopes about the intentional design of programs. Further, such a map provides a profile that distinguishes one program from another and that serves as a basis for comparison when proposing new faculty hires or seeking other kinds of programmatic change.

Second, consider a set of maps developed to trace out genealogies of influence through doctoral committees. Starting with a given PhD candidate, a map could establish ties to the institutional sites from which all the committee members matriculated (a one-degree genealogy) and then to the institutional sites from which all their committee members matriculated (a two-degree genealogy). Without specifying the names of my dissertation committee members, the list of their doctoral programs suggests a lightly associative web insofar as implying my gravitations as a scholar—associations especially impactful during the half-decade following completion of that program. They held PhDs from University of Texas at Arlington, Case Western Reserve University, West Virginia University, Michigan Technological University, and SUNY–Albany. Although this is only a one-degree genealogy, connections run through it as a thin layer of my disposition as a scholar. This alone is not quite sufficient to reach conclusions about a worldview, much less a scholarly agenda. Yet the geographic run-down provides clues toward something more complex and multifaceted as a scholarly identity. To be clear, this suggestion is in many respects consistent with the aims of The Writing Studies Tree, but with an important distinction. The approach I advocate would begin more granularly, with one or two smaller networks approached methodically and comprehensively, the connections collected and plotted as exhaustively as possible, rendered visible cartographically. From this, more fully visible genealogy maps would serve as examples to extend from yet more extensive ties.

A one- or two-degree genealogy map could also build on scholarship such as Andrea Wiggins's (2007) "The Small Worlds of Academic Hiring Networks," which looked at academic hiring networks and the ways job candidates from institutions are employed by institutions with predictable qualities. Coupling data on committee genealogy with data on hiring (though this second data set is far more complicated to gather) would again lend depth to how we understand the interdependence of the two, especially considering the dearth of data presently collected for RCWS in either of these areas.

Finally, the prospective map I find to be most compelling would work by threading together the models I have presented up to this point. Consider a map that provided word clouds based on all the articles authored by faculty or alums of all the programs in the Rhetoric and Composition Doctoral Consortium. To such a map we could add a listing of the most frequently cited references compiled from all the scholarship published out of a given institution. From this, we could begin to see which figures re-surface in the scholarship coming from Purdue, Ohio State, Michigan Tech, or Cincinnati. We could begin to see the patterns in words and phrases of the scholarship itself produced at or in association with these and other institutions, one day spanning across multiple journals, monographs, and teaching materials. To imagine such a project at its nascence would be to attempt this for a single program first. Choose one program. Collect scholarship published by its alumni. Analyze the scholarship for text and citation pattern. And out of this, begin to highlight patterns. I am suggesting here great potential in establishing such maps—maps that incorporate geolocative data along with textual and bibliographic processes detailed in the previous two chapters. At the junctures among these distant reading and thin description practices we now have promising opportunities for seeing the field in dimensions that, to date, we have only begun to explore.

Chapter 6: Network Sense: Patterned Connections Across a Maturing Discipline

> I shall reconsider human knowledge by starting from the fact that *we can know more than we can tell*. (Polanyi, 1966, p. 4)

> There is a growing mountain of research. But there is increased evidence that we are being bogged down as today's specialization extends. The investigator is staggered by the findings and conclusions of thousands of other workers—conclusions which he cannot find time to grasp, much less remember, as they appear. Yet specialization becomes increasingly necessary for progress, and the effort to bridge between disciplines is correspondingly superficial. (Bush, 1945, para. 6)

This book began with sketches of three problems facing rhetoric and composition/writing studies (RCWS), and these operated as driving exigencies for the distant reading and thin descriptive methods theorized and applied by way of spotting turns, graphing citation frequencies, and plotting cartographically institutional–programmatic locations and professional pathways. Recall these three problems:

One: We have over the last three decades witnessed the continuous production of discipliniographies concerned with the field's constitutive activities, its theoretical and methodological underpinnings, and its worldviews, values, and epistemological attachments. Such projects have relied extensively on anecdotal evidence, intuition, and local experiences, on tacit knowledge lodged in what Stephen North (1987) counted as his "10 years of 'living among' the people of Composition" (p. 4). Noting this tendency is not to devalue these forms of evidence, nor to characterize them as lacking rigor or substance. Instead they purposefully tend to strain for a generalizing extensibility, surfacing a locally or regionally bounded perspective to account for larger-scale trends, patterns, or turns. Distant reading and thin description methods aid our corroborating claims about the field in these accounts, presenting augmentative forms of evidence to cases grounded in local experiences and, thus, these methods supply leverage for inquiring into the reach and plausibility of subjective claims about where the field at-large has been and where it is headed.

Two: Data essential to disciplinary patterning, particularly involving graphesis, has to this day been uneven and unsystematic in its collection, maintenance, and open accessibility. Consequently, inquiries concerned with enduring patterns in the field have done little more than tap into idiosyncratic and fleeting forms of evidence: local experience, anecdotes, and glancing impressions, on the one hand, or ethereal, painstakingly gathered data sets that blinker in and out again too soon after they have been procured for one-time claim-making. For example, in attempts to survey the current state of the field, scholars such as Mark Bauerlein (2008), Susan Peck MacDonald (2007), and Michael Bernard-Donals (2008) have keyed on patterns appearing in the titles of CCCC presentations listed in the convention program. This practice suggests that, since NCTE started making the conference program available online, its standing as the best available data-set has caught on. The trend of arriving at conclusions about the field judging by conference paper titles alone certainly raises some unavoidable questions about the gains and the limitations of distant and thin methods. More importantly, the title-skim operation points to the dearth of well-established data available for grounding claims about the field. The methods advanced in this book—as perhaps in any book—are out of necessity limited in their scope of application. And yet, moving forward this project should illuminate an expanded horizon for related projects, noticing that more expansive efforts aimed at data-collection, organization, and maintenance become ever more overdue as the field continues to grow. The neglect of data curation in RCWS indicates with ever-rising urgency a need for a new and sustainable curatorial ethic. Addressing this would do well to begin with the establishment of an information officer among the three consortia of RCWS programs described in Chapter Five. That information officer would keep up to date the directory information related to programs and program leadership. The role of an information officer could be defined and supported in a variety of ways. Funding could come from an annual stipend collected from consortium membership, underwritten by a national organization, such as the National Council of Teachers of English (NCTE), or funded by a donor or sponsor. At the very least, the role would require support and infrastructure sufficient for lists and contacts to be updated annually.

Three: Like all modern disciplines, we continue today to face a reading dilemma that has skyrocketed in the past three decades of disciplinary growth and expansion. More disciplinary material is generated than any one person reading by conventional strategies alone could reasonably, meaningfully engage. Richard Lloyd-Jones (2006) mentioned this quandary in his 1978 chair's address "A View from the Center," an address I will return to later in this chapter. A number of other scholars have engaged the closely related matter of excessive specialization since. One of the first to consider the challenges of specialization for

RCWS was Janice Lauer in her famous 1984 essay "Composition Studies: Dappled Discipline." In that essay, Lauer took up the problem of curricular planning of graduate programs in RCWS. She acknowledged pioneers of the field who, in the 1960s, balanced teaching responsibilities with the problems of how best to pursue training (of themselves and others). The formative work by early scholars in the field led to deeper investigations of the natures of writing and how best to teach them. Lauer noted that these prescient scholar–practitioners did much more than seek answers to early theoretical questions about teaching; they also took risks by venturing into other disciplinary areas to inform their inquiries. Lauer further explained that the interdisciplinary theoretical influences were complemented by an early commitment to multimodality in methods ranging from linguistic and hermeneutical work to empirical studies and so on. Compositionists recognized early on the value in a wide range of disciplinary perspectives and research methods to get at answers to the persistent questions that concerned them. To put it another way, the dappled, fanned-out purview of RCWS meant that for those doing the work of the field to be effective, they needed to create for themselves a *network sense* of the expansive domain. Tendering network sense requires a facility for recognizing and tracing relationships, for engaging in focused reading and exploratory reading, and for noticing connections among programs and people, publications and conferences, difficult questions and myriad stakeholders. Working *effectively* in a dappled discipline involves grasping to the extent one can the meshwork of ties among those who self-identify with the field, their institutional situations, geographical locations, methodological preferences, and areas of specialization. As if this wasn't enough—and Lauer's essay implied it wasn't—RCWS's dappledness also requires familiarity with extradisciplinary domains of knowledge and activity with the potential to shed light on writing practices, processes, research methods, histories, and theories.

I recount these three problems for RCWS because this book's conclusion calls for further development of the ways in which distant reading and thin description methods support, reinforce, and catalyze network sense—an ongoing and unfolding sense of disciplinary networks and their interrelationships. A sense of these networks intervenes into the problems described above. I must avoid too tightly coupling distant reading and thin description methods and the problems listed above in a tidy problem–solution or quandary–remedy relationship. If this project has been successful in showcasing the application of these methods, it will have persuaded you to accept, in addition to a problem-solving function, the generativity of these methods as they promote invention and inquiry by rendering patterns we did not realize existed. Network sense, in that it is a powerful epistemological corollary to distant reading and thin description methods, counters the problem of excessive specialization and provides scholars with formal, often exploratory, tools for the pattern-tracing essential to knowledge production in and across domains.

Text Sense, Felt Sense, Network Sense

In effect, network sense renders as cognizant the multiscale, patterned connections constitutive of a maturing and expansive disciplinary domain. To bring network sense into fuller view, it is instructive to situate the concept in relation to two notable forbearers: *text sense*, developed by Christina Haas (1996) as qualities of textual knowing involving memory, annotation, and attending to formal and informal features, and *felt sense*, developed by Sondra Perl (2004) as qualities of tacit, bodily knowing, capacities of feeling, and registers of intuition. Insofar as text sense focuses on texts and their epistemological extensions, and felt sense keys on inwardly focused contemplative practice, network sense names an epistemological wherewithal, or an awareness, of a collective's activities as they bloom across a conglomerate of language practices, meetings and conferences, referential linkages, and locative markers. Although this collective bloom of activities and practices is distributed unevenly in space and time, it is constitutive of a complex, expanding academic discipline.

In *Writing Technology*, Haas (1996) applied empirical research methods to study the ways writers interact with their texts differently depending on whether those texts are composed using pen and paper or whether they were composed using a computer. Haas used the phrase *text sense* to describe a writer's degree of awareness about the text while in the process of writing it. "Clearly," she wrote,

> writers interact constantly, and in complex ways with their own written texts. Through these interactions, they develop some understanding—some representation—of the text they have created or are creating. [. . .] One of the things that writers come to during the course of text production is an understanding of the meaning and structure of their own written arguments; I call this understanding or representation of one's own text *a sense of the text*. (p. 117)

Haas went on to define "a sense of the text":

> What is a sense of the text? *Text sense* is a mental representation of the structure and meaning of a writer's own text. It is primarily propositional in content, but includes spatial and temporal aspects as well. Although text sense—as an internal

construction—is distinct from the written textual artifact, it is tied intimately to that artifact. Text sense is constructed in tandem with the written text and seems to include both a spatial memory of the written text and an episodic memory of its construction. (p. 118)

Distant and thin methods complement the sense of the text Haas (1996) identified with a sense of the network because these methods afford insights for both readers and writers and are more expansively concerned with a range of activities and materials extensive to identifiable acts of composing. The mental representations of these methods are inscribed, rendered visually, externalized, and expressed as articulations set on visibility and interconnection. Furthermore, the animated index, citation frequency graphs, and maps of scholarly activity from Chapters Three, Four, and Five articulate as permeable the edges among the more than 500 articles published in *College Composition and Communication*, survey data, directories from the three consortia, job listings, and the world at large. Methods for visualizing disciplinary activity generate network sense by illuminating connections among texts themselves and their extensions—the linkages among words and phrases, source materials, and sites of production. Network sense expands upon and is highly compatible with text sense. The sense of the network enhanced by word watching, citation frequency graphing, and mapping adds layers and dimensions to a sense of the text. Rather than singling out any text as an end or product, network sense connects and reconnects texts (also places, people, moments) as nodes in dynamic, shifting compilations of meaning that extend in and across a variety of dimensions.

A second forebearer and influence on network sense, Perl's (2004) notion of felt sense, tends to be individualistic, bodily, and in-dwelt. As such, it is more difficult to locate as empirically verifiable or directly knowable, much less as ready-to-articulate. In fact, what makes felt sense "felt" is the way it operates just beneath the surfaces of direct observation or linguistic expression. Felt sense names the impactful implicit. The notion extends from Michael Polanyi's (1966) important work on tacit, personal knowing in the sciences, and, in this way, it rightly honors a writer's hunches and intuitions, recognizing that, as Polanyi famously framed it, "we can know more than we can tell" (p. 4).

Perl (2004) wrote about felt sense as "a kind of knowing . . . that is tacit because it is embedded in the body and nowhere else" (p. xiv). With respect to this locative definition, network sense proves complementary for its operating as a somatic knowledge, potentially radiant and hosted in and circulating across the body and (potentially) anywhere else. Network sense understands a discipline to be a mega-body writ broadly, extensibly, and organizationally complex, manifesting as a loose and distributed structure of participation.

In their focuses on writers writing, Haas (1996) and Perl (2004) attended to microshifts and focused primarily on a single composition, or a serialized compositional act that culminated in a focused text. By way of differentiation, network sense extends out into a scalar spectrum, working across multiple texts and long periods of time to conceptualize connections and relationships irreducible to individual experience or a text unto itself. Network sense helps us cognize the growing mountain of research insofar as it provides additional means for grasping patterns latent in the accumulating textual materials usually produced by multiple authors in different times and places. We cannot hold it all in our heads, except distantly, thinly. As a suite of tools for tracing associations, distant reading and thin description methods do not inherently favor production or reception (which is to say they are not inherently predisposed to reading or writing). Word watching, graphing citation frequencies, and plotting maps need not be confined to representations of the text or of the text-in-progress while composing. The visual models showcased in this book can encompass just about anything, from texts and textual citations to institutional locations and affiliations, inclusive of programs, departments, colleagues, mentors, friends, and a boundless range of anything else that can be articulated as a linkage. Network sense is as concerned with connections among people and places as with texts and characteristics of texts. In this generous, flexible capacity, network sense is imbricated with knowledge production, a tremendously relevant handle on the field, both for initiates and long-timers.

Network sense further mitigates the negative consequences of excessive specialization. Excessive specialization has commonly been examined as an intellectual problem threatening all the humanities, not only RCWS. Bruce McComiskey (2006), in *English Studies: An Introduction to the Discipline(s)*, characterizes three typical responses in English programs to "radical specialization": *secession, corporate compromise,* and *fusion.* According to McComiskey, secession within English studies, such as one might find when linguistics, creative writing, rhetoric and composition, or other groups of faculty split from English and function as an independent academic unit, "leads to further specialization" (p. 36). Of the three alternatives, McComiskey identified fusion as the model that places the greatest emphasis on becoming a generalist, although he noted concern that such a design is rare and will struggle to get beyond a superficial level of engagement with any one area of specialization. Similarly, in *Refiguring the Ph.D. in English Studies*, Stephen North (1999) discussed the deterioration of the *magisterial curriculum* and noted that English studies increasingly struggles for an identity, arguably right along with any of the sub-fields associated with the humanities that have been saddled by continuing trends toward specialization. For how it heightens awareness of connections and relationships and makes these linkages traceable, distant reading and thin description methods intervene into this muddle and modestly alleviate stressors addressed by McComiskey and North.

Rhetoric and composition/writing studies has long embraced the advantages in a dual disposition that aligns with specialization and generalization simultaneously. The spirit of this intellectual history is evident in Lauer's (1984) essay and also surfaces in Lloyd-Jones's (2006) CCCC keynote address from 1977, "A View from the Center." In his address, Lloyd-Jones attempted both to characterize the field's status and assert its legitimacy while also appealing to his audience, as constituents of the field in that place and time. He opened the address by referring to a commitment to language as the primary trait of RCWS. From there, he introduced and then analyzed a series of metaphors, testing each of them out and working through whether each sufficiently accounted for a deepening structure of RCWS. Choice metaphors included politics, foundations, architecture, skeletal anatomy, and, although he named it only by allusion to a telephone operator, networks.

In keeping with his title, "A View From the Center," Lloyd-Jones (2006) identified as his preferred characterization of the centrality compositionists occupy in the academy the rural telephone operator, Mrs. Peterson, who was highly connected and also highly knowledgeable about the community's inner workings, without being recognized for either. She was a generalist, an intermediary, and a connector, cognizant of the many discourses, relationships, and activities playing out around her. Lloyd-Jones's metaphoric figure occupied a central, conductive role because she developed and enacted a network sense of the complex disciplinary scene, a scene that already in the late 1970s existed as a nexus of pathways reaching far and wide into distributed domains. Lloyd-Jones intimated that this connective aptitude was essential because compositionists tended to occupy roles as "negotiators, explainers, and referees" (p. 50). A high degree of connection was preferable, he argued; without it, we "deserve our present basic position, that is, our traditional place in the damp cellar of the house of the intellect" (p. 50). By implication, Lloyd-Jones raised a question pertinent still today, especially so in the context of trends toward specialization noted by McComiskey (2006) and North (1999): How will compositionists perform their centrality in the future, both in the academy and beyond?[26] This is, of course, a question about actively seeking

---

26 We can look again at the work by Fulkerson (1979, 2005) and Hesford (2006) cited in Chapter One as performances of centrality. Perhaps any claim leveled about disciplinary formation, emergence, stabilization, or fragmentation is a performance of centrality, to some degree, and thus it implies something like a network sense, whatever forms of evidence might ground it.

ways of being both a specialist and a generalist, one who knows a lot about a little and at the same time one who knows a little about a lot.

Lloyd-Jones's (2006) imaginary telephone operator effectively allegorizes the network sense I have set out to define in this concluding chapter. Network sense refers to a connective facility and adeptness at recognizing patterns, relationships, and associations. It is a *sense* that allows us to reconcile a contextualist worldview,[27] rife with an overabundance of information, with intuition and imagination—those experientially shaped faculties for making sense of complex phenomena playing out in the world around us (and the world with *us* in it). Further, network sense is commonly assisted by technological apparatuses that aid inquiry by laying bare traceable associations in a collection of materials. Out of necessity, it is shaped through a blend of active, motivated tracing and assembling and situated experience. In each of the visual models—the animated index and turn-spotting hubs, citation frequency graphs, and scholarly activity maps—we should see the ways these treatments promote a sense of the field as a networked phenomenon. The insights that these models, as new media objects, bear out fall on both sides of the framework I have used to examine distant reading and thin description methods. On the one hand, the models mitigate problems created by small-scope discipliniographies, such as disorganized data and a "growing mountain of research" (Bush, 1945, n.p.); on the other hand, they introduce us to patterns, both known and new, with a generative, heuristic quality useful for posing questions and engaging with them differently than we have before. Other aspects of distant reading and thin description remain to be explored, but in these two aspects—a problem-solving orientation and a heuristic orientation—distant reading and thin description methods are prime for myriad uses in combination with other research methods.

Even with distant reading and thin description methods, certain aspects of disciplinarity will lurk and lurch along, remaining opaque, elusive, and indeterminate; this is unavoidable. Yet, because these methods foreground the hybrid quality of this collective we so steadily refer to as a discipline, they are capable of great flexibility, adaptation, and inclusion. If these forms of knowledge—the animated index and turn-spotting hubs, citation frequency graphs, and scholarly activity maps presented here—bear insights; if in distant reading and thin description, in related model-making and abstracting practices, we might begin to reckon with some of the nonobvious patterns proliferating in an ever more vast arena of scholarly activity; then we can justify expanding these initial efforts, all the while deepening our sense of the discipline as a networked phenomenon.

---

27   See Phelps (1991) *Composition as a Human Science.*

Network Sense in Expanded Practice

> Although I do not argue for a nostalgic return to the bygone days of literary generalists, I do think that a certain amount of institutional power is lost when common purpose dissolves. For with radical specialization, as English studies has experienced in the last half century, we are no longer able to represent ourselves to university administrations or public audiences as having coherent goals (other than the material fact that we work side by side). (McComiskey, 2006, p. 30)

In addition to tracing a dotted perimeter around network sense and suggesting its importance for generating new knowledge in addition to its many responses to the challenges that accompany excessive specialization, I seek to extend an account of its value, to sketch more pointedly who specifically gains from distant and thin methods and the epistemological interventions that follow from them. This section takes up the matter of who is served by network sense and presents selected projections—horizons of possibility—to shed light on how many are served by the visualization approaches featured in this book.

1. Established Professoriate

The established professoriate can apply distant reading and thin descriptive methods and the visual models created by these techniques as devices for deciding how to focus and differentiate curricula, programs of study, and specific courses. Much like an individual article abstract aids in the decision about whether to read or whether an article fits adequately with an established line of inquiry, distant and thin methods span scales of materials to render them more readily identifiable, individually and collectively. Upon grasping patterns of interrelation, we can more fastidiously and responsibly establish explicit ties in the collection of materials we are working with, whether for research, curriculum, or policy-making. I do not intend for this to imply that faculty members need assistance with generating associations and establishing clusters of materials for curricula and courses. Yet, distant reading and thin description intervene productively into what are already established practices. This is especially true in situations when faculty members feel isolated or when they are, like newcomers, venturing into unfamiliar areas, such as when teaching a new class for the first time, or when developing a new project at any stage of a career.

A second contribution of these methods for cultivating network sense can be found in the respect for differences Gary Olson called for at the end of his 2000 essay, "The Death of Composition as an Intellectual Discipline."

Olson explained that the viability of the discipline depended for two decades upon "exciting cross-disciplinary investigations of the interrelations between epistemology and discourse" (p. 24). According to Olson, the field must remain concerned with pedagogy, though not exclusively so. Olson strongly and repeatedly emphasized "intellectual diversity"; he argued that RCWS's disciplinary future depended on specialization that included shared terms. Distant reading and thin description provide a necessary precondition to respect differences and find shared terms in the midst of intellectual diversity—a network sense of the field. For the established professoriate to heed Olson's argument and take seriously the intellectual expansiveness of the discipline, we must be better at knowing *what we know* and better at knowing *what we do not know*. Distant reading and thin description offer devices and incentives for doing so.

2. Newcomers and Initiates

Newcomers to the field continuously face different challenges than does the established professoriate. The takeaways listed above pertain to this group, as well. Graduate students, the clearest sub-group among newcomers, gain from improved findability, from patterns that aid in decidability (e.g., of a program of study), and from a grounding in the many forms of knowledge produced and engaged with by a longer established professoriate. But newcomers also face a more pressing challenge: where to begin. Recalling Heather Love's (2013) interruption of Clifford Geertz's (1977) "turtles all the way down" maxim, we too must facilitate more patient and long-dwelt encounters with *first* turtles. Of course, these methods do not solve this problem outright (i.e., distant reading and thin description are among the many ways of dwelling with first turtles). But they do lay plain layered and connective patterns that, because they can be apprehended, provide a basis for sensing more extensively the connections that hover just beyond the point where one decides to begin. It does not replace or diminish the long list of well-established resources already available to aid in committing these early gestures (e.g., works cited; informal conversations with mentors, advisers, and peers; listserv discussions; special issues of journals; conference themes; and graduate courses). Distant reading and thin description, do, however, add to these resources, providing a greater range of traceable associations than is already available, much less circulating.

"Where to begin" applies to more than the conceptual foraging that usually precedes (and also persists throughout) any sustained inquiry. It also pertains to the pragmatic challenges of identifying and selecting graduate programs to apply to in the first place. Yet, even when the question shifts in this way toward the practical considerations about where to apply, network sense makes a significant difference. Prospective graduate students might, for example, see patterns in the publications produced by faculty or alumni at a particular institution. Using these methods, they can see connections between certain themes and *topoi* in the scholarship produced by current faculty and recent course offerings in the program (from both course descriptions and full syllabi, where they are available). They can also zoom in on programs by region or state. There is little question that much of what I have described is already attempted informally and idiosyncratically by applicants who seek admission to graduate programs in RCWS. The point is that distant reading and thin description methods guide more systematic treatments for surfacing patterns in whatever information is available, and these forms of knowledge serve newcomers just beginning their processes of determining where to start.

These methods also aid in preliminary and ongoing processes of sampling. Network sense brought about by distant and thin methods provides the heuristics one must develop early in any act of inquiry, whether disciplinarily invested or otherwise. Further, these uses can aid students working relatively independently on research projects or it can occupy a greater part in a common course, such as a graduate seminar. To illustrate this more tangibly, consider a graduate seminar focused on the history of computers and writing since 1980. Collectively, students could produce an animated index rendered from all the articles published in *Computers and Composition: An International Journal* or perhaps render the articles into lists of bi-grams separable into 5- or 10-year increments. Next, students could collectively decide on 20 or 25 words and phrases that they would trace back through the scholarly record. Here, data-driven word watching functions as a heuristic and a relay, returning the students to a generative activity. And finally, the students would develop a glossary of short essays, or what I characterized in Chapter Three as deep definition essays, that ground the terms in the record of scholarship and account for the varied connotations, the place of the term and concept in certain arguments, the locations where it operates as a given or commonplace, and so on. A project such as this is highly flexible and could be adapted to a great range of materials, including a selection of articles, a collection of syllabi from a writing program, or a sample of scholarship produced by faculty or alumni in a program during a given time period.

3. Public

These methods and the visual models they produce can also have an effect on general audiences, including people who do not yet realize that such a field as RCWS even exists. This does not mean that one would have to apply the methods to realize the insights the models suggest. For instance, consider the ways maps of programs could touch off greater awareness of the basic presence of writing programs in colleges and universities across the United States and Canada and, increasingly, abroad. The map of the three consortia in Chapter Five is but one suggestive example, and, of course, more of this work is due. With improved handling of data and more regimented surveys or reporting procedures, we would have simple maps showing not only the three consortia but also the locations of university writing centers, writing across the curriculum programs, first-year writing programs, undergraduate minors, and perhaps even programs that emphasize cultural rhetorics or other important disciplinary concentrations. Maps like these prove tremendously useful for making arguments to administrators and other decision-makers about the viability of developing a program or the geographic gap in any similar offerings such that an institution, by beginning an undergraduate major, would distinguish itself from other institutions in the region. Maps of this sort can also help non-academics recognize the vibrancy of the field as it has continued to grow and mature over the last 40 years. Also, such maps, if developed systematically, could have powerful bearing on the attitudes and actions of university administrators and public officials, such as legislators, whose decisions about funding shape higher education.

4. Students

The network sense catalyzed by distant and thin methods has much to offer to students at all levels of study and in many fields of study beyond RCWS. For many of the reasons recounted above—corroboration, findability, patterning—students can apply variations of these methods as a complement to any project involving research and writing. For example, with the availability of TagCrowd and Wordle, a pair of word-cloud applications, students can convert a text they are reading or writing into a visual model that follows a database logic of word watching rather than a narrative logic, thus, reintroducing them to a text by amplifying their text sense. These processes are useful, whether motivated by summary (an abstracting practice in its own right) or by wonder (the pursuit of discovery and possible insight).

Consider the following pedagogical applications of distant and thin methods as a more specific illustration of word watching in a pedagogical context. In the fall 2008, I taught a Studio for Transfer Students class (WRT 195) at Syracuse University where the students created Tagcrowd-based word clouds to assist them in the work of summarizing several texts assigned for the course. They were asked to read the full text, produce a word cloud for it, and then use the cloud as a heuristic to refocus on key vocabulary in the piece. Working with Caleb Crain's (2007) article "Twilight of the Books," students were alerted by this process to the large number of references to "American" and "percent" in the first quarter of the article. The frequent appearance of these two terms served as a powerful reminder that Crain focused almost entirely on examples of a decline in traditional reading among people in the US ("Americans"), and that he introduced quantitative data, much of which is drawn from surveys, to make his case that reading as a print-bound phenomenon has changed significantly in the past decade. In this teaching context, the word clouds alerted students to the forms of evidence (survey statistics) and demographic assumptions.

Similar processes might apply to student writing, as well. Shortly after TagCrowd and Wordle made their services publicly available, many graduate students, myself included, created clouds rendered from their dissertation prospectus or from individual chapters or articles they worked on. On the surface, these processes might seem to serve only hermeneutic invention. But reflective word watching also confronts the writer anew with the openness of the text and its possibilities, thus matching distant and thin methods with *proairetic invention*, a counterpart to hermeneutic invention that privileges a generative approach within an "ecology of invention" (Brooke, 2009, p. 63).

A distant and thin process I applied to the entire collection of seminar papers I produced in two years of doctoral coursework at Syracuse University illustrates one final example of how these methods might serve students. Just before preparing for qualifying exams, defining my reading areas, and formally developing a proposal, I aggregated into a single list all the works cited from papers and projects I produced throughout coursework. By compiling and sorting the citations into a single list, I found concentrations (i.e., patterns) that might have otherwise been unapparent to me. This proved a generative complement to the processes I was already relying upon, involving memory and my own felt sense about intellectual influences and inspiring readings. Absent distant and thin methods, my reflection on coursework would have undoubtedly resulted in overlooking relationships among many items in the pool of citations. In a situation such as this, we gain much from a smaller scale network sense—an awareness of the interconnections across and among our own materials, ever extensible into potential adjacencies.

Consider how an approach like this could ground a research project (whether for undergraduates or graduate students) in which students selected a figure in RCWS (or another field) to explore that person's scholarship based on the most frequently cited authors or works enlisted throughout an entire career. For instance, taking all the monographs, chapters, and scholarly articles produced by, say, Geneva Smitherman, Louise Wetherbee Phelps, Victor Vitanza, or Sharon Crowley, what patterns, and surprises, would we begin to see in their work? This is one more tangible example of the ways distant and thin methods and the generative elucidation of connective patterns—and resultant network sense—can make possible.

Thickening Agents for a More Durable, Dappled Discipline

Foremost, I have written this book with newcomers to the field in mind. I am committed to making RCWS visible, durable, and responsive, given changes in how invitation into the discipline works. Such invitational conditions are not as they once were. Localist discipliniographies, a dearth of well-curated data, and growing mountains of research complicate contemporary invitational conditions. They make it more difficult to identify the field: These are the precarious edges at the thresholds for RCWS, as for many emerging disciplines.

Up to this point, I have argued that network sense finds genesis and anchorage in the distant and thin methods introduced and applied in this book. Network sense capacitates a wide berth for disciplinary inquiry. It honors the necessarily tacit, felt, and text senses of identifying with a discipline as an experiential aperture for continuously re-knowing the field. For as strong a case as can be made for network sense, or for the distant and thin methods that bring it about, situated experience and context-specific engagements remain essential to disciplinary knowledge, action, and participation. Nevertheless, the approaches advanced in this book combine as thickening agents the explicit and traceable connections that are all the more available to us in the abstracting practices I have sketched related to word watching, citation frequency graphing, and scholarly activity mapping. By boosting visibility, providing wide-scope perspectives, and insisting on the ever-refreshed curation of disciplinary data sets, distant and thin methods support the thicker and more specialized work of continuing as a dappled discipline. They ask us to notice that the bases for knowing a sprawling and aging disciplinary formation inevitably evolve, as they must if we are to honor the groundbreaking work of forebearers and to forecast a future horizon hospitable to a durable disciplinary locus of knowledge and activity. As such, this book assumes durability and disciplinary development are implicit goods.

And it is on this note about persistence that we should begin—albeit upon this book's concluding—to see parallels between the returns and consequences of distant and thin methods and questions about the field's durability. If we accept as a legitimate omen the vulnerabilities of the field's knowledge, as Stephen North did in 1987, we begin to realize the need for a different curatorial ethic than the current one that has, for far too long, gotten us by with knowing enough of the field at large. Such a curatorial ethic is not easy to establish or pin down with a definition; the premise itself is bound to be fraught with controversy and with pitfalls. Everything from the utopian dreams of capturing some fleeting totality of the field to the well-known challenges of power, authority, and agency in establishing a grand database—these problems mix and mingle in the very suggestion of an improvable curatorial ethic. Still, there is room for improvement.

One framework for this curatorial ethic is available in The Long Now Foundation, an organization spearheaded by sustainable systems champion Stewart Brand and British composer Brian Eno, among others. The Foundation has taken up the challenge of long-term thinking on a global scale by committing vast resources to the development of a 10,000-year clock. Called "The Clock of the Long Now," the time-keeping device will be built to renew awareness of our own active roles in shaping the future. Michael Chabon (2006) explained the clock this way:

> The point of the Clock is to revive and restore the whole idea of the Future, to get us thinking about the Future again, . . . and to reintroduce the notion that we don't just bequeath the future—though we do, whether we think about it or not. We also, in the very broadest sense of the first person plural pronoun, inherit it. (para. 1)

While I am not proposing a similar clock for RCWS, I am suggesting that we take a hint from The Long Now Foundation's interest in a collective inheritance and in the shared responsibility that it produces for us—now in the first decades of the 21st century and for those who will be doing RCWS's work in 50, 100, or 300 years. Chabon continued,

> Can you extend the horizon of your expectations for our world, for our complex of civilizations and cultures, beyond the lifetime of your own children, of the next two or three generations? Can you even imagine the survival of the world beyond the present presidential administration? (para. 3).

Whether or not we can "extend the horizon" of expectations beyond our own careers, the lives of the students we teach, or whether or not we can imagine the continuation of the field beyond the terms served by the current organizational leaders, perhaps we can at least realize the generative returns distant and thin methods provide for aiding us in grappling with large-scale and many-lives-long patterns, patterns that are often nonobvious to us at the smaller, more local (and often default) scales of engaging the field. Until we do a better, which is to say more effortful and sustaining, job of grasping the "complex ongoing event," why should we expect anything other than more graceless turnover and fragility? Distant and thin methods and the network sense they promote create the invitational conditions to answer the problems listed at the beginning of this section. They thicken and strengthen conditions compatible with specialist ventures. And they also inch us closer to a full, ethical realization of long-term, future-oriented thinking for the discipline.

References

Ackerman, John. (2007, March). Plotting the growth of rhetoric and composition. Presented at the Conference on College Composition and Communication, New York, NY.

Adler-Kassner, Linda & Wardle, Elizabeth. (2015). *Naming what we know: Threshold concepts of writing studies*. Logan: Utah State University Press.

Alexander, Jonathan & Wallace, David. (2009). The queer turn in composition studies: Reviewing and assessing an emerging scholarship. *College Composition and Communication, 61*(1), W302.

AlfredoCreates.com. (2017). Bar chart. *The noun project*. Retrieved March 31, 2016, from https://thenounproject.com/term/bar-chart/347787.

Anderson, Chris. (2004, October 1). The long tail. Retrieved April 12, 2016, from http://www.wired.com/2004/10/tail/.

Anderson, Chris. (2008). *The long tail: Why the future of business is selling less of more* (Rev. ed.). New York, NY: Hachette Books.

Ball, Philip. (2006). *Critical mass*. New York, NY: Farrar, Straus and Giroux.

Barton, Ellen. (2008). Further contributions from the ethical turn in composition/rhetoric: Analyzing ethics in interaction. *College Composition and Communication, 59*(4), 596–632.

Batelle, John. (2005). The search: How Google and its rivals rewrote the rules of business and transformed our culture. New York, NY: Porftolio.

Bauerlein, Mark. (2008, January 28). Where are rhetoric and composition going?. *The Chronicle of Higher Education*. Retrieved September 23, 2017, from http://www.chronicle.com/blogs/brainstorm/where-are-rhetoriccomposition-going/5650.

Bazerman, Charles. (1992). The interpretation of disciplinary writing. In Richard Harvey Brown (Ed.), *Writing the social text* (pp. 31–38). New York, NY: Aldine de Gruyter.

Berlin, James A. (1982). Contemporary composition: The major pedagogical theories. *College English, 44*(8), 765–777. http://dx.doi.org/10.2307/377329.

Berlin, James A. (1987). *Rhetoric and reality: Writing instruction in American colleges, 1900–1985*. Carbondale: Southern Illinois University Press.

Bernard-Donals, Michael. (2008, April). *Why composition needs rhetoric*. Presented at the Conference on College Composition and Communication, New Orleans, LA.

Berthoff, Ann E. (1986). Abstraction as a speculative instrument. In Donald A. McQuade (Ed.), *The territory of language* (pp. 227–237). Carbondale: Southern Illinois University Press.

Bialostosky, Don. (2006). Should college English be close reading? *College English, 69*(2), 111–116. http://dx.doi.org/10.2307/25472195.

Bishop, Wendy. (1998). A rhetoric of teacher-talk: Or how to make more out of lore. In Christine Farris & Chris Anson (Eds.), *Under construction* (pp. 217–233). Boulder: University Press of Colorado.

Booth, T. Y. (1986). I. A. Richards and the composing process. *College Composition and Communication, 37*(4), 453–465. http://dx.doi.org/10.2307/357915.

Boulton, Andrew & Zook, Matthew. (2013). Landscape, locative media, and the duplicity of code. In Nuala C. Johnson, Richard H. Schein & Jamie Winders (Eds.), *The Wiley-Blackwell companion to cultural geography.* Chichester, England: Wiley-Blackwell.

Brereton, John C. & Gannett, Cinthia. (2011). Learning from the archives. *College English, 73*(6), 672–681.

Brooke, Collin G. (2009). *Lingua fracta: Toward a rhetoric of new media.* Cresskill, NJ: Hampton Press.

Bush, Vannevar. (1945, July). As we may think. *The Atlantic.* Retrieved March 16, 2016, from http://www.theatlantic.com/magazine/archive/1945/07/as-we-may -think/303881/.

Butler, Paul. (2008). *Out of style: Reanimating stylistic study in composition and rhetoric.* Logan: Utah State University Press. Retrieved September 23, 2017, from http://digitalcommons.usu.edu/usupress_pubs/162.

Butler, Paul. (Ed.). (2009). *Style in rhetoric and composition: A critical sourcebook.* Boston, MA: Bedford/St. Martin's.

Campbell, John. (1991). *Introductory cartography* (2nd ed.). Dubuque, Iowa: William C Brown Pub.

Carter, Michael. (1990). The idea of expertise: An exploration of cognitive and social dimensions of writing. *College Composition and Communication, 41*(3), 265–286. http://dx.doi.org/10.2307/357655.

de Certeau, Michel. (1988). *The practice of everyday life.* (Steven Rendall, Trans.). Oakland: University of California Press.

Chabon, Michael. (2006, January 22). The future will have to wait. *The long now.* Retrieved June 16, 2016, from http://longnow.org/essays/omega-glory/.

Chamberlain, Elizabeth. (2016). *You are how you cite: How academics might reach wider publics with new hyperlink citation practices* (Unpublished doctoral dissertation). University of Louisville, Kentucky.

Clary-Lemon, Jennifer. (2014). Archival research processes: A case for material methods. *Rhetoric Review, 33*(4), 381–402. http://dx.doi.org/10.1080/07350198.201 4.946871.

Clayton, Lenka. (2002). Qaeda, quality, question, quickly, quickly, quiet [Video]. Retrieved February 9, 2016, from http://www.lenkaclayton.com/qaeda-quality -question-quickly-quickly-quiet/.

Committee on the Major in Writing and Rhetoric. (2008). Writing majors at a glance [2009 listing]. *National Council of Teachers of English.* Retrieved April 16, 2016, from http://www.ncte.org/cccc/committees/majorrhetcomp.

Connors, Robert. (1997). *Composition-rhetoric: Backgrounds, theory, and pedagogy.* Pittsburgh, PA: University of Pittsburgh Press.

Corder, Jim. (1995). Turnings. In Christina G. Russell & Robert L. McDonald (Eds.), *Teaching composition in the nineties: Sites of contention* (pp. 105–117). New York, NY: Harper.

corroborate, v. (n.d.). *OED online*. Oxford University Press. Retrieved February 4, 2016, from https://en.oxforddictionaries.com/definition/corroborate.

Coupland, Douglas. (2008). *Microserfs*. New York, NY: Harper Perennial.

Craggs, Samantha. (2016, January 8). Canadians more polite than Americans on Twitter, study says. Retrieved February 4, 2016, from http://www.cbc.ca/news/canada/hamilton/news/canadians-polite-twitter-1.3395242.

Crain, Caleb. (2007, December 24). Twilight of the books. *The New Yorker*. Retrieved April 4, 2016, from http://www.newyorker.com/magazine/2007/12/24/twilight-of-the-books.

Cramer, Peter. (2007, April). Archipelago rhetorica: The ambivalent discourse of anti-disciplinarity in rhetorical studies. Fifth annual meeting of the Cultural Studies Association, Portland, OR.

Crowley, Sharon. (1998). *Composition in the university: Historical and polemical essays*. Pittsburgh, PA: University of Pittsburgh Press.

Derrida, Jacques. (2000). *Of hospitality: Anne Dufourmantelle invites Jacque Derrida to respond*. (Rachel Bowlby, Trans.). Stanford, CA: Stanford University Press.

Detweiler, Eric. (2015, October 27). "/" "and" "-"?: An empirical consideration of the relationship between "rhetoric" and "composition." *Enculturation*. Retrieved September 23, 2017, from http://enculturation.net/an-empirical-consideration.

Dickson, Alan Chidsey, Mejía, Jaime Armin, Zorn, Jeffrey & Harkin, Patricia. (2006). Responses to Richard Fulkerson, "Composition at the turn of the twenty-first century." *College Composition and Communication, 57*(4), 730–762.

Diggles, Tim. (2005, November). Composition and cultural rhetoric program colloquium. Syracuse, NY: Syracuse University.

Drucker, Johanna. (1998). Figuring the word: Essays on books, writing and visual poetics. New York, NY: Granary Books.

Drucker, Johanna. (2010). Graphesis: Visual knowledge production and representation. Poetess Archive Journal: The Journal of the Initiative for Digital Humanities, Media, and Culture, 2(1), 1–50.

Drucker, Johanna. (2014). *Graphesis: Visual forms of knowledge production*. Cambridge, MA: Harvard University Press.

Dunn, John & Mueller, Derek. (2013). Report on the 2012 survey of programs. *Master's Degree Consortium of Writing Studies Specialists*. Retrieved October 1, 2017, from http://www.mdcwss.com/docs/2012surveyreport.pdf.

Emig, Janet. (1983 [1977]). The tacit tradition: The inevitability of a multi-disciplinary approach to writing research. In Dixie Goswami & Maureen Butler (Eds.), *The web of meaning* (pp. 145–156). Upper Montclair, NJ: Boynton/Cook.

Ericson, Matthew. (2004, September 2). The words speakers use. *The New York Times*. Retrieved February 9, 2016, from http://www.nytimes.com/imagepages/2004/09/02/politics/campaign/20040902_words.html.

Ericson, Matthew. (2011, April 17). The words they used. *The New York Times*. Retrieved February 9, 2016, from http://www.nytimes.com/interactive/2008/09/04/us/politics/20080905_WORDS_GRAPHIC.html.

Ericson, Matthew & Bostock, Mike. (2012, August 28). At the republican convention, the words being used. *The New York Times.* Retrieved February 9, 2016, from http://www.nytimes.com/interactive/2012/08/28/us/politics/convention-word -counts.html.

Faris, Michael. (n.d.). Queer rhetorics citation mapping. Retrieved February 9, 2016, from http://michaeljfaris.com/queerrhetorics/index.html.

Farmer, Frank. (2013). After the public turn: Composition, counterpublics, and the citizen bricoleur. Logan: Utah State University Press.

Fitzgerald, Kathryn. (2001). A rediscovered tradition: European pedagogy and composition in nineteenth-century Midwestern Normal schools. *College Composition and Communication, 53*(2), 224–250. http://dx.doi.org/10.2307/359077.

Flynn, Elizabeth A. (2007). Reconsiderations: Louise Rosenblatt and the ethical turn in literary theory. *College English, 70*(1), 52–69.

Foster, David. (1988). What are we talking about when we talk about composition? *JAC, 8*, 30–40.

Fulkerson, Richard. (1979). Four philosophies of composition. *College Composition and Communication, 30*(4), 343–348. http://dx.doi.org/10.2307/356707.

Fulkerson, Richard. (1990). Composition theory in the eighties: Axiological consensus and paradigmatic diversity. *College Composition and Communication, 41*(4), 409–429.

Fulkerson, Richard. (2005). Composition at the turn of the twenty-first century. *College Composition and Communication, 56*(4), 654–687.

Fuller, Alex. (2017). Pattern. *The noun project.* Retrieved March 31, 2016, from https://thenounproject.com/term/pattern/97737.

Geertz, Clifford. (1977). *The interpretation of cultures.* New York, NY: Basic Books.

Gebhardt, Richard. (1987). Editor's note. *College Composition and Communication, 38*(1), 19–20.

Gere, Anne. (1997). Intimate practices: Literacy and cultural work in U.S. women's clubs, 1880–1920. Urbana: University of Illinois Press.

Gladwell, Malcolm. (2007). *Blink: The power of thinking without thinking.* New York, NY: Back Bay Books.

Goffman, Erving. (1974). *Frame analysis: An essay on the organization of experience.* Boston, MA: Northeastern University Press.

Goggin, Maureen Daly. (2000). Authoring a discipline: Scholarly journals and the post-World War II emergence of rhetoric and composition. New York, NY: Routledge.

Graban, Tarez Samra. (n.d.). Visualizations. *Metadata mapping project.* Retrieved September 25, 2017, from http://allicrandell.net/mdmp/ecologies-and-ontologies /visualizations/.

Haas, Christina. (1996). Writing technology: Studies on the materiality of literacy. New York, NY: Routledge.

Harmon, Katharine. (2004). *You are here: Personal geographies and other maps of the imagination.* New York, NY: Princeton Architectural Press.

Harris, Jonathan. (1997). *A teaching subject: Composition since 1966.* Upper Saddle River, NJ: Prentice Hall.

Harris, Jonathan. (2004). Wordcount. Retrieved February 9, 2016, from http://number27.org/wordcount.

Harvey, David. (2001). *Spaces of capital: Towards a critical geography*. New York, NY: Routledge.

Hayles, N. Katherine. (2007). Narrative and database: Natural symbionts. *PMLA, 122*(5), 1603–1608.

Heilker, Paul & Vandenberg, Peter. (Eds.). (1996). *Keywords in composition studies*. Portsmouth, NH: Heinemann.

Heilker, Paul & Vandenberg, Peter. (Eds.). (2015). *Keywords in writing studies*. Logan: Utah State University Press.

Hesford, Wendy S. (2006). Global turns and cautions in rhetoric and composition studies. *PMLA, 121*(3), 787–801.

intermezzo. (n.d.). Retrieved April 13, 2016, from http://intermezzo.enculturation.net/.

Irmscher, William F. (1987). Finding a comfortable identity. *College Composition and Communication, 38*(1), 81–87. http://dx.doi.org/10.2307/357589.

Jockers, Matthew L. (2013). *Macroanalysis: Digital methods and literary history*. Urbana: University of Illinois Press.

Johnson, Jim. (1988). Mixing humans and nonhumans together: The sociology of a door-closer. *Social Problems, 35*(3), 298–310. http://dx.doi.org/10.2307/800624.

Johnson, Karen E. (2006). The sociocultural turn and its challenges for second language teacher education. *TESOL Quarterly, 40*(1), 235–257. http://dx.doi.org/10.2307/40264518.

Johnson, Steven. (2001). Emergence: The connected lives of ants, brains, cities, and software. New York, NY: Scribner.

Jones, Ed. (2017). Database. *The noun project*. Retrieved March 31, 2016, from https://thenounproject.com/term/database/8859.

Kitchin, Rob. (2014). Big data, new epistemologies and paradigm shifts. *Big Data & Society, 1*(1). http://dx.doi.org/10.1177/2053951714528481.

Kopelson, Karen. (2008). Sp(l)itting images; or, back to the future of (rhetoric and?) composition. *College Composition and Communication, 59*(4), 750–780.

Korzybski, Alfred. (1962). *Time-binding: The general theory*. Lakeville, CT: Institute of General Semantics.

Kuhn, Thomas S. (1996). *The structure of scientific revolutions* (3rd ed.). Chicago, IL: University of Chicago Press.

Lancashire, Ian & Hirst, Graeme. (2009, March). Vocabulary changes in Agatha Christie's mysteries as an indication of dementia: A case study. Paper presented at the 19th Annual Rotman Research Institute Conference, Cognitive Aging: Research and Practice, Toronto, Ontario.

Lang, Doug. (1980). *Magic fire chevrolet*. Washington DC: Titanic Books.

Lanham, Richard. (2012). *A handlist of rhetorical terms* (2nd ed.). Berkeley: University of California Press.

Larson, Richard L. (1988). Selected bibliography of scholarship on composition and rhetoric, 1987. *College Composition and Communication, 39*(3), 316–336.

Latour, Bruno. (2007). Reassembling the social: An introduction to actor-network-theory. Oxford, UK: Oxford University Press.

Lauer, Claire. (2009). Contending with terms: "Multimodal" and "multimedia" in the academic and public spheres. *Computers and Composition, 26*(4), 225–239. http://dx.doi.org/10.1016/j.compcom.2009.09.001.

Lauer, Janice M. (1984). Composition studies: Dappled discipline. *Rhetoric Review, 3*(1), 20–29.

Lefebvre, Henri. (1992). *The production of space*. (Donald Nicholson-Smith, Trans.). Cambridge, MA: Wiley-Blackwell.

LeFevre, Karen Burke. (1986). *Invention as a social act*. Carbondale: Southern Illinois University Press.

Lloyd-Jones, Richard. (2006). A view from the center. In Duane Roen (Ed.), *Views from the center: The CCCC chairs' addresses, 1977–2005* (pp. 45–53). Boston, MA: Bedford/St. Martin's.

Love, Heather. (2010). Close but not deep: Literary ethics and the descriptive turn. *New Literary History, 41*(2), 371–391. http://dx.doi.org/10.1353/nlh.2010.0007.

Love, Heather. (2013). Close reading and thin description. *Public Culture, 25*(3 71), 401–434. http://dx.doi.org/10.1215/08992363-2144688.

Lynch, Paul. (2012). Composition's new thing: Bruno Latour and the apocalyptic turn. *College English, 74*(5), 458–476.

Lyotard, Jean-Francois. (1984). *The postmodern condition: A report on knowledge*. Minneapolis: University of Minnesota Press.

MacDonald, Susan Peck. (2007). The erasure of language. *College Composition and Communication, 58*(4), 585–625.

MacDonald, Susan Peck. (2010). *Professional academic writing in the humanities and social sciences* (2nd edition). Carbondale: Southern Illinois University Press.

Manovich, Lev. (2001). *The language of new media*. Cambridge, MA: The MIT Press.

Manovich, Lev. (2007). Database as symbolic form. In Victoria Vesna (Ed.), *Database aesthetics: Art in the age of information overflow* (pp. 39–60). Minneapolis: University of Minnesota Press.

Marback, Richard. (2009). Embracing wicked problems: The turn to design in composition studies. *College Composition and Communication, 61*(2), W397–W419.

Massey, Lance & Gebhardt, Richard. (Eds.). (2011). *Changing of knowledge in composition: Contemporary perspectives*. Logan: Utah State University Press.

Masters, Thomas M. (2004). *Practicing writing: Postwar discourse of freshman English*. Pittsburgh, PA: University of Pittsburgh Press.

Mathieu, Paula. (2005). *Tactics of hope: The public turn in English composition*. Portsmouth, NH: Heinemann.

Mauk, Jonathon. (2003). Location, location, location: The "real" (e)states of being, writing, and thinking in composition. *College English, 65*(4), 368–388. http://dx.doi.org/10.2307/3594240.

McComiskey, Bruce. (2006). *English studies: An introduction to the discipline(s)*. Urbana, IL: National Council of Teachers of English.

McLemee, Scott. (2003, March 21). Deconstructing composition. *The Chronicle of Higher Education*. Retrieved January 12, 2017, from http://www.chronicle.com /article/Deconstructing-Composition/6127/. [Paywall]

Meryl Norton Hearst lecture series: The digital turn. (n.d.). *UNI calendar of events*. Retrieved September 29, 2017, from https://www.uni.edu/unicalendar/meryl -norton-hearst-lecture-series-digital-turn/08-04-2014.

Meyer, Jan H.F. & Land, Ray. (2003) Threshold concepts and troublesome knowledge: Linkages to ways of thinking and practicing. In Chris Rust (Ed.), *Improving student learning—Theory and practice 10 years on* (pp. 412–424). Oxford, UK: Oxford Centre for Staff and Learning Development.

Miles, Libby, Pennell, Michael, Owens, Kim Hensley, Dyehouse, Jeremiah, O'Grady, Helen, Reynolds, Nedra, Schwegler, Robert & Shamoon, Linda. (2008). Commenting on Douglas Downs and Elizabeth Wardle's "Teaching about writing, righting misconceptions." *College Composition and Communication, 59*(3), 503–511.

Miller, Benjamin. (2014). Mapping the methods of composition/rhetoric dissertations: A "landscape plotted and pieced." *College Composition and Communication, 66*(1), 145–176.

Miller, Benjamin, Licastro, Amanda & Belli, Jill. (2016, January 1). The roots of an academic genealogy: Composing the writing studies tree. *Kairos: A Journal of Rhetoric, Technology, and Pedagogy, 20*(2). Retrieved February 9, 2016, from http://kairos.technorhetoric.net/20.2/topoi/miller-et-al/index.html.

Miller, Susan. (1993). *Textual carnivals: The politics of composition*. Carbondale: Southern Illinois University Press.

Monmonier, Mark. (1993). Mapping it out: Expository cartography for the humanities and social sciences. Chicago, IL: University of Chicago Press.

Monmonier, Mark. (1996). *How to lie with maps* (2nd ed.). Chicago, IL: University of Chicago Press.

Moretti, Franco. (2000, January/February). Conjectures on world literature. *New Left Review*, (1), 54–68. Retrieved September 23, 2017, from https://newleftreview .org/II/1/franco-moretti-conjectures-on-world-literature.

Moretti, Franco. (2005 [1983]). *Signs taken for wonders*. New York, NY: Verso.

Moretti, Franco. (2007). Graphs, maps, trees: Abstract models for a literary history. New York, NY: Verso.

Moretti, Franco. (2013). *Distant reading*. New York, NY: Verso.

Morris, Charles E. (2006). The archival turn in rhetorical studies; Or, the archive's rhetorical (re)turn. *Rhetoric & Public Affairs, 9*(1), 113–115. http://dx.doi.org/10 .1353/rap.2006.0027.

Muchiri, Mary N., Mulamba, Nshindi G., Myers, Greg & Ndoloi, Deoscorous B. (1995). Importing composition: Teaching and researching academic writing beyond North America. *College Composition and Communication, 46*(2), 175–198. http://dx.doi.org/10.2307/358427.

Mueller, Derek N. (2012, January 15). Views from a distance: A nephological model of the CCCC chairs' addresses, 1977–2011. *Kairos: A Journal of Rhetoric, Technology, and Pedagogy, 16*(2). Retrieved February 4, 2016, from http://kairos .technorhetoric.net/16.2/topoi/mueller/.

Mueller, Derek N. (2015). Mapping the resourcefulness of sources: A worknet pedagogy. *Composition Forum, 32*(Fall 2015). Retrieved April 13, 2016, from http://compositionforum.com/issue/32/mapping.php.

Mueller, Derek N., Williams, Andrea, Phelps, Louise Wetherbee & Clary-Lemon, Jennifer. (2017). *Cross-border networks in writing studies.* Anderson, SC: Inkshed/Parlor.

Musaplated, PT. (2017). Bear. *The noun project.* Retrieved March 31, 2016, from https://thenounproject.com/term/bear/147784.

National Center for Educational Statistics. (n.d.). Classification of instructional programs (CIP): Detail for CIP code 23.13. Retrieved January 3, 2017, from https://nces.ed.gov/IPEDS/CIPCODE/cipdetail.aspx?y=55&cip=23.13.

North, Stephen M. (1987). *The making of knowledge in composition: portrait of an emerging field.* Upper Montclair, NJ: Heinemann.

North, Stephen M. (1999). *Refiguring the Ph.D. in English studies: Writing, doctoral education, and SUNY-Albany's fusion-based curriculum.* Urbana, IL: National Council of Teachers of English.

Nystrand, Martin, Greene, Stuart & Wiemelt, Jeffrey. (1993). Where did composition studies come from? An intellectual history. *Written Communication, 10*(3), 267–333. http://dx.doi.org/10.1177/0741088393010003001.

Odell, Lee. (2006). Diversity and change: Toward a maturing discipline. In Duane Roen (Ed.), *Views from the center: The CCCC chairs' addresses, 1977–2005* (First edition) (pp. 145–155). Boston, MA: Bedford/St. Martin's.

Olson, Gary. (2002). The death of composition as an intellectual discipline. In Gary Olson (Ed.), *Rhetoric and composition as intellectual work* (pp. 23–31). Carbondale: Southern Illinois University Press.

Paul, Christiane. (2007). The database as system and cultural form: Anatomies of cultural narratives. In Victoria Vesna (Ed.), *Database aesthetics: Art in the age of information overflow* (pp. 95–109). Minneapolis: University of Minnesota Press.

Pemberton, Michael A. (1993). Modeling theory and composing process models. *College Composition and Communication, 44*(1), 40–58. http://dx.doi.org/10.2307/358894.

Pepper, Stephen C. (1942). *World hypotheses: A study in evidence.* Oakland, CA: University of California Press.

Perl, Sondra. (2004). *Felt sense: Writing with the body.* Portsmouth, NH: Heinemann.

Phelps, Louise Wetherbee. (1991). *Composition as a human science: Contributions to the self-understanding of a discipline.* New York, NY: Oxford University Press.

Phelps, Louise Wetherbee. (2016, April). Surprised by research: The mystery of presence. Presented at Conference on College Composition and Communication, Houston, TX.

Phelps, Louise Wetherbee & Ackerman, John M. (2010). Making the case for disciplinarity in rhetoric, composition, and writing studies: The visibility project. *College Composition and Communication, 62*(1), 180–215. http://dx.doi.org/10.2307/27917890.

Phillips, Donna Burns, Greenberg, Ruth & Gibson, Sharon. (1993). College composition and communication: Chronicling a discipline's genesis. *College Composition and Communication, 44*(4), 443–465. http://dx.doi.org/10.2307/358381.

Pilsch, Andrew. (2016). After "the" "text": A review of comparative textual media. *Enculturation*. Retrieved September 23, 2017, from http://enculturation.net /comparative-textual-media.

Polanyi, Michael. (1966). *The tacit dimension*. Garden City, NY: Doubleday/Anchor.

Porter, James E., Sullivan, Patricia, Blythe, Stuart, Grabill, Jeffrey T. & Miles, Libby. (2000). Institutional critique: A rhetorical methodology for change. *College Composition and Communication, 51*(4), 610–642. http://dx.doi.org/10.2307/358914.

Prior, Paul. (1998). Writing/disciplinarity: A sociohistoric account of literate activity in the academy. New York, NY: Routledge.

Reiff, Mary Jo. (2011). The spatial turn in rhetorical genre studies: Intersections of metaphor and materiality. *JAC, 31*(1–2), 207–24.

Reynolds, Nedra. (2004). *Geographies of writing: Inhabiting places and encountering difference*. Carbondale: Southern Illinois University Press.

Rice, Jeff. (2006). Networks and new media. *College English, 69*(2), 127–133.

Rice, Jeff. (2007). *The rhetoric of cool: Composition studies and new media*. Carbondale: Southern Illinois University Press.

Rice, Jeff. (2008). Urban mappings: A rhetoric of the network. *Rhetoric Society Quarterly, 38*(2), 198–218. http://dx.doi.org/10.1080/02773940801958438.

Rice, Jeff, Brown, Jim, McGinnis, Michael, Grant, David & Mueller, Derek. (2009, March). *Choragraphies of composition*. Presented at the Conference on College Composition and Communication, San Francisco, CA.

Richards, I. A. (1994). Speculative instruments. In Theresa Enos & Stuart Brown (Eds.), *Professing the new rhetorics: A sourcebook* (pp. 8–39). Englewood Cliffs, NJ: Prentice Hall.

Rickert, Thomas. (2004). In the house of doing: Rhetoric and the kairos of ambience. *JAC, 24*(4), 901–927.

Ridolfo, Jim. (n.d.). *Rhet Map*. Retrieved September 29, 2017, from http://rhetmap .org/.

Roen, Duane. (Ed.). (2006). *Views from the center: The CCCC chairs' addresses, 1977–2005*. Boston, MA: Bedford/St. Martin's.

Rosling, Hans. (2006, February). *The best stats you've ever seen*. Retrieved January 11, 2016, from https://www.ted.com/talks/ hans_rosling_shows_the_best_stats_you_ve_ever_seen?language=en.

Saper, Craig. J. (2001). *Networked art*. Minneapolis: University of Minnesota Press.

scale, n.1. (n.d.). *OED Online*. Oxford University Press. Retrieved February 15, 2016, from https://en.oxforddictionaries.com/definition/scale.

Shepley, Nathan. (2013). Rhetorical-ecological links in composition history. *Enculturation*. Retrieved January 20, 2016, from http://enculturation.net/rhetorical -ecological-links.

Sheridan, David M. & Inman, James A. (Eds.). (2010). *Multiliteracy centers*. Cresskill, NJ: Hampton Press.

Sirc, Geoffrey. (2002). *English composition as a happening*. Logan: Utah State University Press.

Smit, David W. (2004). *The end of composition studies*. Carbondale: Southern Illinois University Press.

Soja, Edward W. (1989). *Postmodern geographies: The reassertion of space in critical social theory*. New York, NY: Verso.

Stevens, Anne H. & Williams, Jay. (2006). The footnote, in theory. *Critical Inquiry, 32*(2), 208–225. http://dx.doi.org/10.1086/500701.

Stoian, Oliviu. (2017). Scale. *The noun project*. Retrieved March 31, 2016, from https://thenounproject.com/term/scale/320134.

Tag cloud. (2015, September 1). *Wikipedia*. Retrieved January 21, 2016, from https://en.wikipedia.org/w/index.php?title=Tag_cloud&oldid=678980330.

Taylor, D. R. Fraser. (Ed.) (2005). *Cybercartography: Theory and practice*. Amsterdam, Netherlands: Elsevier.

Taylor, Mark C. (2003). *The moment of complexity: Emerging network culture* (2nd ed.). Chicago, IL: University of Chicago Press.

Thaiss, Chris & Porter, Tara. (2010). The state of WAC/WID in 2010: Methods and results of the U.S. survey of the international WAC/WID mapping project. *College Composition and Communication, 61*(3), 534–570.

The digital turn. (n.d.). Retrieved February 4, 2016, from https://sites.google.com/a/uni.edu/thedigitalturn/.

Threshold concepts in digital rhetoric. (n.d.). *Digital Rhetoric Collaborative*. Retrieved February 4, 2016, from http://webservices.itcs.umich.edu/mediawiki/DigitalRhetoricCollaborative/ index.php/Threshold_Concepts_in_Digital _Rhetoric. [Login required]

Tinberg, Howard. (2006). In the land of the cited. *Pedagogy, 6*(3), 397–403.

Tinnell, John. (2011). Transversalising the ecological turn: Four components of Felix Guattari's ecosophical perspective. *The Fibreculture Journal, 18*. Retrieved September 23, 2017, from http://eighteen.fibreculturejournal.org/2011/10/09/fcj -121-transversalising-the-ecological-turn-four-components-of-felix-guattari %E2%80%99s-ecosophical-perspective/.

Tirrell, Jeremy. (2012, May 15). A geographical history of online rhetoric and composition journals. *Kairos: A Journal of Rhetoric, Technology, and Pedagogy, 16*(3). Retrieved May 23, 2016, from http://kairos.technorhetoric.net/16.3/topoi/tirrell /index.html.

Torok, Joseph. (2013, May 22). *Visualizing Present Tense: Graphing and mapping a corner of the discipline* (Unpublished master's project). Eastern Michigan University, Ypsilanti, MI.

Ulmer, Gregory L. (1994). *Heuretics: The logic of invention*. Baltimore, MD: Johns Hopkins University Press.

Unsworth, John. (2005, November 11). New methods for humanities research. Retrieved January 12, 2017, from http://www.people.virginia.edu/~jmu2m/lyman .htm.

Volk, Tyler. (1995). *Metapatterns*. New York, NY: Columbia University Press.

Weinberger, David. (2007). Everything is miscellaneous: The power of the new digital disorder. New York, NY: Times Books.

Weinbren, Grahame. (2007). Ocean, database, recut. In Victoria Vesna (Ed.), *Database aesthetics: Art in the age of information overflow* (pp. 61–85). Minneapolis: University of Minnesota Press.

What are your most used words on Facebook? (2015, November 17). Retrieved September 29, 2017, from http://en.vonvon.me/quiz/550.

Wiggins, Andrea. (2007). *Exploring peer prestige in academic hiring networks* (Unpublished master's thesis). University of Michigan, Ann Arbor, MI.

Wiley, Mark, Gleason, Barbara & Phelps, Louise Wetherbee. (1995). *Composition in four keys: Inquiring into the field.* Mountain View, CA: McGraw-Hill.

Williams, Raymond. (1985). *Keywords: A vocabulary of culture and society* (Rev. Sub. ed.). New York, NY: Oxford University Press.

Winterson, Jeanette. (1998). *Sexing the cherry* (Reissue ed.). New York, NY: Grove Press.

Wood, Denis. (1992). *The power of maps* (Rev. ed.). New York, NY: The Guilford Press.

Wood, Denis. (2010a). *Rethinking the power of maps.* New York, NY: The Guilford Press.

Wood, Denis. (2010b). *Everything sings: Maps for a narrative atlas.* Los Angeles, CA: Siglio.

Wood, Denis. (2013). *Everything sings: Maps for a narrative atlas* (2nd edition). Los Angeles, CA: Siglio.

Writing Studies Tree. (n.d.). Retrieved February 9, 2016, from http://www.writing studiestree.org/.

Yancey, Kathleen Blake. (2004). Made not only in words: Composition in a new key. *College Composition and Communication, 56*(2), 297–328. http://dx.doi.org/10 .2307/4140651.

Yau, Nathan. (2010, April 7). Watching the growth of Walmart – now with 100% more Sam's Club. Retrieved September 23, 2017, from http://flowingdata.com /2010/04/07/watching-the-growth-of-walmart-now-with-100-more-sams-club/.

Young, Richard E., Becker, Alton L. & Pike, Kenneth L. (1970). *Rhetoric: Discovery and change.* New York, NY: Harcourt, Brace & World.

Zebroski, James T. (2007). The turn to social class in rhetoric and composition: Shifting disciplinary identities. *JAC, 27*(3–4), 771–793.

Index

A